£25.00

D1357727

Cambridge Human Geography

PHENOMENOLOGY, SCIENCE AND GEOGRAPHY

Cambridge Human Geography

Edited by

BRIAN ROBSON

Professor of Geography, University of Manchester

PETER HAGGETT

Professor of Urban and Regional Geography, University of Bristol

DEREK GREGORY

Lecturer in Geography, University of Cambridge, and Fellow of Sidney Sussex College

Cambridge Human Geography will provide an important new framework for the publication both of the fresh ideas and initiatives often embodied in postgraduate work and of the more substantive research and wider reflective output of established scholars. Given the flux of debate within the social sciences as a whole, the series will seek to attract authors concerned to address general issues of the conflicting philosophies within and between the political science and 'liberal' approaches. Much of this interdisciplinary debate will be developed through specific studies: of production and economic restructuring; of the provision and management of public goods and services; of state investment and collective consumption; of human agency; and of the man–environment interface. The central aim of the series will be to publish quite simply the best of new scholarship within the field of human geography.

PHENOMENOLOGY, SCIENCE AND GEOGRAPHY

Spatiality and the human sciences

JOHN PICKLES

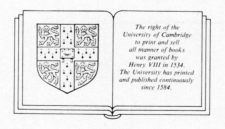

The right of the University of Cambridge to print and sell all manner of books was granted by Henry VIII in 1534. The University has printed and published continuously since 1584.

CAMBRIDGE UNIVERSITY PRESS

Cambridge

London   New York   New Rochelle

Melbourne   Sydney

Published by the Press Syndicate of the University of Cambridge
The Pitt Building, Trumpington Street, Cambridge CB2 IRP
32 East 57th Street, New York, NY 10022, USA
296 Beaconsfield Parade, Middle Park, Melbourne 3206, Australia

First published 1985

Printed in Great Britain at the University Press, Cambridge

Library of Congress catalogue card number: 84-12164

British Library Cataloguing in Publication Data
Pickles, John
Phenomenology, science and geography.—
(Cambridge human geography)
1. Anthropo-geography—Philosophy
I. Title
304.2′01   GF21

ISBN 0 521 26540 1

Contents

Preface

The modern human sciences have at least two broad conceptions of praxis. On the one hand, there is a confidence in method and technique; a confidence strengthened in the rapid and major advances that occurred in these areas during the 1950s and 1960s. On the other hand, there is a growing recognition that extra-logical and extra-methodological issues influence the nature of scientific claims, particularly in the social realm, and that these influences are more significant than had previously been recognized or acknowledged. Ideology, language, social relationships, and cultural attitudes have now been shown to be important and necessary concerns for the practising methodologist.

In the first case the human sciences recognize the importance of method and technique. In the second case the multiplicity of possible forms of evidence and interpretations has created an atmosphere of uncertainty in regard to any single technique or methodology. With the rise of what has been called 'the philosophical revolution' it has become increasingly clear that without the necessary reflective concerns and procedures any practising science merely perpetuates the taken-for-granted world of the status quo, and denies to the scientific enterprise its primary role as a critical enterprise. But in such reflection the scientist has few methodological procedures and guidelines to follow, and, in turning to philosophy for such guidance, the scientist again comes across a confusing multiplicity of views and interpretations. Indeed, the reintroduction of a necessary reflective component in all empirical science may still seem heretical to those who learned about the objectivity of method as the critical goal of empirical science, and for whom the exorcism of metaphysics had long been proclaimed as the goal of practically engaged positivist science; and positivism has been, by and large, the modus operandi of the social sciences throughout much of the present century. Thus, the methodologically sophisticated sciences found it difficult to understand that the call to reflexivity was not also a call to anti-science. In part, the social sciences failed to understand what the physical sciences had long been aware of: that method and understanding are integrally and necessarily related: that, as Heisenberg had shown, the looking and the seen are fundamentally inseparable.

Without the recognition that perception and conception cannot be divorced – that no innocent eye is available to us – and without the acknowledgement that science is necessarily a methodically constrained way of knowing the world, science claims to itself a privileged position. Method and technique become arbiters of social understanding and truth, instead of establishers of certainty. In that move extra-scientific forms of knowing and dwelling in and with the world are relegated to secondary positions. From this point on we begin to live in a world where man is patterned as machine, information processor, or gene pool. When such reductions occur, not only do we run the danger of forgetting the nature of human being, but science itself can no longer say anything at all about human experience *as such*. The human sciences thereby give up the very object domain on which they sought to found themselves, and the world in which such science predominates becomes a world where the being of beings is given over in favour of the things themselves. The ontological difference is forgotten, and thereby human be-ing is impoverished. In such a forgetful attitude science increasingly becomes concerned with its technique and praxis; with its way of answering questions, instead of with its way of asking and arriving at acceptable questions.

Generally such issues are consigned to the cloisters of occasional courses on the history and theory of the particular discipline at issue. But in this way the fundamental and grounding ontological understanding for any discipline is left largely untended. This is no less true of geography.

In such forgetfulness of the world in favour of things in the world, the important question becomes why and how such a fascination with the ontical world of material nature, and with the practice of fixing and mending, becomes so predominant within the sciences themselves. The issue is a broad and difficult one.

In this work only a preliminary foray into this question has been attempted, yet such a foray has been a necessary one. Geographic discourse has long delimited the realm of the possible and the acceptable too narrowly. Man and earth and the creation of man's world have always been, and remain, central to the geographer's view of the world. Such understanding has been confined largely to the 'real' world; a world of things and matter, and relationships between things and thinglike beings. Yet if geographers are truly interested in understanding "the earth as the world of man" (Broek, 1965, 79) it must be acknowledged that such concerns are inherently philosophical in that they deal with, or presume, the nature of what it is to be human, how worlds are created and maintained, and how meaning provides a framework for action.

The crucial question for the human sciences is not which approach of the many available and currently being practised is most useful or productive, but on what basis is each of these approaches grounded, and what assumptions do we carry along with them by accepting their particular requirements and their implicit models of man, social organization, culture, history, and world. I do not argue that on a priori grounds we can or should reject any single perspective. Such a decision is for the individual or group to determine in the context of specific issues and research frameworks. But I do argue that knowledge of that still shrouded world of a priori frameworks of meaning, or what John McPhee refers to as 'the Big Picture', is essential for any authentic and professional research tradition, and ultimately then for any discipline.

Without an understanding of 'the Big Picture', science itself no longer understands itself and its moves are made perpetually in the dark. The danger is obvious to any observer of the contemporary scene, where science is tied increasingly to technology, and ultimately to social and individual control. Science becomes scientism, and scientists, insofar as they are incorporated into the production of technologies, become dangerous. Such a relationship between science, technology, and policy determination can only be legitimated on the basis of good arguments, and cannot be accepted by default. Such a claim is not a rejection of science, but a revitalization and radicalizing of its essential and necessary nature.

In contemporary geography the work of the past three decades has left the discipline reeling from a profusion of techniques and competencies, as well as a wealth of new and well-tried approaches. Yet it might be argued that the nature of the 'geographical object', should such exist, has been lost sight of. The discipline and its practitioners are concerned less with the core of the discipline, than with the most effective means to move to its fringes and to facilitate accretion there. Admittedly this is the realm of new and ground-breaking work, but it can be such only with a finely honed and carefully articulated sense of disciplinary purpose and identity. Without such identity, 'approach' comes to mean technique, the definition of the 'geographical' remains superficial and therefore un-satisfactory, and disciplinary rigour divorced from any understanding of the nature of the phenomena becomes merely mathematization. Mathematization, divorced from a conscious thematization of the phenomena of disciplinary concern is, as we have already seen, an ideological view of science, ungrounded in good reasons and rational argument. It is also a view where the human subject is likely to be lost in favour of some more readily delimited object of inquiry.

Where the essential core and objects of concern of any science are to be clarified through historical investigation, ontological analysis, and empirical investigation, a reflective attitude is required. The world in which we live is our fundamental object of concern. Such a world is not derived from scientific study, but from our living in it. The geographical perspective is one of which we have prior knowledge and experience. Our task as scientists is, following Husserl, the rational reconstruction of an irrational world. More simply our task is to give an account of the earth as the world of man.

The advantage of a formal approach to such a reflective geography is our ability to problematize the world as given to us 'immediately'. Such a world is always historically constituted. It can always be other than it is. The taken-for-granted and the immediate are, as Heidegger has shown us, not two separate forms of experience, but are intimately related through our learning and socialization into the tradition of the community. It is the task of all reflective inquiry – traditionally called philosophy – to show how this world of possibilities has been concretized as this particular world in which we live. It is the task of a reflective geography to show how the experience of space and place, of land and life, and of our ties with the earth as the world of man, have been constituted through the unfolding of the traditions of the past to create for us the world of the present and the possibilities for a future.

The pursuit of the ideas laid out in this work owes a great deal to colleagues and friends. The Department of Geography at the Pennsylvania State University played host to these reflections from November 1978 until August 1983. Over a period of five years the department, along with the Interdisciplinary Graduate Program in the Humanities and the Department of Philosophy, proved to be a congenial and tolerant home to several of us for whom the accepted forms of practice and discourse proved inadequate. The willingness and flexibility of these geographers to engage philosophical issues, and of the philosophers to work with geographers, has been invaluable. In particular those students and faculty who participated in formal and informal seminars in the university have greatly helped in the articulation of these concerns.

Two colleagues, in particular, travelled parallel paths. Donald Kunze and Noriyuki Sugiura will soon have their own books in print, and therein we will bring this part of our combined journey to a happy and timely, if temporary close. The plans for the continued journey are underway.

Travelling requires that the pilgrim be well prepared for the arduous and unknown nature of the journey. In this task I owe sincere gratitude and respect to three of my teachers. Joseph Kockelmans taught me philosophy, and a great deal more. His influence and ideas, and his guidance through the works of Husserl, Heidegger, and Merleau-Ponty, provide the warp on which the weft of this work hangs. Roger Downs has been a source of constant encouragement, good advice, and critical interest throughout the project. He has spared no effort in the careful questioning and articulation of the ideas in this work. Peter Gould has been a perfect agent provocateur, and has helped enormously through his interest in my project. Greg Knight and Peirce Lewis have both been formative and critical influences on this work. I have learnt much about the philosophy of Husserl and Heidegger from Thomas Seebohm, Theodor Kisiel, and David Carr, as well as from Joseph Kockelmans, in part through the Summer School in Phenomenology organized annually at the Pennsylvania State University. Roger Downs, Joseph Kockelmans, Peter Gould, Greg Knight, Derek Gregory and Peter Haggett have been most kind and helpful in reviewing the manuscript. Of course, while I owe much, all errors and misinterpretations are my own responsibility.

Finally, we all hear about the magic moments of graduate school when for a time geographers, philosophers, sociologists, psychologists, and others, come together around central issues and common questions. At those times the spirit of inquiry kindles the spirit of discovery. In this process many are involved, only few can be explicitly acknowledged, but all can be thanked.

Ohio University
Athens, 1983

Acknowledgements

The author and publisher are grateful for permission granted to quote extracts from material as follows:

D. T. Herbert and R. J. Johnson (eds.), *Geography and the Urban Environment*, vol. 1 © John Wiley & Sons Ltd. 1978. Reprinted by permission of John Wiley & Sons Ltd. H. Arendt, *The Human Condition* © University of Chicago Press 1958. Reprinted by permission of University of Chicago Press. J. J. Kockelmans, *Martin Heidegger: A First Introduction* © Duquesne University Press 1965. Reprinted by permission of Duquesne University Press. M. Merleau-Ponty, *Phenomenology of Perception*, trans. C. Smith. Reprinted by permission of Routledge and Kegan Paul Ltd, London and Humanities Press Inc., Atlantic Highlands, NJ. M. Heidegger, *The Piety of Thinking*, trans. J. G. Hart and J. C. Maraldo. Reprinted by permission of Indiana University Press. Martin Heidegger, *What is a Thing?*, trans. W. B. Barton and V. Deutsch. Reprinted by permission of Gateway Editions Ltd. *Husserl: Shorter Works*, ed. P. McCormick and F. Elliston. Reprinted by permission of University of Notre Dame Press. From *Waiting for the Barbarians* by J. M. Coetzee. Copyright © J. M. Coetzee 1980. Reprinted by permission of Penguin Books. M. Billinge, 'In search of negativism: phenomenology and historical geography', with permission from *Journal of Historical Geography* 3 (1) 1977. Copyright: Academic Press Inc. (London) Ltd. The following extracts are reprinted by permission of Harper & Row, Publishers, Inc.: Specified excerpts, passim, from *Being and Time* by Martin Heidegger, translated by John Macquarrie and Edward Robinson. Copyright © 1962 by SCM Press, Ltd. Specified excerpts, passim, from *The Question Concerning Technology and Other Essays* by Martin Heidegger, translated by William Lovitt. English language translation copyright © 1977 by Harper & Row, Publishers, Inc. Specified excerpts, passim, from *On the Way to Language* by Martin Heidegger, translated by Peter D. Hertz. Copyright © 1971 in the English translation by Harper & Row, Publishers, Inc. Specified excerpts, passim, from *Poetry, Language, Thought* by Martin Heidegger, translated by Albert Hofstadter. Copyright © 1971 by Martin Heidegger. Specified excerpts, passim, from *Identity and Difference* by Martin Heidegger, translated by Joan Stambaugh. Copyright © 1969 in the English translation by Harper & Row, Publishers, Inc.

I

Introduction

1 Science and man

The human sciences have, in the past decade, become the focus of radical reflection to a hitherto unprecedented degree.[1] Methodological disagreements of the 1940s and 1950s have been replaced by profound and wide-ranging discussions of origins, aims, and ethics in science and of the role of science in a broader societal context. Practitioners of a particular discipline may have the impression that their own disciplinary turmoil is unique among the sounder, bolder, better established social sciences, but this is not the case. Current concern for reflective issues regarding the practice of human science and the need to treat these philosophically is not confined to any one science, nor is it absent from any such science.[2]

Several issues are fundamental to these reflective concerns. Modern technological science and society raise issues of freedom and control, of individuality and humanity. Corresponding to these concerns is the recognition of political, moral, and ethical dimensions of inquiry and particularly the relationship between science and technology and the politics of control. Recognition of such issues is widespread, and solutions range from advanced cybernetics (Wiener, 1954; Beer, 1974) to anarchy (Feyerabend, 1979). Hannah Arendt (1958, 2–3) views the situation in the following terms:

This future man, whom the scientists tell us they will produce in no more than a hundred years, seems to be possessed by a rebellion against human existence as it has been given, . . . which he wishes to exchange, as it were, for something he has made himself. There is no reason to doubt our abilities to accomplish such an exchange, just as there is no reason to doubt our present ability to destroy all organic life on earth. *The only question is whether we wish to use our new scientific and technical knowledge in this direction, and this question cannot be decided by scientific means; it is a political question of the first order and therefore can hardly be left to the decision of professional scientists or professional politicians.* [italics added]

Certainly there is a sense in which the sciences have lost their relationship to everyday life. Through increasing sophistication and mathematization, coupled with intense specialization, the sciences have become meaningless to the non-specialist. Yet, because of their increasing ties with technology, business, and government, the sciences have begun to influence everything man does (see Kockelmans, 1982).

The crisis of the sciences goes beyond even these claims, however, for the crisis is also an internal one. Questions have arisen about the basic relationship of science to its subject-matter. This relationship has become insecure, leading to reflections on the basic structures of the sciences. Such reflections seek to dispel the insecurity over basic concepts or to secure those foundations anew in a more original understanding of the subject-matter. The clarification of this primary field of subject-matter requires methods different from those of the empirical sciences themselves. Since the empirical sciences are incapable of providing such self-clarification empirically, in crisis scientific research turns to philosophical reflection.[3] It is, Heidegger (1927) claims through such reflections that genuine progress in the sciences can be said to occur. Yet such progress differs between the sciences themselves. As concrete possibilities of man speaking about the world in which he exists, the sciences stand in different relations to man. If they are not to be merely conventional enterprises, justified only by the prevailing tradition, then they must constantly seek to bring their subject-matter to an original experience before it is hidden by the essential objectifying and thematizing methods of each particular scientific inquiry (Heidegger, 1927, 10; Kockelmans, 1965, 16).

Whereas any one science may seek to clarify its own original experiences and basic concepts through philosophical reflection, it can hardly turn to the history of philosophy to help clarify its problems, since this history suggests that philosophy's own methods may themselves be unreliable and questionable. In any case, adopting philosophical views uncritically would be to adopt a method a priori. If we are to recapture original experiences, we must let ourselves be guided by the things themselves which appear to us immediately. "Because this procedure is the fundamental principle of phenomenology, we may say that phenomenology can perhaps provide an appropriate method for ontology" (Kockelmans, 1965, 18). Correctly conceived phenomenology does not adopt any particular position, standpoint, or world-view in regard to the state of affairs. It is not, in this sense, a world-view philosophy or an -ism. Rather, it is the name for a method which allows *original experiences* to be seen.

2 Science and phenomenology

When we talk about the realms of nature and of man we often take those realms to refer to the domains of objects investigated by the two main groups of empirical sciences, natural and human science. Increasingly we tend to understand nature and man in terms of the scientific claims these sciences make about them. But if this were fully the case, then we would only have access to both nature and man insofar as they are objects thematized in the empirical sciences. But, these sciences, in disclosing a particular field of subject-matter and in objectifying and thematizing, are necessarily limited in their scope. If they perform their proper function as objectifying, thematizing enterprises, something essential always remains closed to them.

What if it were the case that, in separating man from nature, the empirical sciences are unable to comprehend an original and undivided context of subject-matter, which consequently remains hidden? Because these sciences necessarily reduce nature and man to the domain of objects, this hidden subject-matter cannot be brought out by attempts to unify the domains of objective physical and human science (see Kockelmans, 1970b, 48). Something else is needed. Phenomenology seeks precisely to disclose the world as it shows itself *before* scientific inquiry, as that which is pre-given and presupposed by the sciences. It seeks to disclose the original way of being prior to its objectification by the empirical sciences. In this way the basis for a philosophy of the sciences is first created, serving (1) to provide the foundation for the genesis of the empirical sciences from pre-theoretical experience, (2) to elucidate their way of approaching the pre-given reality, and (3) to specify the kind of concept formation which accrues to such research. That is, we can undertake a phenomenology of original experiences in the everyday world, of the human and natural sciences themselves, and of the history and nature of the objects of these sciences and how those objects are constituted.[4]

Phenomenology indicates primarily a principle of method, which can best be formulated in Husserl's phrase: "Back to the things themselves." This expression does not mean that one should return to naive realism; but it indicates that in philosophy one should renounce all principles and ideas that are insufficiently explained or incorrectly founded, all arbitrary ways of thinking and all prejudices, and be guided only by the things themselves. Of course, philosophy does not intend to stop with the description of what immediately manifests itself to us. It intends to penetrate, by way of what shows itself immediately, to that which at first is still hidden and which constitutes the meaning and ground of what is immediately manifest. This is in the last instance the being of be-ings. (Kockelmans, 1965, 18)

It is from this philosophical background that the present work develops its major themes. On the one hand, the issue of science and its over-reaching nature in modern society is to be brought into question. The self-grounding claims of empiricism are challenged, and the physicalist and objectivist prejudices of positivism overcome. On the other hand, this is not to be construed as a rejection of science and the scientific method. Instead, through phenomenology we seek to ground the empirical sciences in such a way that they are no longer merely instrumental procedures, increasingly meaningless to or divorced from everyday life. Furthermore, we seek to show that the human sciences are not merely conventional enterprises, nor are they to be situated automatically within a 'meta-physics' as such, but rather they are to be grounded within a meta-theory appropriate to the domain of the phenomena with which each science is concerned. This is to be achieved, not by the a priori adoption of one more perspective on science, but by a thorough attempt to understand the nature of science as such. Here the limits and possibilities of science are constantly to be kept in view, and philosophy is to be given its proper place, not as hand-maiden to scientific knowledge, but, in the context of reflections on science, as meta-reflections on the sciences and their ground.

3 The plan of this work

Specifically, this work asks several basic questions concerning the nature of science and of geographical inquiry. In a preliminary fashion it asks: How can we have a truly human science? How can we have a truly human science of geography? And, how can we understand the nature of geography and its central problematics, particularly its concern with space and place, in this regard? The work is divided into *four* parts.

Part I, Geography and Traditional Meta-physics, shows how geographical inquiry is founded on an unexamined ontology of physical nature and a positivistic objectivism. The resultant objectivism and epistemological subjectivism have distorted the discipline's own conception of its subject-matter and its basic concepts. In particular, they have resulted in the unquestioned adoption of a conception of spatiality most appropriate for the physical sciences, but one which is of little value in describing the spatiality characteristic of man.

Part II, Geography and Phenomenology, shows how this underlying metaphysical position and fundamental ontology of physical nature has influenced the approaches to and interpretations of phenomenology in geography. 'Geographical phenomenology ' is distinguished from *phenomenology* and *phenomenological geography*, and the claims that have been made regarding 'geographical phenomenology' are explicated.

Part III, Phenomenology and the Question of Human Science, seeks to retrieve phenomenology in order to counter positivist claims concerning science and to deny the objectivism and subjectivism of contemporary human science. We also show the essential relationships between positive empirical science and descriptive phenomenological science, and use phenomenology to ground the sciences, (i) in original experience, (ii) through clarification of their basic concepts, and (iii) by the delimitation of the regions of the phenomena with which the sciences deal. Finally, this section shows how the character of science is essentially abstractive, reductive, objectifying, and thematizing. The final chapter of Part III seeks to ground science in human experience in such a way that Part IV can retrieve spatiality as an appropriate and necessary conception for geography as *human science*.

Part IV, Human Science, Worldhood and Spatiality, clarifies the nature of human science and provides a more balanced view of science than the overly empiricist one with which we now deal. Here we also determine the realm of concern for a geographic science and retrieve the genuine experience of, the basic concepts for, and the constitution of a science of human spatiality.

4 'Geographical phenomenology'

In the process of its adoption, interpretation, and critique in the geographical context, phenomenology has been radically *adapted* from the perspective of traditional geographical concepts and frameworks of meaning. At the same time this 'phenomenology' – as presented in the early writings of Relph, Tuan, Mercer and Powell, and Buttimer – has often become the *only* phenomenology to which subsequent writers turn.[5] As a result we need to ask if this 'phenomenology' is a sound and viable interpretation of phenomenological principles as such. We need to reconsider the precise and original meaning of phenomenology, and to distinguish this from what has been called 'phenomenology' or what I will refer to as 'geographical phenomenology'. The former refers to the project of Edmund Husserl and its subsequent development. The latter refers to the interpretations and adaptations of this project as they have entered the geographic literature.[6] To clarify the manner in which they *do not overlap* is central to this work.

The ground thus laid, we will proceed to an investigation of phenomenology and its relation to science. We will suggest ways in which a phenomenological geography may be possible and whether and in what way it can be like Husserl's phenomenological psychology, or whether the relationship between phenomenology and geography must be thought in a different way. At this stage phenomenological geography will have gone far beyond 'geographical phenomenology', and will have dealt with many of the major problems which have presented themselves in superficial analyses.

The clarification of these geographical interpretations will be important, particularly if the distinction between 'geographical phenomenology' and *phenomenology* as such can be reasonably substantiated, for three principal reasons:

(a) The justification for, and predominant philosophy of, 'humanistic geography' is claimed to be phenomenology and existentialism. I shall argue that if, from this perspective, phenomenology, and thus the relationship between scientific and extra-scientific ways of being-in-the-world, are misunderstood, and consequently if Husserl's claims about the lifeworld are misinterpreted (taken one-sidedly to be the content domain or subject-matter of phenomenology and a phenomenological geography), then serious questions arise about the claims of the humanist enterprise itself. If the seminal papers introducing phenomenology to the discipline distorted its nature, and subsequent discourse developed *in terms* of these claims, then the project itself, even where it goes beyond phenomenology, must be questioned.

(b) On the other hand, the rather easy manner in which opponents have criticized *phenomenology* will also have to be re-examined. This re-examination will be particularly important where criticism is based largely on the claims geographers have made about phenomenology, and where the *delimitation* of phenomenology has been used as a means to justify another viewpoint or perspective. For example, its alleged subjectivism is used to justify idealism (Guelke, 1978) and positivism (Hay, 1979); it is seen to be limited to concern for the lifeworld and social meaning and is used to justify critical theory (Gregory, 1978a) and structural marxism (Smith, 1979); and most recently its supposed individualism is claimed to justify the 'complementarity' of other 'non-phenomenological' approaches, such as a Durkheimian perspective (Jackson, 1981).

(c) If claims (a) and (b) can be substantiated, and if the actual claims of phenomenology can be presented, then many of the arguments currently seen to be problematic within the discipline can be re-thought. Some will – as Martin Heidegger suggested in a broader context – be seen as quasi-problems. Other issues which are now unquestioned and taken for granted will become questionable. We might then be able to see the possibilities for phenomenology and its relevance to a science of geography, including an empirical science of geographical relationships.

What is at stake here, to paraphrase Kockelmans (1971, 142), is the question whether or not phenomenological geography will be able to make an important contribution to empirical research in the realm of geography. Will phenomenology assist in explicating geography's basic assumptions and, in that sense, secure geography's very foundations by carefully analysing the invariable structures and interpretatively clarifying the essential characteristics of our various modes of orientation towards the world on the basis of the phenomena immediately given in experience?

The task before us is not to re-think what others have previously thought, but to think through and about what they have taken as given and to think that which they have failed to think. The important problem is not the collecting and posing of ideas already seen, but the laying out of what, in these attempts, was not seen.[7]

The 'critical' remarks made in this work should be seen in this context. The arguments do not seek to show what is 'wrong' with contemporary branches of geography, or to take a stand for or against particular approaches to them. The main concern of this work is to articulate what has remained unsaid in what has been said, and to do this from the point of view of the question of how and in what ways *human* science is possible, and how such a science might take the spatiality characteristic of man as its object of concern. The remarks made regarding particular approaches and branches or sub-fields of the discipline do not seek to criticize the positions developed, but, through critical reflections, to determine whether and in what ways their aims have or have not been achieved.

5 The disciplinary context

Methodological debates in geography have seldom enthralled me because, with few exceptions, they persist outside the context of philosophical currents of thought and in ignorance of the personal biases of the contestants. The high level of the debate is largely shadow play. In childhood, one boy is good at sums, another likes to write letters home. As professional geographers, these differences in talent and temperament are elevated to the Olympian level of methodological controversy. (Tuan, 1974, 55)

Phenomenology . . . offers ambiguity rather than clarity of several fundamental issues. (Buttimer, 1976, 291)

How is the phenomenologist to develop an ontologically and epistemologically sound foundation for a science of geographical phenomena within the horizon of a tradition where the meaning of phenomenology has been pre-judged, and its essential characteristics assumed beforehand? In particular, how is discourse to begin where all is not what it seems? Not only do we have a pre-established horizon of meaning within the discipline, but those discussing phenomenology have themselves denied beforehand the importance of a careful laying out of the actual claims of the position. Argument has sought to emphasize the 'spirit' of the enterprise (Buttimer, 1977, 181) in the context of substantive applications (Tuan, 1977a, 180), rather than emphasize the ontological coherence and unity of each position, many of whose detailed requirements are relaxed in the substantive work offered to us (Relph, 1973, 234). Underlying this situation are two important features.

First, empirical science is distrusted or rejected because the claims of positivism and the properties of positive science are confused. Second, the intimate relationship between phenomenology and science has not been understood. As a result Husserl's entire project has been treated only in caricature form and thus to the empiricist seems to make no sense: the phenomenological method seems to be unfounded in any purposeful aim; philosophy, phenomenological science and empirical science cannot be clearly understood in their necessary inter-connections or distinguished in their essential differences; lifeworld is unrelated to the project for which it was the culmination and ultimate, if problematical, ground. Consequently the theoretical development of this perspective has from the very beginning been restricted to a criticism of scientism, positivism, or naturalistic empiricism (for example, Entrikin, 1976); no scientific alternative to reductionistic science has been sought (Gregory, 1978a; 1978b). Only by emphasizing the humanities and by understanding lifeworld in a naive fashion can any formal inquiry continue as such.

The consequences of misunderstanding Husserlian phenomen-ology, and thus of the misinterpretation of subsequent phenom-enologies, such as those of Heidegger, Merleau-Ponty and Schütz, have been severe. For example, such misunderstanding results in the virtually complete rejection of Husserlian phenomenology in Ley's evaluation of epistemological options for social geography (Ley, 1978, 44). Here, despite the actually rather tenuous links of 'phenomen-ology' in humanistic geography with the Husserlian project, Ley argues that humanists have:

inappropriately overassociated phenomenology with Husserl's transcendental idealism, not recognizing that contemporary phenomenologists in the social sciences draw their inspiration not from Husserl but rather from philosophers with an eye to social science such as Schütz and Merleau-Ponty, who were not prepared to sacrifice existence for essence, for whom perceptions were always considered in context, in the concrete world of everyday life. (Ley, 1978, 44)

In this way Husserl's gradual move towards a position of transcendental idealism in order fully to ground his earlier, more realistic phenomenology is taken to be the necessary reason for the rejection of his particular and founding approach to phenomenology. Yet this rejection ignores the very great importance of Husserl's early phenomenology on subsequent phenomenological perspectives, including that of Schütz. In these earlier works, especially in *Ideas*, Husserl lays out the fundamental structure of phenomenology as method, and its relationship to the sciences and empirical sciences. In *Phenomenological psychology* he tries to show how mundane phenomenology is to be seen as different from his developing transcendental philosophy with which he sought to ground it. We, like Heidegger, may choose to reject this move to transcendental phenomenology as leading to emphasis on a transcendental subject who, in the final analysis, is wordless. But also like Heidegger we cannot reject Husserl's descriptive phenomenology underpinning every empirical science of relations. If we seek to question the accuracy of his account of the nature of science we must at least answer his claims for phenomenology as method with a thorough-going critique of phenomenology, rather than with its superficial and unexamined dismissal. This has not been attempted by geographers, and yet it is crucial to an understanding of descriptive, eidetic phenomenology.

However, my concern here is not to prefigure Chapters 3 to 6, but to hint sufficiently at the position towards which this argument is working, such that partial claims made in this introduction can be clarified initially in terms of the geographic literature from which they arise and which they will reflect back upon to inform the practice of geographic inquiry. Thus in what follows I shall seek *first* to lay out how geographers have conceived of phenomenology as well as to clarify the a priori categories through which they have interpreted it. In other words, I am interested here in what has been said of phenomenology and how what has been said itself points to something more fundamental (Chapter 3). *Second*, I shall move to investigate how 'geographical phenomenology' has been broadly accepted and how a critique of it has taken shape. This too will direct us towards important taken-for-granted principles and judgements which are to be made explicit *and* problematic (Chapter 4). *Third*, I shall retrieve the phenomenological project from 'geographical phenomenology', showing how it is fundamentally linked to science, and is tied necessarily to empirical science. This will entail a retrieval of Husserlian and Heideggerian conceptions of phenomenology, and will provide a foundation for science and allow phenomenology to be seen as a *method* of a particular kind (Chapters 5 and 6).

In spite of the breadth of these claims, however, we must agree with Paul Ricoeur that "[there] can be no question of viewing the whole of Husserlian phenomenology within this limited space" (1967, 13). Indeed, for the geographer interested in questions of science and its grounding, such a purview is here unnecessary and is, in any case, impossible given Husserl's explicit and constantly repeated claim that phenomenology is an on-going research programme with different forms and paths to be taken depending upon the circumstances and the phenomena under consideration.[8] Because Husserlian phenomenology is motivated throughout by the necessity to overcome modern irrationalism and scepticism, the project seeks, in principle, to be a complete one and is not easily severed into distinct parts. As phenomenological, Husserl's works must be taken as a whole, paraphrase is difficult, and summaries must themselves be phenomenological – not a simple task for an expository treatise. In Husserl's own terms, severing the carefully constructed arguments with which he formulates the pathways through the project requires phenomenological justification. Without it we fall into the irrationality of relativism and scepticism.

In the present context we shall, in fact, now follow Husserl into transcendental phenomenology, where he seeks to provide a fully apodictic grounding for philosophy. We shall remain within the mundane realm of descriptive, eidetic phenomenology, where Husserl seeks to ground the sciences of formal and material regions in their formal and eidetic ontologies. Questions of the viability of the project of transcendental phenomenology, whether or not this implies a transcendental idealism, and whether, as a consequence, it nullifies Husserl's claims for descriptive phenomenology are complex, and are not easily resolved. There is a good deal of philosophical discussion concerning these matters, and they require something more than the eclectic borrowing and relativism of philosophical views that the human sciences have generally brought to the argument. For the purposes of this work the question will be bracketed as a philosophical, rather than a scientific concern. That the question regarding the independence of phenomenological grounding of science from the grounding of philosophy has indeed been answered in a positive manner will be obvious from the arguments developed here. That is, whether or not Husserlian transcendental phenomenology ultimately fails (and if it does it will not be because of the rather naïve criticisms geographers have raised, which Husserl has usually answered beforehand), descriptive, eidetic phenomenology remains important for the self-reflexive component of science, including empirical science. And, if it does fail, this ontology can still be founded in a transcendental phenomenology which is not idealistic, as shown in different ways by Scheler, Heidegger, and Merleau-Ponty.

It is precisely on the question of transcendental phenomenology and the move to transcendental idealism that Husserl and Heidegger disagree. It will be necessary at some point, therefore, to suggest how Heidegger seeks to make this move away from Husserl, to show how he retrieves descriptive phenomenology, and to clarify how this is important for the sciences. All this is preparatory for an ontology of human spatiality.

PART I

Geography and traditional meta-physics

Whatever and however we may try to think, we think within the sphere of tradition. Tradition prevails when it frees us from thinking back to a thinking forward, which is no longer a planning.

Only when we turn thoughtfully toward what has already been thought, will we be turned to use for what must still be thought. (Heidegger, 1969a, 41)

2

Geographical discourse and its central themes

6 Basic concepts of science and the method appropriate to ontology

In every scientific discipline and in every theoretical perspective certain basic concepts determine the way in which we get an initial understanding of the subject-matter which underlies all the objects a science takes as its theme. All positive investigation is guided by this understanding, yet it is generally taken for granted. Only on the basis of such concepts and such perspectives do facts have the meaning they do, and, in the ideal case, do geographers, sociologists, anthropologists, and other scientists, constitute the various disciplines. Only by clarifying these basic concepts and making them transparent do the sciences become genuinely grounded. "But since every such area is itself obtained from the domain of entities themselves, this preliminary research, from which the basic concepts are drawn, signifies nothing else than an interpretation of those entities with regard to their basic state of Being" (Heidegger, 1927, 10).

Geographers have been aware of these fundamental concepts, and occasionally have attempted to make them explicit.[1] More recently there have been some attempts to provide a theoretical basis for questioning such taken-for-granted concepts and perspectives, thereby making them problematical.[2] The manner of such reflections has, however, generally been expository, and only sometimes *critical* (Gregory, 1978a). Until recently criticism has generally not been philosophical as such, but has remained within the realm of the sciences themselves, where texts are taken at face value and arguments constructed from textual, rather than ontological, analyses. This is most clearly seen in Hartshorne (1939; 1959), Fischer, *et al.* (1969), Johnston (1979), and James and Martin (1981), where the explicit aim is to present accurately what geographers have claimed, taking those claims at face value.[3]

In suggesting that the empirical sciences fail to clarify, ontologically and adequately, the ways in which they themselves interpret entities in the world, we do not thereby criticize the empirical sciences.

We must always bear in mind, however, that these ontological foundations can never be disclosed by subsequent hypotheses derived from empirical material but that they are always 'there' already, even when that empirical material simply gets *collected*. If positive research fails to see these foundations and holds them to be self-evident, this by no means proves that they are not basic or that they are not problematic in a more radical sense than any thesis of positive science can ever be. (Heidegger, 1927, 50)

In direct contrast to this view the geographic tradition has generally accepted Hartshorne's (1939; 1959) arguments regarding the logic of methodology. In this view methodology adds nothing to our knowledge of reality, but only to our understanding of such knowledge. The determination of the nature, scope, and purpose of geography is primarily a problem in empirical research. Methodological reflection is, therefore, to be achieved through reliable description of geography as seen through the eyes of geographers of the past as well as of the present. The aim of methodology is not to defend a position once taken, nor to project a new orientation, but rather to clarify our mutual understanding of what we have inherited through careful and literal textual exegesis (Hartshorne, 1959, 6–10).

Such a logic merely recovers the commonplaces and established discourse of the discipline. It does not clarify such discourse by problematizing the basic concepts and making transparent those which are usually taken for granted. Instead, such an approach seeks a *reconstructed* logic, which investigates the status of geography as it chances to find it, in order to discover its 'method'. Is it possible, however, that methodological research might run ahead of the positive sciences themselves, in such a way that a *productive* logic might disclose some area of concern for the first time and, in thus arriving at the structures within, make it available as a realm of inquiry for the positive sciences (Heidegger, 1927, 10)?[4]

It is this critical conception of logic (necessarily based upon some clear understanding of the heritage to which Hartshorne refers) that we seek here. We seek first, to clarify and open for question the basic concepts we use in geographic discourse and the a priori frameworks of meaning with which we operate, and second, to articulate such a productive logic on which human science can be adequately grounded, which is not at the same time an a priori logic of 'nature'.

We faced two initial problems. The first has been to suggest in what way traditional methodological debate within geography has been

inadequate. The second is to show how geographers have consequently and unreflectively adopted an ontology of physical nature as
the fundamental and underlying logic of geographical discourse and
inquiry. It is to the second of these that we now turn.

7 Objectivism and subjectivism

What, then, constitutes the basic concepts and the taken-for-granted
framework of meaning with which this work is primarily concerned? It
is nothing less than the tradition in geographical thinking itself, with a
mode of inquiry which has predicated itself on and has developed from
a particular world-view or metaphysical interpretation of man and
world. This we can call the Cartesian or Newtonian world-view, and
presupposes what Heidegger has called a pro-posing, positing form of
thinking and interpreting the world, "which *secures* beings as objects
over against itself and *for itself*" (Welte, 1982, 92).[5] Western
metaphysics has increasingly become such a pro-posing, positing
thinking of objects, where along with the objectivity of the objects the
subjectivity of the subjects is developed. The subjectivity so implanted
grows throughout Western thinking, culminating in Nietzsche's Will-
to-Power, and differently in modern science and the technological
domination of the world that follows from it, epitomized by the
nuclear age (see Heidegger, 1977a). If we can accept with Heidegger
that in different ages man and world are appropriated differently, then
the manner in which man and world are appropriated one to the other
in *this* age constitutes the most fundamental level at which the taken-
for-grantedness of the world operates. It is this fundament alone which
allows us to clarify fully the nature of man and world, and to delimit
the manner in which science can operate as a valid and true domain of
discourse within limits.

There is one element common to all true phenomenologies since
Husserl and that is their rejection of the traditional metaphysical
assumption of the separation of subject and object as the description of
the fundamental state of affairs. We exist primordially not as subjects
manipulating objects in the external, 'real', physical world, but as
beings in, alongside, and toward the world. Within that world we can,
of course, discover intramundane beings or entities, and through a
formal process of abstraction we can establish a world of subjects and
objects for purely theoretical reflection. But generally and primarily we
exist – that is, *ek-sist*, or stand out – toward a world.[6]

If, as I have claimed, the greater part of this work is to deal with phenomenology, and by implication with that process of *ek-sistence*, and if this has yet to be achieved in geographical inquiry, then I must show, (a) how geography presumes the categories of traditional metaphysics, remaining ensconced in an ontology of physical nature where the world is only and always a world of subjects and objects, and (b) how the rejection of this state of affairs has resulted in a by-passing of phenomenology itself in favour of a world of subjects. This is the aim of this and the following two chapters.

Furthermore, it is necessary to show how the epistemological dilemma to which this situation has led cannot be transcended from within. Nothing less than an overcoming of the subject–object dichotomy of Western thinking will allow us to move beyond the relativism and dogmatism of contemporary geographical science, *and only in this way* will we be able to retrieve the scientific project – as the appropriate domain for a pro-posing, positing or objectifying activity – in a rational and coherent manner for the human sciences. Only in this way can we fully appreciate the *nature* and the *limits* of the project of positive science.[7] Only in this way can a coherent and meaningful research programme concerned with human spatiality and worldhood be developed. To demonstrate how and why this is the case is the aim of the rest of the work.

8 Positivism and naturalism

No discussion in the philosophy of human science in the second part of the twentieth century can ignore the vast influence of positivism and its more narrowly defined variants, naturalism, scientific realism, and logical empiricism. Yet the reader of such philosophies might be excused for wondering whether further discussion of positivism was necessary; whether the spectre of positivism had not already and finally been exorcised in the myriad works dealing with it; whether scientists had not long since moved to post-positivist modes of thinking, adapting and sifting from several traditions, synthesizing an epistemologically more tenable self-understanding. And, of course, to some extent this is true. Modern social science has become increasingly aware of its own assumptions, and works proliferate to provide 'post-positivist' modes of explanation. Indeed, by 1972 Mercer and Powell (1972, 48) could claim that non-positivist movements in the social sciences "have paid their way handsomely, and are unquestionably well-founded on coherent and highly reputable philosophical premises . . ." In geographic thought the past two decades have indeed turned accepted premises and practice topsy-turvy, and have produced a heady, and at the same time a somewhat tragic, sense of uncertainty in contemporary attempts to provide firm epistemic grounding to the research enterprise (Cox and Golledge, 1981; Couclelis, 1982).[8]

In what sense, then, does a work concerned with the geographic enterprise need to begin, once again, with the question of positivism? Two reasons can be given: one somewhat superficial, the other rather more profound. In the first case, the spectre of positivism has *not* been exorcised. While repeated attempts to bury it have had some success, neo-positivists have continued to argue for reconstituted positivist positions, which seek (in the final analysis) merely to sideline the more critical of those arguments levelled against it (see Golledge, 1973; Hay, 1979; Couclelis, 1982; and Johnston, 1982). Beyond this, positivism has become in its varied forms *the* accepted method and philosophy of scientific inquiry. This is even embedded within the language of the social sciences, where positivism is the scientific method, adherence to empirical truth, and logical consistency (Walmsley, 1974, 97; Bird, 1977, 108).

The second reason to question positivism is one which Habermas (1971) explicitly recognizes when he refers to the need to enter into historical reflection on the social sciences if one is to come to terms with positivism.

8a The a-historical nature of positivism

Under the influence of positivism the modern human sciences have consciously cut themselves off from their historical tradition, in particular from their immediate roots in the nineteenth century, or they have appropriated that tradition *in terms of* the established concepts of the present.[9] In the 1930s and 1940s especially, the disappearance of this entire dimension of awareness was precisely the sign of membership in an advanced guard that had finally freed itself from a pre-, pseudo-, or non-scientific past, in which many contemporaries in other disciplines were still held captive (Lenzer, 1975, xviii).

For Habermas (1971), positivism marks the end of the theory of knowledge, its place being taken by the philosophy of science. Positivism cuts off the transcendental inquiry into the meaning of knowledge as such, which it sees as meaningless in view of the achievements of modern science, in terms of which knowledge is now implicitly defined. Positivism still expresses a philosophical position with regard to science, since the scientistic self-understanding of the sciences does not coincide with science. As a result, "[positivism] is philosophy only insofar as is necessary for the immunization of the sciences against philosophy" (Habermas, 1971, 67). Consequently, the critique of positivism must be explicitly tied to the renewal of this lost process of reflection. This has to be historical since positivism's elimination of the historical dimension was itself the process by which it abandoned reflection:

I am undertaking a historically oriented attempt to reconstruct the history of modern positivism with the systematic intention of analyzing the connections between knowledge and human interests. In following the process of the dissolution of epistemology, which has left the philosophy of science in its place, one makes one's way over abandoned stages of reflection. Retreading this path from a perspective that looks back toward the point of departure may help to recover the forgotten experience of reflection. That we disavow reflection is positivism. (Habermas, 1971, preface)

Eugene Gendlin, in his accompanying 'Analysis' to Martin Heidegger's *What is a thing?*, refers to the problem of overcoming the dominance of axiomatic science and the thing-model in Western thinking:

There is a current tendency among some groups to denigrate scientific conceptual methods without actually grasping their nature, and to reject pseudo-explanatory models altogether. In line with this tendency we might wish to reject the thing-model in favor of a reaffirmation of life and human creativity. But if we do only that we will fail to move beyond the thing-model, because *without examining it fully, we will not notice how it pervades the way we think, meet, and deal with almost any thing.* Thus, we might reject the mechanistic thing-like ways of thought where we do see them clearly, and yet we will operate with them and with nothing else in all we do and see. (Gendlin, 1967, 262–3)

In this mode of calculative thinking we tend to see poems and myths as things, using them only as tools or data, forgetting their poetic and essentially non-thing-like nature. We fail to grasp the essential characteristics of plants and animals because we approach them as 'living things' – as a thing or body with mysterious added-on traits of life. Works of art are considered as things with aesthetic traits somehow added on, in the extreme interpretation, by the viewer himself.[10] Similarly we often view personality, and even ourselves, as 'personality structures', or as a 'self' (as if it were a thing inside) having personality contents or traits, as if a subject were a structure with parts, a container with things inside, or a subject bearing traits. This way of thinking leads to a great many separations: subjects and objects; inside and outside; feelings and situations; individuals and interpersonal

relationships; individual and community; the time moment now and a
time moment later; symbol and knower; body and mind; and so on.
These divisions are not separate issues since each involves the same
type of conceptualization of things, each separately located; a unit
thing existing here and now in a certain unit of space and at a moment,
i.e., unit bit of time (Gendlin, 1967, 262–3). Only by studying this
thing-model in depth – that is, by re-awakening the questions to which
it is the answer – can we really get beyond it, and can we really
understand its limits and its possibilities:

we cannot simply accept our present approach unexamined, neither can we
simply reject it – for in doing so we would still be using it constantly,
implicitly, in spite of ourselves. We must examine this approach as we have it,
realizing that it has developed as a series of answers to a series of questions
asked long ago, settled long ago, and now no longer asked. Our now
unquestioned, implicit approach was once a new answer to a question that
was then open. If we find our way back to those questions we will see them,
not only as live questions and as they were answered at that time, but we will
be, thereby, in a position to answer them differently. Regaining these
questions as live and open is the only way to get behind our unexamined
assumptions, to see how they are now our basis, and to change them.
Heidegger calls this 're-opening' a question, or taking a question that is now
'quiescent' and 'setting it into motion' again. (252)

8b The Enlightenment and positivism

The emergence of a science of behaviour as foundational for the
development of empirical human science is generally linked with the
changing ideas we call the Enlightenment. These changes removed
from science the Cartesian restriction to the study of natural
phenomena and sought to explicate the possibility of a science of
human behaviour. For human nature and society to be encompassed
within the realm of science presumed a radical revision of attitudes
towards the passions and the rational. Thus, the realm of the
individual and the social came to be seen as rationally explicable; the
realm of the empirical to constitute a, if not the, major source of
knowledge. Science was broadened to include human nature, declaring
that it too was amenable to methodical investigation (Rossides, 1978,
49–51; see also, Copleston, 1964, 15).[11]

Science, then, can rationally understand and control phenomena –
eventually even people themselves. Metaphysics and theology were
brought under the control of reason, and institutions appealing for
justification to metaphysics or theology were reformed or replaced.[12]

Science was to provide the standard for this critique. It embodied three presuppositions: (1) eighteenth-century natural law was applicable to the human sciences, giving rise to natural science conceptions of human affairs; (2) law-like processes in human affairs were assumed; and (3) the interest in natural science conceptions of human affairs was in the service of the specific and concrete ideal of control and the re-making of human society or human nature.

This ideal entailed a changed conception of the relationship between fundamental conceptions and facts. According to Heidegger (1967, 67) the greatness of sixteenth- and seventeenth-century science was that scientists were also philosophers: "They understood that there are no mere facts, but that a fact is only what it is in the light of the fundamental conception and always depends upon how far that conception reaches." With positivism facts are thought to be sufficient. Concepts are necessary evils, but should be avoided if possible, to be left to philosophy. Discourse which cannot be reduced to factual argument and exemplification is unclear and suspiciously regarded. But it should be noted that even in the heyday of positivism

this attitude only prevails where average and subsequent work is done. Where genuine and discovering research is done, the situation is no different from that of three hundred years ago. The age also had its indolence, just as, conversely, the present leaders of atomic physics, Niels Bohr and Heisenberg, think in a thoroughly philosophical way, and only therefore create new ways of posing questions and, above all, hold out in the questionable. (67)

With the development of logical positivism, clarity and method became primary goals; the logical and the mathematical became the exemplary modes of expression. As a result philosophy was no longer seen as a body of wisdom, aimed at truth and the meaning of life, for this is the business of science. Instead the role of philosophy is to make propositions clear; as an analytical discipline it is to be the hand-maiden of science (Kaplan, 1968, 10).

Once the criteria and standards of what constitutes knowledge and progress in the natural sciences had been adopted by the social sciences, all preceding systems of thought and theories were automati-cally regarded as pre-scientific; belonging to the realm of social philosophy, metaphysics and unscientific speculation. They had been superseded by scientific methodologies, theories, and research meth-ods. The construction of laws, generated and testable through empirical observation and capable of prediction, was central. Such methods 'clearly' differentiated science from, for example, religion. It was less obvious that not only religion was being dismissed from the category of 'knowledge'. The deliberation procedures by which the positivist model itself was created also did not conform. Thus, A. J. Ayer's claim that statements were in principle verifiable or nonsense, which by its own definition must be nonsense, was illustrative of the general absence of reflection on positivism's own presuppositions. Indeed, positivism's own methodology entailed the impossibility of self-justification; its commitment to empirical confirmation negated the possibility of any confirmation of itself, and its claim of the fundamental irrationality of value commitments equally negated any personal defence of its own commitment to its methods of science (Nicholson, 1980, 22).

8c Naturalism and idealism

The attack on positivism which has developed and continued since its inception has focussed primarily upon approaches to social theory which seek to reduce the domain of human relations and meaning to physical and bio-physical explanation, to discuss human behaviour in terms of analogies drawn from natural science (Hughes, 1977, 37). Positivism was thus linked to other conceptions viewed with equal disfavour: materialism, naturalism, mechanism. Furthermore, while positivism embedded within it a naturalistic reductionism, opposition to positivism in idealistic terms raised further problems, notably of relativism.

Dilthey focussed upon these two perspectives in the historical sciences, seeing them as world-views deriving ultimately from thinking and the experience of life in general.[13] "Man is determined by nature" in the sense that he is subject to the forces of life in nature, by the outward world and the world of his body (Dilthey, 1957, 52).[14] Naturalism is thus a permanent concept, constantly tending to find explanations for the spiritual in the physical and so collapsing the two. Because the sciences of the spirit are based on experience acquired by living and understanding, this reduction makes them unattainable. Naturalism is thereby caught in a restless dialectic; it tries to derive a phenomenon which exists only in man's consciousness, from his physical nature. But the two are not the same. "The impossibility of comparing these two facts eventually leads to the positivistic correlation of the physical and the spiritual . . . However, this correlation must meet strong doubts, and finally, the ethic of original naturalism reveals its insufficiency for making the evolution of society comprehensible" (54).

On the other hand, there is idealism – "the idealism of freedom" – which presupposes the realm of the free responsible individual, bound by laws but inwardly free. This world-view is derived from the facts of consciousness; the conception of a formative intellect that forms matter into world, and the recognition that logical thinking is independent of nature. In this situation, knowledge of the world derives from categories of the mind, and if we wish to know reality and the world of man, these must be the focus of scientific concern.

Stepping outside of this polarity between naturalism and idealism, Dilthey argued that, by contrast, the human studies (or historical sciences) must concern themselves with the phenomenon of 'life' in all its richness, seeking to develop independent methods appropriate to their subject-matter. The great scientific thinkers do not transfer methods to different spheres of phenomena, rather they adjust their knowledge to the nature of the subject-matter: "We conquer nature by submitting to it" (89).[15]

Instead of accepting Dilthey's injunction, geographers have accepted the mid-nineteenth-century neo-Kantian call, "Also muss auf Kant zuruckgegangen werden!",[16] for a return to Kant, through which a philosophical foundation and justification for the positivistic conception of science might be found (see Heidegger, 1967, 59–60). It is, in large part, to this neo-Kantianism that geographers have turned, and it may be no coincidence that geography as a field of formal study in the universities appeared in Germany about this time.[17] The neo-Kantianism of Windelband and Rickert is of particular importance because of the influence of their distinction between the idiographic and the nomothetic and the influence they held over geographers such as Hettner.[18]

This dominance of positivism as a particular approach to science in the mid-nineteenth century was a dominance of 'fact' in issues regarding the truth. Facts cannot be argued over; they are the highest appeal in matters of truth and untruth. From this perspective "[what] is proved by experiments in the natural sciences and what is verified by manuscripts and documents in the historical–cultural sciences is true, and is the only scientific verifiable truth" (Heidegger, 1967, 59).

9 Kantian ontology of material nature

The success of the natural sciences was a result precisely of the adoption of an a priori framework and descriptive methods which allowed the domain of physical entities to be captured as physical. And thus, "the positive outcome of Kant's *Critique of Pure Reason* lies in what it has contributed towards working out what belongs to any Nature whatsoever . . . His transcendental logic is an *a priori* logic for the subject-matter of that area of Being called 'Nature'" (Heidegger, 1927, 10–11).

Fischer *et al.* (1969, 48–9) suggest that Kant's influence in geography "is seen in the thought and writings of the many prominent geographers of subsequent generations". Hartshorne (1939) clearly thought his influence to be of paramount importance, particularly as it affected Hettner. Two works give explicit treatment to Kantian and neo-Kantian thought (May, 1970 and Livingstone and Harrison, 1981 respectively), Kantian and neo-Kantian conceptions of space have been treated by Richards (1974) and Entrikin (1977), and the influence of such thought on other geographers and social theorists such as Dilthey (Rose, 1981), has been considered.

Livingstone and Harrison claim that "the recent reassertion within the discipline, during the 1970s, of a subjectivist, largely anti-positivist, orientation can be interpreted as an implicit acceptance and manifestation of the continuing influence of the spirit and purpose, if not the detailed substance, of Kant's critique" (1981, 359), indeed, that most of the philosophical sources of subjectivism in human geography are related to the transcendental critical philosophy of Kant (360).[19] But, with the exception of work by Hartshorne and Lukermann, the importance of a Kantian ontology of material nature, its relation to Newtonian concepts of space, and its influence on geography has not been explicitly discussed. Although geographical inquiry has been influenced to a large extent by Kantian geography,[20] despite this long association, few geographers have grasped the implications of applying a Kantian ontology devised for Newtonian physics to the human sciences.

10 Conceptions of physical space and geography

The unexamined adoption of the Kantian ontology of physical nature which occurred in this way, became, in the mid-nineteenth century, the domination of what Whitehead (1925) called "the intellectual 'spatialization' of things". In this tradition "[the] selection of the geometry of classical physics by geographers as the structure of the space associated with the occurrence of geographic events is not a controversial point" (Sack, 1973, 16). Geographic space, for Sack (16, n. 1), is to be retained for this three-dimensional Euclidean space. "To claim that geographic space should refer to several or all synthetic spaces is to make the term practically meaningless . . ." Multi-dimensional and non-Euclidean spaces are to be called non-geographic synthetic spaces. From this perspective Sack (1980a, 313–14) has argued that a general framework can be established within which the multiple meanings of space geographers use – action spaces, awareness spaces, personal spaces, physical, economic, political, and social spaces – can be based on "the grander and more enduring viewpoints that all people have the potential to possess". This general framework incorporates different modes of thought which "affix their own meanings to *geographic* or physical space or the space of the earth's surface". We know that the nature of this space has been decided by Sack (see, 1973). Its resolution in terms of a primordial physical space to which subjective meanings and subjective spaces accrue is fully developed in his *Conceptions of space in social thought: A geographic perspective* (1980b). For us, however, the spatiality characteristic of man's mode of being in the world remains a question, as does how this spatiality relates to the Euclidean or other geometries of world-space.

Sack's distinction between geographic and non-geographic spaces may be a practically useful one, and it may clarify the use of the term in question. It nonetheless presupposes the fundamental issue which gave rise to the formulation of multi-dimensional and non-Euclidean spaces for geographic inquiry in the first place. The distinction presupposes the fundamental nature of the geographic, taking it arbitrarily to refer to the physical space of science. The question, what is the fundamental nature of *geo-graphus* is not asked, instead its meaning is assumed in an implicit manner. Yet it is precisely this issue which the talk is about. If geography is the description of the earth taken as a physical body, then Sack is correct, and other uses of the term 'geographic space' are misleading. If, on the other hand, geography is the description of the earth taken as the home of man, and if description is to be phenomenologically rigorous, then, unless the phenomena of the earth as the home of man are found to be the same as the earth taken as a physical body, Sack's definition must be abandoned. As we will see, this is to be the case, if for no other reason than that the theoretical conception of earth as a physical body, to which Sack gives primacy, is ontologically derived and scientifically thematized from earth as home.

If positivism, based on an ontology of physical nature, provides the background for much thinking in contemporary geography, what kind of discipline, subject-matter, and methodological debates might we expect? In the first place we can expect to find a discipline seeking a stable foundation, to determine once and for all its basic orientation, its fundamental approach, method and content area. On this foundation theory and laws can be constructed. Secondly, we would expect this foundation to be closely related to an ontology of physical nature. Thus, it might conceive of itself in terms of a Cartesian or Newtonian world-view. Thirdly, we might expect to find attempts to subordinate all other and different conceptions of subject-matter, approach and method to its own. If the basic concepts of this world-view were taken to be space and spatial relations, then we might expect a particular form of 'space' to be taken for granted – that is, a Newtonian space, structured primarily according to Euclidean principles. That space would be physical, eternal, and independent, and 'in it' even the human world would operate and be investigated and described according to the principles of mechanics.

We should, of course, expect a social physics to develop along with a complete and pervasive spatial analytic, predicated on the same Newtonian foundation. Such thinking would take human spatiality to be the same as, or a modification (or distortion) of, the spatiality appropriate to the physical world. We should not be surprised, then, to find epistemological problems arising within geographic discourse when geographers seek to humanize the physical conceptions of space with which they operate.

If any commonalities can be discerned throughout the changing emphasis in twentieth-century geography they include: (1) an emphatic concern with material nature, (2) an increasing emphasis on space as the focus of geographic concern and the arena of material nature, and (3) a constantly renewed attempt to create a sound and respectable science of geography. These three themes – material nature, space, and science – go hand in hand. The development of a scientific geography entailed the formalization of space in a particular way because both were predicated on a physical conception of the world. The geographic literature suggests that these concerns are of recent interest, dating from the work of Schaefer and the subsequent work of Bunge, Harvey, and others. But this is to confuse what science is with analytical perspectives on it, such as positivism and logical empiricism. Schaefer and Harvey introduce geographical science from a logical empiricist perspective, Schaefer being influenced directly by the Vienna School through Bergmann.[21] But before them Davis, Semple, Barrows, Ackerman and Hartshorne, among others, had each sought to found a scientific geography upon different fundamental conceptions.[22]

The process was gradual. Davis, Barrows, and their contemporaries, gradually developed basic ideas and orientations from which the 'spatial school' of logical empiricism would develop in the 1950s. It is only recently that the influence of this tradition on the thinking of spatial analysis has been retrieved from the reconstructed histories of the period (see, for example, Guelke, 1977). But this is not the same as arguing that the concepts of spatial analysis were already implicit in previous frameworks, and that spatial analysis simply formalized such themes. These frameworks articulated some of the necessary conditions for the possibility of such an analytic; they did not already contain it, nor did they implicitly presuppose it.

10a *The emergence of geography as an abstract, theoretical science*

The development of a formal 'scientific' perspective in geography along the lines prescribed by logical empiricism occurred ostensibly in 1953 when Schaefer responded to Hartshorne's claims in *The nature of geography* (1939). However, Guelke (1977) has shown how Hartshorne's own work had already delimited the realm of the geographical to areal differentiation, a definition that "obscured important choices open to geographers". Thus, by 1945, in developing a monistic conception of geography through the 'logical' interdependence of regional and systematic approaches to the discipline, Ackerman (1945) could claim that: (1) geography is areal differentiation,[23] (2) distribution and correlations between distributions are fundamental, and (3) significant correlations include those between features in space. In this view, space remained unproblematical, regardless of the character of the 'features' with which one is concerned. Here "[space] is the basic organizing concept of the geographer" (Whittlesey, 1957, 28), and everything else about a region but its spatial relationships could be ignored (Schaefer, 1953, 228; see Gale, 1977, 267).

With the general acceptance of the spatial viewpoint which followed, and its self-conception as a geometry of space, a radical change occurred in the subject-matter of the discipline. The formerly close relationship between spatial geographies and geographies concerned with place and the horizonal nature of the region was severed. When the implicit spatial dimension and the geometry of space it sought to articulate were made explicit, the two were seen as different enterprises: one scientific, the other descriptive and hence 'non-scientific'. The concern for place in the tradition that Broek and Sauer, for example, represented,[24] was either incorporated into a Newtonian framework as location, devoid of properties other than those stipulated, or it was relegated to the descriptive, historical, and hence unscientific (a position that, surprisingly, many of its practitioners accepted without argument). In this sense, place was less amenable to a general treatment than a formal conception of space. Instead spatial interaction, focussing on "circulation and the connections between areas rather than on the nature of areas themselves", was to be *the* concern of geography (Ullman, 1954, 283).

The concern for idiographic inquiry and the difficulties for a science of the so-called 'unique' had been raised by Hartshorne, and had remained a common focus of argument within the discipline. Places as empirical entities (no other possibility was raised) were seen to be unique and therefore not readily amenable to a true science (Schaefer, 1953). Traditional emphases on landscape and man–land relationships were subjugated to a spatial perspective. The geographer was offered only a narrow choice: space, a nomothetic approach and science, *or* place and landscape, concerned with the unique and mere description.[25] The choice was between describing the unique or seeking general, i.e. scientific, laws (Guelke, 1977, 383).

If science was to be chosen then precision was important (for example, Burton, 1965); if a precise science was to be constructed, it needed a stronger philosophical basis (for example, Harvey, 1969b). Such a science needed to articulate its basic concepts, a requirement achieved by work such as that by Ullman (1954) and Nystuen (1968), who sought to clarify and define the basic concepts peculiar to the distinctively spatial point of view: situation, circulation, connections, complementarity and distance (Ullman, 1954); direction, orientation, distance, connection and relative position (Nystuen, 1968). Problems were to be articulated within a theoretical context of dimensional tensions and relations between point, line and area activities.[26] Underlying all of this was a fundamental conception of geography as an abstract, theoretical science of space and spatial relationships. Kohn (1970, 212), in reviewing the 1960s as a decade of progress in geographical research and instruction, noted that "[the] emergence of geography as a more abstract, theoretical science appears to have been the most over-riding development in geographical research during the 1960's". This science deals with five crucial problems: it studies distributions, seeks to perfect technique, studies the process of distribution and the covariation reflected in spatial relations, and seeks to show the full evolutionary pattern of earth–space relations (Ackerman, 1958, 28ff).

The excitement which accompanied the development of geography as a theoretical-deductive science during the 1950s and 1960s, where parallels with Kuhn's 'revolutionary science' were made (see, Berry and Marble, 1968; Kohn, 1970, 212, n. 5), was accompanied by a "great increase . . . in articles dealing abstractly with the spatial structure and

relations of natural and cultural phenomena and with the analysis of
the spatial aspects of human behaviour" (Kohn, 1970, 212). Following
major works, such as those by Hägerstrand (1953), Bunge (1962), and
Haggett (1965), attempts were made to institutionalize this conception
of the geographic and to re-write the historical concerns of the
discipline. In 1970 Taaffe sought to review the discipline in order to
"present a view of the field of geography in the U.S. in the late
1960's".[27] In practice this report reduced all other perspectives to
spatial organization, making them *partial components* of it. The
traditional view of geography as giving an orderly description of man's
world becomes the study of spatial organization expressed as patterns
and processes. Its antecedents – the ecological studies of man–
environment interrelations, studies of cultural landscapes, and
locational studies emphasizing the geometries of movement, size,
shape and distance – "[all] these are represented in the theme of spatial
organization, expressed as both pattern and process. Geographic study
of the spatial organization of any area necessarily considers man-
environment relationships and cultural landscapes" (Taaffe, 1970, 6).
Man–environment relations and the areal perspective can both be seen
within the perspective of the spatial framework. The questions of
geography are questions about location and geometry (Sack, 1972, 78).
Not only is the spatial perspective a development *from* the old
positions, but in their earlier

emphasis on maps and relations between mapped phenomena whether
physical, social, economic, or political, *they* [geographers] *were implicitly
using spatial expression* as a selection criterion. Most geographers were not
really trying to synthesize everything in an area, nor were they trying to
synthesize all phenomena of significance to man; they were only trying to
synthesize those phenomena of significance to man which had significant
spatial expression. (Taaffe, 1974, 7)

But, if the "core of geographic questions is the geometric properties
of geographic distributions" (Sack, 1972, 78) and the concern with
geometric connections of facts is the "*sine qua non* of geographic
discourse" (Sack, 1974a, 449), then it is a geometry of the human world
that is sought, through the empirical application of the spatial
perspective.

Two problems must inevitably arise. On the one hand, there is no
theoretical guideline to distinguish between the ontographic, ecological, and chorological conceptions of geographic inquiry *and* a more
radical social physics (see Sack, 1972; 1973; 1974a). If spatial
organization and interaction, conceived geometrically, are fundamental, and if the ontology of material nature and Newtonian space on

which they are predicated is unquestioned, then modelling such spaces is an exercise in social physics (a fact that Curry has consistently argued). On the other hand, if this implication is rejected it becomes necessary to incorporate elements of human behaviour and under-standing – perception, cognition, preference – in the process of modelling spatial behaviour. But, where this also takes place without re-thinking the initial claims about space and interaction, epistemo-logical problems inevitably arise.

10b Social physics

Given the foregoing, it is not surprising that social physics was readily accepted within the discipline. Its adoption began with the assumption that:

the dimensions of society are analogous to the physical dimensions and include numbers of people, distance and time. Social physics deals with observations, processes and relations in these terms. The distinction between it and mathematical statistics is no more difficult to draw than for certain other phases of physics. The distinction between social physics and sociology is the avoidance of subjective descriptions in the former. (Stewart, 1956, 245)

Furthermore, it assumes that any science seeks to reduce the dominant principles with which it operates to the smallest number (Warntz, 1957, 2), instead of describing a phenomenon with whatever principles are appropriate to it. In this framework

emphasis is upon population potentials, product supply potentials, demo-graphic energy, time accessibility and the like. In many cases all that has been necessary is to substitute such quantities as 'number of people', 'size of income', or 'quantity produced' for mass in the equations of mechanics with time and distance retained as 'social dimensions' in the explanation of various regularities amongst social and economic phenomena. This augurs well for the development of a truly macro-economic geography based on field quantity theory. (2–3)[28]

By 1968 Berry and Marble took for granted the value of social physics, combined with computer technology, for revitalizing location theory and the spatial tradition. Indeed, had there not been a long history of attempts to describe human phenomena in terms of physical laws, especially within a Newtonian or Darwinian framework?

In geographic studies this attempt is represented by the use of gravity models to describe spatial interaction and the generalization of gravity concepts in potential models, designed as general summaries of the interdependencies existing simultaneously among all places in large areas. Such models have been argued by their proponents to correlate highly with the spatial distributions of a wide variety of social and economic phenomena in economically advanced countries. (Berry and Marble, 1968, 3)

Central to the resultant models was the assumption that interactions or movements between places are proportional to the product of the masses of those places and inversely proportional to some exponent of the distance separating them. Interest in social physics was strong (3), and remains so.

Recently Allen and Sanglier (1981a; 1981b) – two physicists – have explicitly returned to the theme of social physics, and have developed dynamic models of central place systems derived by analogy from the evolutionary 'dissipative structures' in the physical sciences (Allen and Sanglier, 1981b, 167). Here the focus is on the interdependencies of the self-organization of a central place system. The evolution of the system is deterministically modelled, but caters for the indeterminacy of instability when structural changes occur. "These considerations . . . introduce the concepts of 'memory' or 'history' into the 'explanation' of the state of a system, as well as an 'uncertainty' or 'choice' as to its future evolution" (167). The physical domain of entities is personalized and given a social character. The outcome is a purely physical model dealing with physical entities, on the basis of which claims about the collective nature of individual actions and the difficulties of living in an interdependent society are to be made.

Gale's (1977, 267) doubt as to whether 'geography as geometry' has any more substantive weight today than, say, 'geography as mapping' is only justifiable superficially, as he realizes himself. Both remain significant themes within geographic discourse, and in large measure "recent developments in the theory of human geography can be viewed as the interplay between those concepts rooted in social physics and those construed in terms of social engineering" (269).

Social physics treats people and their actions as analogous to physical particle flow; independent entities governed by laws with the same epistemological status as physical laws. Social engineering is goal oriented, where goals provide the structure for actions, behaviour, and their evaluation, and where the aim is to identify effective instrumental strategies (see Olsson, 1972; 1975). On these twin pillars rests the analytic of contemporary spatial geographies.

11 Physical space, cognitive behaviouralism and the turn to subjectivity

The spatial analytic that has developed in geography and regional science presupposes the primacy of theoretical reflection as a mode of being-in-the-world, and this in turn leads it to accept the primacy of space and spatial projections of the world and the corresponding projection of entities in space(s). In this way the spatial analytic has attained its present level of mathematical sophistication.

Cognitive behaviouralism is historically allied closely with this 'region' of concern, and presupposes its implicit regional ontology (see Cox and Golledge, 1981, xxvi, n. 2). For Harvey (1969a), geography is concerned with spatial distribution and location theory. However, its mechanistic models have proved somewhat unsatisfactory. Since "locational patterns in human geography are the physical expression of individual human actions, locational analysis must therefore incorporate some notions regarding human decision making" (35). Such notions can either be in the form of idealizations of rational economic man giving rise to normative location models (Weber, von Thunen, Lösch), the incorporation of empirical evidence in the form of stochastic probability distributions (Wilson, Curry), or the incorporation of the cognitive processes involved in the act of decision. In this way the parameters of a spatial analytic are to be broadened to incorporate psychological variables, conceived in a similarly 'mechanistic' manner:

We know that decisions are affected by attitudes, dispositions, preferences, and the like. We know, too, that mutual processes may mediate the flow of information from the environment in such a way that one individual perceives a situation differently from another even though the external stimuli are exactly the same. Each individual may be thought of as making decisions with respect to his attitudes and in the context of his perceptions. We also know that an individual's attitudes and dispositions may be affected, often cumulatively over time, by the constant bombardment of stimuli from the environment around him and by cultural conditioning. (Harvey, 1969a, 36)

Golledge (1979, 109) illustrates the fundamental position of such an ontology most clearly.[29] He claims that 'sets of primitives' were necessary for the development of inquiry into spatial form and process. The world is composed of more-or-less permanent objects and is external to individuals. This is the 'objective' or 'external' reality – "at once *substantial, relatively stable*, and *composed of many discrete things*" which obeyed sets of natural laws" (109) – existing in time and space, and independent of mind. This Newtonian world could then yield its 'definitive structures' and their spatial form could be discovered. On this Newtonian stage human actions passed as "but fleeting events in the on-going flux of existence" (110), and their only substance and stability was one imposed insofar as they were assumed to be *repetitive* and *relatively invariant* events. Explanation was achieved through correspondence of aggregate patterns of relations between actions and the definitive structures of either human or natural environments.

It was also necessary to assume that each individual places himself and others in a common external environment; one which exists and will continue to exist independent of its human inhabitants or their awareness of it. This entails that "each being requires a means for constructing a system of relations among objects in external reality", and must be able to construct some spatio-temporal network to incorporate them: "*Internalized reflections of the external flux must also have some structure and some commonalities*" (110).

The presumption of the interior and exterior worlds in the theoretical attitude is clearly evident in the work of cognitive mapping. Theory in this area deals with four sets of variables: "the spatial environment itself, the information or stimulus set, the intervening cognitive processes, and the group and individual differences in the operation of these processes" (Downs and Stea, 1973, 7). The machine and computer analogy are common: "Cognitive mapping is a process composed of a series of psychological transformations by which an individual acquires, codes, stores, recalls, and decodes information about the relative locations and attributes of phenomena in his everyday spatial environment" (9). These transformations themselves have spatial attributes where the sender and receiver of information can be identified as to their location and the efficacy of the behavioural mechanism related to relative location (Golledge, 1981, xvi).

The central theme is the intervention of cognitive processes between man and his environment, which allow him to give meaning to what he sees: "to add distinctions and relations to the physical or objective properties of environments" (Golledge, 1973, 62). Research indicates that what exists in the 'objective' environment, and what people conceive the environment to be, differ (62). Spatial structure and behavioural patterns could not be understood without some knowledge of "the perception of spatial reality retained in the human mind" (Cox and Golledge, 1981, xvi). Such spatial information is 'stored mentally'.

Problems peculiar to the researcher attempting to search for theory in geography arise from the fact that he must be interested not only in the external physical environment and the internalizing of human actions, but also with the interface between the two. This raises the entire problem of how to represent cognitive and physical worlds, and how to use behavioural processes to explain overt activity in the physical world. (Golledge, 1973, 64)

In this way a one-sided concern with things, instead of with the mode of being of the phenomenon itself, has led geography to the epistemological dilemma of how an external, objectively existing 'reality' can be known by a consciousness arbitrarily understood as a 'thinking substance'.

Golledge must and does necessarily arrive at this fundamental question: "we are faced with the inevitable and perplexing question – what is reality?" – a question he has repeatedly raised, but one to which he has been unable to provide any satisfactory answer. While he claims that: "intervening between a constant but changing external world and a chaotic mass of unique sensate beings are the internalized reflections of the external flux or the isomorphisms of this flux produced by the minds of the sensate beings" (Golledge, 1979, 114), questions still remain. What relationship exists between objective reality and the world inside our heads? How can we determine the nature of the relationship between man in the world and the world in man? How can we determine what is assimilated by individuals from this objective reality, and to what do we accommodate ourselves (Golledge, 1979)? What is distance? What does proximity imply? How does environmental information accumulate over time? From the information that is received from an individual, how can we spatially represent what is known? What is the philosophical distinction between real and perceived environments? (Cox and Golledge, 1981, xx). What is the nature of the image or cognitive map? How does a person 'know' the 'real' world? How can we adequately prove the reality of the external world? To what extent is reality to be known in itself? What does 'reality' then mean? How can we determine appropriate real measures against which to measure the representation of reality?

12 The mode of being characteristic of geographical objects

In *Explanation in geography* Harvey (1969b, 191) claims that "[the] whole practice and philosophy of geography depends upon the development of a conceptual framework for handling the distribution of objects and events in space". Here and elsewhere Harvey defines geography as the study of the location, relationship and movement of objects in space; as the study of the present-at-hand, whether these objects are things, people or events. Their overriding property is their character as objects or things as physical entities. This is to be a spatial science of the present-at-hand of entities, for which Kant's a priori ontology was developed. "At its simplest this amounts to defining some co-ordinate system (such as latitude and longitude) to give absolute location to objects and events . . ." (191).

In a slightly different manner Tuan (1974, 56) has argued that geographers are not divorced from the world as with some sciences, but rather that the world is too much with us. We might say that geography has shown a one-sided concern with intramundane beings or things, instead of with the problem of the whole, or the being of those beings. Such thinking, focussed on things considered one-sidedly in their appearance as objects of theoretical knowledge, has led generally, and in geography in particular, to confusion of being with the thing-object (or *res*). *Res* is 'reality' in this context, and the ontological understanding of man within this conception is as *present-at-hand* and as 'real'; in essence, as a thing. In this way attention is immediately diverted away from the starting point for all research in originally given experience (Heidegger, 1927, 201), and into the sort of thinking that Golledge in particular, and behavioural theory in general, typifies.

Where reality is thus associated with the problem of the external world, it is seen to be a question for theoretical and contemplative inquiry 'in' consciousness.

Thus, insofar as reality has the character of something independent of consciousness and of something in-itself, the question of the meaning of reality becomes necessarily linked with the question of whether reality *can* be independent of consciousness, *and* whether consciousness is able to transcend itself and to know the real world the way it is in itself. (Kockelmans, 1969, 8)

Kockelmans has shown how these problems arise in a broader context:

whoever conceives of the world independent of man necessarily throws man back upon himself. If one then speaks of knowledge of the world, he must interpret such knowledge as a special process taking place 'within' consciousness. And the more univocally one maintains that knowledge is really 'inside' consciousness and has by no means the same kind of being as the intramundane things, the more reasonable and urgent the question concerning the clarification of the relationship between subject and object appears to be. (8–9)

Of course behavioural geographers may argue that we do not need to think of a subject's 'inside' and its 'internal representations' as some sort of container or as enclosed entities. But when one asks what this 'inside' might be, in which knowing is enclosed and through which world and behaviour are mediated, there has been no further answer.[30]

"[No] matter how this inner sphere gets interpreted, if one does no more than ask how knowing makes its way 'out of' it and achieves 'transcendence', it becomes evident that the knowing which presents such enigmas will remain problematical unless one has previously clarified how it is and what it is" (Heidegger, 1927, 60–1).

The unasked question in all these deliberations concerns the mode of being characteristic of the knowing subject. If knowledge is seen as a special mode of man's orientation toward the world, then it no longer makes sense to conceive of knowledge as a process by means of which the 'subject' creates 'for and in himself' 'representations' of something that is 'outside' the knowing subject. The question of how these 'representations' can be measured against the 'external reality' similarly makes no sense. Indeed, for a being which is essentially intentional the question of the existence of the world and possibilities for proving it make no sense. They make sense only for a subject which is worldless, or unsure of its world, and even then the questions themselves presuppose that world (Heidegger, 1927, 202–3; Kockelmans, 1969, 9–10).

Knowing the world is first grounded in being-in-the-world, and as such is constitutive for man's being. This is not the theoretical world of objects divorced from a context of concern, but one of concernful involvement or fascination with the world. Entities in this world of involved concern are not merely just there, as present-at-hand, but are constantly and always at hand – ready-to-hand, to be used in the pursuit of some task, defined in terms of their appropriateness for pursuing the particular task; defined by the tasks man engages in, not by theoretically fitting the components, tools and tasks together. Thus, in laying out this world of involved concern Heidegger (1927, 68–9) can say that "[what] we encounter as closest to us is the room; and we encounter it not as something 'between four walls' in a geometrical spatial sense, but as equipment for residing. Out of this 'arrangement' emerges, and it is in this that any 'individual' item of equipment shows itself. *Before* it does so, a totality of equipment has already been discovered."

We reach the point at which we must begin to disclose the way in which we are to conceive of man's world as other than a world of physical entities in geometrical space. We must consider the method appropriate to such disclosure (phenomenology) and show how even this has entered geographical inquiry through the lenses of objectivism, the underlying ontology of the present-at-hand, and a turn to subjectivism. Here, epistemological problems have developed from attempts to relate human understanding and behaviour to a world of physical entities, through a spatiality appropriate to the physical sciences. Attempts to overcome these problems resulted in a radicalization of the turn to the subject, and the consideration of the personal and private domains of experience in the hope of better explaining how man 'operates' in this world of the present-at-hand. In crude terms, the parameters of the models have been extended to incorporate increasingly subjective and individual characteristics. In 'humanistic geography' rigorous models are no longer used at all, but their questions, their underlying presuppositions, and the ontologies with which they operate, remain little changed. Either an objectively existing independent real world is still presupposed (and so perpetuates the behaviouralist problematic), or independent multiple realities are presumed, or the possibility of any intersubjectively known world is denied, resulting in a radical subjectivism and ultimately in relativism.

PART II

Geography and phenomenology

Phenomenology is always the name for the procedure of ontology, which essentially distinguishes itself from all other, positive sciences.

It is true that someone engaged in research can master, in addition to his own positive science, phenomenology as well, or at least follow its steps and investigations. But philosophical knowledge can become genuinely relevant and fertile for his own positive science *only when*, within the problematic which stems from deliberation on the ontic correlations in his area, he comes upon the basic traditional concepts and, furthermore, questions their suitability for that which is made the theme of his science. Then, proceeding from the demands of his science and from the horizon of his own scientific inquiry, which lies, so to speak, on the frontiers of his basic concepts, he can search back for the original ontological constitution of that which is to remain and become *anew* the object of his science. The questions which arise in this way methodically thrust beyond themselves insofar as that which they are asking is accessible and determinable only through ontology. (Heidegger, 1976, 21)

3

The interpretation of phenomenology in geography

If science is not to degenerate into a medley of ad hoc hypotheses, it must become philosophical and must enter upon a thorough criticism of its own foundations. (Whitehead, 1925, 24–5)

13 The phenomenological basis of geography

As to whether or not geography should be considered a science, and if so, what sort of science it would be, geographical inquiry has always been rather tentative, and its claims generally ambiguous. Particularly in the United States, geography's historical roots in the physical ontology of Davisian physiography, and later in the biological ontology of Barrows' spatial ecology, suggest a one-sided foundation in the physical and biological sciences. The recognition of a much older European tradition in the influential works of Sauer and Hartshorne was important for a discipline seeking to unify its developing and yet disparate realms of inquiry and discourse. Geographers variously trained as geologists, botanists, cartographers, and increasingly as economists, sought to come to some understanding of the common ground they occupied (see James and Martin, 1978). The subsequent methodological debates left many disenchanted with the possibility of providing any such unifying basis to their own activities.

Spatial analytics similarly sought to redefine the discipline as a spatial science within which various systematic issues could be addressed and through which the common interests of several fields could be expressed. But spatial analytics was unable to provide such a framework given its own assumptions regarding social physics and the rejection of other established methodologies and forms of evidence. This was clear in its outspoken positivism and reduction of all phenomena to a world of Newtonian mechanics, in predetermined Euclidean spaces.

With spatial analytics varied disciplinary concerns were broken down in favour of a universalist position. On the one hand, a form of geographic reductionism developed, which I will call 'spatialism' (Chapter 5), where the world is reduced to and explained only in terms of the methodological perspectives consistent with a science of space and spatial relations. 'Regional science' departments were proposed and some were set up, seeking to realign the disciplinary matrix more 'accurately' with the changing state of affairs and interests. On the other hand, disciplinary boundaries were seen as merely conventional; within a spatial focus the particular perspectives of any one discipline were interpreted as parochial boxes, outmoded conventions to be transcended.

In this context the questions, "what are the phenomena with which geography deals?", and "from what perspectives can geographers claim a common view?", provide the necessary backcloth against which to see the rise of phenomenological discourse. Geography was not to be so lightly discarded (see the special issue of the *Annals* of the Association of American Geographers, 1979). Geographers may not have a common perspective or methodology (although it was long argued that the *map* was one such unifying factor), but they had something better; a sound phenomenological base in experience to which formal geography 'responded'.

The phenomenological basis of geography takes several forms in geographical literature: 'phenomenological foundations' (Relph, 1976b); 'immediate experience of life' (Relph, 1976b, 1); 'geographical consciousness' (Van Paassen, 1957); 'geographical experience' (Dardel, 1952); 'everyman as geographer and personal geographies' (Lowenthal, 1961); 'life-world' (Buttimer, 1976). Interest in these domains is prompted clearly by what Gregory (1978a, 123) refers to as geography's "traditional attachment to particular places and the people that live in them". Such claims have a long and respectable tradition within the field; Sauer's seeing the land with the eyes of its own inhabitants; Wright's geosophy; Whittlesey's 'sense of terrestrial space'; Lowenthal's man as "artist and landscape architect, creating order and organizing space, time and causality in accordance with our apperceptions and predilections" (Lowenthal, 1961, 260). Each in some way seeks to uncover the 'spirit' or 'character' of a place (Gregory, 1978a, 137). Each, in some way, points to a particular phenomenological basis to geographic understanding.

Yet geographers claim a peculiar affinity with their subject-matter, one which is not generally shared in other sciences; that the everyday experience of the world is already in some sense geographical. The geographer's task is to describe and thematize this 'geographical experience'. The same, of course, can be said for economics, sociology and political science, where man is obviously an economic, sociological and political agent also, but implicit in these perspectives is a prior abstraction and thematization from the everyday world. Geographers, on the other hand, seem to claim that it is the everyday world as such, and its constitution as this very world, my world, or culturally variable modes of existence, which is geographical. Thus, while the phenomenological basis for the discipline and the foundations of geographical knowledge "lie in the direct experiences and consciousness we have of the world we live in" (Relph, 1976a, 4), these experiences derive from a "geographical consciousness":

On the one hand the geographer develops this consciousness and makes society more aware of geography, but on the other hand the rise of geographical science is dependent upon the existence of a prescientific and natural geographical consciousness . . . geographers and geography exist only in a society with a geographical sense. (Van Paassen, 1957, 21)

For Lowenthal (1961, 242) "anyone who inspects the world around him is in some measure a geographer". Consequently formal geography becomes a mirror for this basic human experience (Relph, 1976a, 4). Furthermore, it is concerned with phenomena that cannot be merely observed, but which "must be lived to be grasped as they really are . . ."

Such phenomena of experience are the substance of our involvements in the world and constitute the foundations of the formal body of knowledge we term 'Geography'. (Relph, 1976b, 1)

These claims raise important issues about geography and science, and the nature and importance of a phenomenology. In such a world phenomenology takes on the role merely of an *archaeology*, wherein the hidden layers are investigated to reveal the hidden artifacts of everyday geographical experience. Geographical experience is prior to geographical science – ontologically and historically – in its broadest perspective, as 'formal' geography. Formal geography is a thematization of this experience. Phenomenology is the act of recovering and mediating that original geographical experience. Such a position (if a tenable description of the state of affairs) has immediate consequences for the interpretation of phenomenology. As archaeology its principal aim is retrieval. Abstraction and reduction are redundant since that experience (as geographical) exists prior to the scientist's attention to it. The geographer's task is to describe it (naively in the natural attitude).

Phenomenology immediately becomes a very different enterprise, and we begin to see why its adaptation into geography has been problematical. This phenomenology is not the Husserlian project, nor any derivation of it, but is a form of scientific realism based on a return to a prior phenomenology – a description of extant phenomena as they really are (that is, as they *appear*). That is, we turn to a Kantian and Machian conception of phenomenology.

Relph seeks to clarify the main features of these foundational experiences of places, spaces and landscapes which constitute 'Geography' "that everyone has, regardless of whether they know anything of *Geography* as a formal science" (Relph, 1976b, 1–2). Here Relph seems to misinterpret Dardel's claims, on which his argument is based, which in fact points in the opposing direction.

Geography is not initially a form of knowledge, geographical reality is not at first sight an 'object', geographical space is not a blank waiting to be coloured and filled in. Geographical science presupposes a world that can be understood geographically and also that man can feel and know himself to be tied to the Earth. (Dardel, 1952, 46, in Relph, 1976b, 1)

If it is the case that formal geography merely 'discovers' its objects fully constituted in this prior 'geographical experience', those objects remain unproblematical – places, spaces, and landscapes are pregiven in experience to be described and manipulated by formal science. No explanation of the constitution of scientific objects, nor of 'objects in general' need be given by the geographer. No account of the a priori framework of meaning by which the geographical perspective on a pre-given lifeworld is itself constituted is necessary – the geographical is itself an a priori category of experience, discovered in the world. But Dardel, unlike Relph, does not suggest this. He claims that geographical science presupposes not a geographical world, but a world that can be understood or constituted geographically. Its phenomenological basis, from which geographical science constitutes its own particular 'objects' is man and Earth.

These are critical issues, and pose severe problems for the geographer and phenomenologist. Here, geographical science does not constitute or project its particular perspective as one scientific world, or its particular entities from that perspective. The geographer seeks instead to describe the geographical experience – *as itself a phenomenon*. If this is the case, we might expect that the interpretation of phenomenology – whose history in geography is currently our primary concern – will (a) confine itself to the mundane attitude, (b) emphasize descriptive methodology, and de-emphasize or misinterpret the nature of the phenomenological reduction, bracketing and abstraction, (c) focus upon the original experience prior to its scientific thematization, and ignore phenomenology's primary concern with the foundation of the sciences and the constitution of their objects of concern, (d) be concerned with lifeworld *as object* of study and as everyday mundane lived experience, and (e) begin to refer to the task of the phenomenologist (independent of (a) through (c)) as the decription of "things as they are".

14 Geographical phenomenology

If it is true that "by our theories you shall know us" (Harvey, 1969b, 486) then in recent years geographers might begin to be known to some extent as phenomenologists, for phenomenological inquiry has impressed a distinctive signature on the discipline and has markedly weakened the hold of positivism on geography (Gregory, 1978a, 131). In just over a decade, primarily through the orientation of humanistic perspectives, explicit reflections upon phenomenology have entered the geographic literature and, as Gregory (123) claims, have been deeply felt. These reflections have, however, been superficially conducted (123). Walmsley (1974, 104), Billinge (1977, 62–3), and Hay (1979, 16) are also correct in pointing out that phenomenology has been slow to develop in geography and that "phenomenologists we have by no means become" (Billinge, 1977, 67). Phenomenology in geography has been characterized by "much preaching and little practice" (Johnston, 1979, 138), and the role of the phenomenological method is even smaller in the more recent work of two of its founders: Tuan and Buttimer (Entrikin, 1976, 615). Yet such arguments belie the impact of geographers' claims about phenomenology, and the manner in which discourse within the discipline has changed as a result of it. In some form or another, phenomenology is developed within the geographic literature to which the interested reader can be referred.[1] Recent work portrays quite sophisticated understanding of aspects of the project.[2] Some of the excesses and misinterpretations have been discussed, and opposing traditions have been defined in regard to this approach.[3] Reviews of these perspectives have also appeared.[4] Recently papers which seek to consider the possibility and desirability of incorporating phenomenological insights into various sub-fields of the discipline have appeared.[5]

Superficially, at least, there seems to be little need either to explicate further the basic concepts of phenomenology or for arguments questioning the viability of the approach. Geographical phenomenology stands as the primary foundation of humanistic concerns,[6] it is seen as an important if limited perspective by critical theorists and marxists,[7] and in the past decade other positions such as neo-positivism and idealism have sought to define themselves in opposition to phenomenology.[8] If we can accept this as the state of affairs then we probably should also accept the much repeated injunction to phenomenologists to begin to produce 'substantive work', 'examples' or 'actual research findings' rather than yet further programmatic statements. It is time to step down into the arena; the ground having been laid 'geographical phenomenology' must – the argument goes – begin to produce phenomenological geography of substance.

14a Phenomenology and 'practical' research

Calls for phenomenologists to produce practically useful research rather than further develop theoretical arguments concerning phenomenology are not restricted to its critics and opponents. From the very beginning, concern for the pragmatic aspects of phenomenological principles has characterized geographical interpretations. For Relph (1973, 234):

> It is important to note that I am not concerned here with what constitutes pure phenomenology . . . nor with extremist statements of any nature, for these are necessarily rigid and stress polarities and differences. Statements like those of Edmund Husserl for phenomenology . . . are certainly essential for the development of a coherent methodology, but in applying them to the investigation of substantive issues many of their detailed requirements need to be relaxed if the study is to avoid being pedantic and scholastic.

Relph (1977, 178) sees in programmatic statements "a serious danger of introducing misleading impressions and confusions", which could be avoided by showing by example the insights that phenomenology offers. As a result he would "much prefer to see substantive applications rather than discussions of the possible uses of phenomenology". Tuan (1977a, 180) entirely agrees with him, in support of which he offers his own examples of applications of the phenomenological method (1971a, 192, n. 2). Buttimer (1977, 181) frankly admits that she herself has "paid less attention to the 'letter of the phenomenological law', as it were, than to capturing something of its spirit". Seamon (1980a, 89) would also prefer to "speak to the spirit of phenomenology than to its letter", and both he and Buttimer (1977, 182–3) emphasize pedagogic technique and 'encouragement' over the discussion of phenomenological principles; widespread discourse about its use, rather than a form of inquiry which might relegate it to the archives "where only the well-read and the philosophically inclined may touch it!"[9]

In this way, while much basic information concerning the history, principles and claims of phenomenology has been presented and is now generally accepted within the discipline, phenomenological principles and their application to inquiry concerning the human subject have been justified by rejecting philosophical reflection. From the very beginning the appropriate mode of discourse for evaluating phenomenology was denied. It was rather one approach to a particular factical subject-matter for evaluation alongside the other approaches and topics of the social scientist, and treated as an "adjunct or preamble to scientific procedures, a means of adding to and improving accounts of overt behaviour" (Relph, 1977, 178; see also Buttimer, 1977). It was treated more as a guiding motivation than as a rigorous methodological conception, and its evaluation proceeded in terms of already given categories. Fundamentally then its transcendental and ontological status was denied from the beginning. It is, I think, to this that Relph refers when he claims that:

it is inconsistent with the major tenets of phenomenology to accept existing concepts and explanations of phenomena; on the contrary the aim is to suspend belief in such explanations and to elucidate the variety of our direct, pre-scientific experiences of the lifeworld. It could be that phenomenological approaches will lead to the identification of time-space rhythms of some form, but these cannot be assumed beforehand, nor if they are discovered will they have the same ontological status as those discussed by Hägerstrand. (1977, 179)

Phenomenology as a philosophy requires "perseverance, commitment, critical insight and imagination", it cannot be an easy crutch for a particular methodological perspective (179). By treating it as an adjunct to empirical science, in the manner of Buttimer and Tuan, several of its most important claims have been ignored and attendent necessary assumptions have been relaxed.

15 Approaches to geographical phenomenology

The literature within geography and other fields is replete with warnings about the difficulties of pinning down one conception of phenomenology or of explaining clearly its nature as a method. In part this is true, for there are several phenomenologies (see Spiegelberg, 1978), and even Husserlian phenomenology was conceived of as an on-going research programme to which Husserl claimed only to provide a series of "introductions".[10] It is important to distinguish this sense of an on-going programme developing through time, and therefore difficult to fix at any one point in time, from the claims of geographers where difficulties result from their own limitations.[11] This should be understood in a context where the material is difficult, much of the translated material is poorly translated or, where well translated, is sometimes difficult to follow, and most remains untranslated. Only in recent years has much Continental philosophy, and phenomenological works in particular, become readily accessible in English.

In the human sciences, but also in philosophy, Husserlian phenomenology has been interpreted and criticized from the perspective of only partial reading of the entire opus of Husserl's work. Static phenomenology has generally been criticized for reasons which Husserl himself had bracketed for the time being, to be explicated only later in genetic phenomenology particularly with the introduction of the constitution of internal time consciousness.[12] Consequently it is only recently that several early and fundamental misinterpretations have begun to be clarified. Criticism from these perspectives has been common within the philosophical literature, and they will have to be addressed. For the moment I will bracket them and show simply how such confusion is already present at the inception of phenomenological ideas into geography.

15a The necessary distinction between humanism and phenomenology

The introduction of phenomenological principles into geography is directly related to the development of a series of perspectives seeking a more humane or humanistic geography, emphasizing that "thread to geographic thinking which, at its best, produces an acute sensitivity to place and community, to the symbiotic relations between individuals, communities and environments" (Harvey, 1974, 22).[13]

Relph (1970), Tuan (1971a), and Mercer and Powell (1972) claim their central philosophical basis to be phenomenology. Relph seeks in phenomenology the possibility of grounding a more humane geography; Tuan's 'humanistic geography' is grounded in the application of the phenomenological method to geographical experience, in the sense that it is one of the humanist's roles to serve as intellectual middleman by 'decomposing' and 'simplifying' experience, such as that expressed in art, so that it can be systematically ordered and may yield to scientific explanation (Tuan, 1976, 274). Buttimer seeks to recapture the dynamism of the lifeworld to develop a "more experientially grounded orientation within the discipline" (Buttimer, 1976, 290). Entrikin (1976) sees all of these claims underpinned by existential phenomenology, which he equates with humanism.[14] More recently Ley (1981) has pointed to 'the philosophies of meaning' – phenomenology, existentialism, interactionalism and surrealism – as attempting to provide a philosophical grounding for humanistic work, while Ley and Samuels (1978, 9) claim that these philosophies of meaning offer a means for reconciling social science and man's lived experience. Phenomenology, through its emphasis on intentionality, may thus contribute towards a solution for the preoccupation of geographers with the 'objective' (Ley, 1979, 216).

Yet, as Relph (1977, 179) argues, however sympathetic to humanist principles phenomenology may be it does not necessarily lead to humanism. This association and the resulting confusion in these initial and subsequent works must be sorted out if we are to evaluate the claims made, or the claims that we can make, about phenomenology.

In geography, Smith (1979, 366–8) has provided the most strident clarification of the confusion between phenomenology and 'humanistic geography', a confusion which "flatters humanism". Phenomenology, he argues, is characterized correctly as eclectic, but incorrectly when it is said to be a humanism; phenomenology is a method, humanism an attitude (336–7).

In so far as phenomenology has degenerated into humanistic geography or worse, behavioural geography, its outlook is even narrower. Relph himself claims that humanistic geography has tended to be exclusive, restricted and conservative (1977, 178–9). It is no accident that Yi-Fu Tuan has come to view humanistic geography as simply another 'subfield in our discipline' (1977a), and that Entrikin sees humanist geographers as seeking a 'prescientific awareness of our environment,' (1976, 625). The ambiguity of 'prescientific' – conceptual priority expressed in the language of temporal priority – is particularly revealing in the context of humanism. (336–7)

He continues, echoing Harvey's (1974, 24) denunciation of 'parochial humanism':

For at its worst, humanism deals with the future as it deals with science, by denying it. The denial, however, turns back on itself; in a world where science's monopoly on knowledge is rapidly expanding, humanism must either compete with science – a battle lost before begun – or accept a diminishing jurisdiction. The destruction of place occurs at the behest of objective societal forces that neither humanism nor, in the end, phenomenology, can fully apprehend. (367–8)

For my present purposes it will be necessary to bracket the claims of humanism insofar as they are independent of claims concerning phenomenology. In large measure, of course, they are *not* independent. Phenomenology in geography is suffused with humanist claims and language. For the present I wish only to make clear in what ways phenomenology does not also necessarily equate with humanism. In the end I hope to make this claim more radical and, through Heidegger, to show: (1) how, if it knows itself properly, phenomenology can never be a 'humanism', and (2) how geographers have confused claims about immanence and transcendence, and why their claims to describe the experience of lived immediacy fail, and fall into a subjectivism, unless mediated in some way.

15b Existentialism

Phenomenology is associated with existentialism in many of the social sciences, particularly in psychology, from which geographers have drawn extensively.[15] Both geographers and psychologists have relied primarily on secondary sources where this association has occurred.

Historically phenomenology was introduced to the general public, particularly in France, England and America, through the works of existentialist philosophy, as the logical forerunner of existentialism; existential phenomenology was seen as the proper culmination of Husserlian and Heideggerian phenomenology (see Madison, 1977). In many secondary works today, particularly in psychology, from which geographers such as Relph, Tuan, Buttimer and Seamon have drawn, this is still the case (see Kockelmans, 1971). Radnitzky (1973, 222) attributes this general state of affairs to American usage "which tends to lump together existentialist philosophy and phenomenology", while Ricoeur (1973a, 122) shows how the idiosyncratic misinterpretation of phenomenology in the Anglo-Saxon world generally, has taken Heidegger's analyses of "care, anxiety and being-toward-death in the sense of a refined existential philosophy. They do not notice that these analyses belong to a meditation on the 'worldhood of the world' and that they essentially are aimed at destroying the claim of a knowing subject to be the measure of objectivity."

Phenomenology has been taken as *existential phenomenology* by Tuan, Relph, Buttimer, Mercer and Powell, and Entrikin. Buttimer (1974, 37) explicitly claims that existential phenomenologists "try to deal with 'embodied intentionality' in its culturally variable modes of expression", adding that phenomenology and existentialism seek to "explicate the whole of lived experience" drawing from scientific and non-scientific sources. Jackson (1981, 303) claims that "it is the existential phenomenologists (Merleau-Ponty, Heidegger [sic] and Sartre) who have most effectively reinterpreted Husserl's thought, abandoning his idealist tendencies", and Johnston (1979, 139) claims that geographers have encountered difficulties in the separation of the two perspectives. Thus Entrikin (1976, 615) can claim that:

the fundamental philosophy of the humanist approach is existential phenomenology [which] is more significant to understanding the application of phenomenology and existentialism to the human sciences than either of the philosophies alone. The combination of the phenomenological method with the importance of understanding man in his existential world is the basis for the change of approach evident in many of the human sciences.

That is, a phenomenological human science is concerned with the world of man informed by an existentialist perspective. It should be pointed out, however, as Gibson (1974, 47) has done: (1) that what emerges is generally not a description of existentialism or of phenomenology, but a distillation of several positions – including strong influences from *Lebensphilosophie* – resulting from a fundamental rejection of positivistic methodologies. Thus Gibson claims that Buttimer refers not to what "she knows of existentialism and phenomenology, but something quite different, her personal vision of what geography ought to become"; and (2) "[while] most contemporary existentialists are also phenomenologists, many phenomenologists are not existentialists". Existentialism (as a movement of related philosophies) and phenomenology (as a systematic philosophy and method of analysis) must be treated separately – at least initially – if we are to understand the specific claims of phenomenology.

16 The view of science

The relationship between phenomenology and science is not at all well understood by geographers. As a result of its association with existentialism and idealism within a humanist context, phenomenology has been seen variously as anti-science (Johnston, 1978), as an adjunct to empirical science (Buttimer, 1976), and even as functionally related to positivism (Tuan, 1975b). Confusion is exacerbated because of the failure of geographers to distinguish between empirical science and science, and between empirical science and positivist perspectives on it. Positive, empirical and positivist or logical empiricist science have been presumed to be the same (see Pickles, 1982). Similarly objective science has been confused with objectivism, and natural science with naturalism. Philosophical arguments concerning the transcending of subject–object dichotomies have been taken as criticisms against objectivation in human science (Mercer and Powell, 1972; Buttimer, 1976), and thus abstraction in science has been rejected. Consequently science as an abstractive, objectifying enterprise has been rejected in favour of humanistic inquiry.

Even where distinctions are attempted they are often ambiguous regarding the relationship of science and phenomenology. Smith (1979, 367) has criticized phenomenology precisely because it has been "loath to explain the scientific experience of reality". Given all of these confusions, geographers still fundamentally misunderstand phenomenology in the sense that they fail to recognize or even allow room for phenomenology as a philosophy or perspective on science, a phenomenology of science and phenomenology *as* science.

Even as recently as 1980 Ley, in recognizing some of these arguments, claims that "[aligned] to the criticism of trivial and unique subject matter has been the charge that humanistic perspectives do not engage in the scientific parade of objectivity, classification, and the development of theory and ultimately laws" (Ley, 1980a, 4). He argues that this position derives entirely from within the positivist perspective, "and as such its presuppositions would be unacceptable to social scientists who do not subscribe to a naturalist epistemology". In summarily rejecting this criticism as positivistic, and moving immediately to a justification of interpretative understanding, Ley fails to recognize the necessary relationships between phenomenology and empirical science, and the nature of empirical science and the scientific enterprise itself.

Essentially four views of the relationship between phenomenology and science can be identified in the geographic literature: (1) phenomenology is opposed to positivism, as a critique of the over-objectifying tendencies in human science; (2) phenomenology is characterized as anti-science; (3) phenomenology is a founding and grounding enterprise for empirical science; and (4) phenomenology is the study of phenomena as they give themselves in lived experience.[16]

16a Phenomenology as criticism

Relph (1970, 195) claims that phenomenology opposes many "assumptions and methods of physical science, especially those of positivistic science and scientism", but is not to be seen as "some type of irrational antiscience". Instead of opposing science, phenomenology opposes the presumption that science is *the* privileged form of knowing and the corresponding "dictatorship . . . of scientific thought over other forms of thinking".

Concerned to overcome the 'objectifying reductionism' of nine-teenth- and early twentieth-century science, phenomenology sought to explicate the whole of lived experience, drawing from scientific and non-scientific sources (Buttimer, 1974, 37). Thus it has been seen as a form of criticism seeking to counter the "overly objectifying and abstractive tendencies of some scientific geographers", while it seeks to provide a basis for the abstractions of science (Entrikin, 1976, 616). Entrikin's important rider to these claims has, however, generally been ignored or not understood: "Implicit in this view is that phenomen-ology provides the 'essential' basis for science but does not replace science" (621). Had this claim been better understood it is doubtful that Buttimer's (1976, 278) arguments about science and the separation of subjects and objects would have gained such currency within the discipline.[17]

Fundamental to this interest in phenomenology as critique of positivism and objectivism in human science is the seeking of a more humane geography (see Parsons, 1969). Thus, Buttimer (1976, ab-stract, 277) can say that "scientific procedures which separate 'subjects' and 'objects', thought and action, people and environment are inadequate to investigate this lifeworld". The question as to how the immediacy of lifeworld can be studied at all without reduction and abstraction, that is, without some mediation, is not raised. Instead concern with the integrity of lived experience and the objectivism of positivist science has resulted in the rejection of the fundamental principle of positive science – the positing of objects for a subject (taken as the community of scientists, for whom claims must be intersubjectively verifiable). Buttimer simply confuses the nature of scientific inquiry with the objects of its concern. By definition positive science is a proposing–positing activity requiring distanciation and hence objectivation of the scientist from that which is inquired about – the object.[18] Her argument is really aimed not at science, as such, but at the treatment of its objects of concern. She argues: "One must reject any scientific cause–effect models of subject and object, and concept-ualize the relationship between body-subject and world as reciprocally determining one another" (Buttimer, 1976, 283). Because of the separation of body and mind implicit in these models "scientific procedures fail to provide adequate descriptions of experience" (283). Phenomenology as critique of positivism becomes phenomenology as anti-science very easily from this point.

16b Phenomenology as anti-science

Three basic issues characterize Relph's understanding of phenomenology in his concern "with the reorientation of science and knowledge along lines that have meaning and significance for man" (Relph, 1970, 193). Phenomenology seeks to "explore the original worlds of man's experience while rejecting the approaches of mechanistic science" (194). He seeks to reorient geographic inquiry away from objectivist science and positivism, and thereby to provide a philosophical background for a more humane geography through inquiry into the relevance and claims of phenomenology. He includes empirical science in this critique, and his arguments here will begin to orient us to the nature of geographic discourse surrounding phenomenology. The study of landscape is beyond the methods of science (195); phenomenology shows how limited quantitative *and* positivist approaches are to the study of geographic problems (196); phenomenology is "an attempt to formulate some alternative method of investigation to that of hypothesis testing and theory development" (193). In the first and second of these claims Relph merely articulates frustration against the universalistic claims of the 'quantitative revolution' and the spatializing of the discipline under the aegis of the newly emerged spatial analytic. In the third, however, he makes a claim decisive in the subsequent unfolding of geographic interpretations of phenomenology; one which has been adapted and repeated throughout the subsequent debate concerning the nature of phenomenology (see, Jackson, 1981, 302; Johnston, 1979, 135; Moriarty, 1981, 484). Since this claim is so important it will be worthwhile to reflect carefully upon it.

Relph (1970, 193) claims that one basic issue in phenomenology is "an attempt to formulate some alternative method of investigation to that of hypothesis testing and the development of theory". He cites several works by phenomenologists to substantiate this and the preceding two claims. We must ask: (a) What is said here? (b) Do the references support this claim? And, (c) is the claim itself tenable?

(a) What is said here? Relph's claim as given seeks only to establish the possibility of a method where phenomena can be given directly in apodicticity, and where hypothesis testing and inductive–deductive reasoning are unnecessary. Insofar as apodictically self-evident description involves no construction and causal generalization, theory is unnecessary.

(b) Do the references support the claim? Only Tymieniecka refers to the matter of hypothesis testing and theory development, and this somewhat loosely. In other words, we are not quite sure what precisely she means when she claims – because the phenomenological approach is self-grounding and apodictic "the evidence from direct insight obviates the hypothetico-causal approach" (Tymieniecka, 1962, 19). Relph, and the whole tradition following him, take this literally to mean that phenomenology, insofar as it is seen as phenomenological description seeking to describe phenomena in their apodictic givenness, has no use for the hypothetico-causal approach. But this does not imply that the approach is to be cast aside, rather it presupposes that with which phenomenological description is itself concerned. That is, phenomenology is concerned with how phenomena are originally given, the constitution of what is acceptable as evidence and the a priori framework of meaning from which a hypothesis and a causal relationship can be framed as meaningful and relevant. Phenomenology seeks to ground the sciences. Geography as an empirical science, including landscape study within a research programme, can develop a phenomenological geography. Phenomenological geography will be a descriptive, eidetic science; empirical geography will be hypothesis testing seeking to establish formal, functional and causal relationships.

(c) Is the claim tenable? Relph's claim holds *only* insofar as it refers to a phenomenological geography. For Relph (1970) and the tradition following him, the claims made are actually about empirical geography.

It is ironic that of all geographic interpretations of phenomenology, Relph's is the most accurate in seeing phenomenology as an apodictic descriptive method. Unfortunately he does not clearly explicate its foundational role for an empirical science of relations, and his particular claim has been taken as the primary justification for the separation of two conceptions of geographic inquiry: a descriptive enterprise, in a poetic sense; and a rigorous enterprise, in the sense of scientific, hypothesis testing and theory development (Johnston, 1979; Moriarty, 1981). Thus Buttimer (1976, 281) suggests that recent work on perception in geography could "be described as 'scientific' in phenomenological language", while the phenomenological method is seen as an important 'preamble' to scientific procedures (Buttimer, 1976, 289). In Tuan's (1974, 57) terms spatial analysis and other positivist techniques can adequately describe the upper levels of social reality, but the deeper we probe into this reality the less well suited are these objective (i.e., scientific) methods, and we need to resort increasingly to the methods of phenomenological description.

More loosely framed arguments – representing the bulk of secondary geographical literature – take an even more disjunctive view of the relationship between phenomenology and science: there is no relationship. Guelke (1978, 54) distinguishes between the 'scientist', and his abstracting enterprise, and the 'phenomenologist' who seeks to "grasp the dynamism of the lifeworld". For him "if a geographer comes across a fountain while walking through a city and writes a poem about the meaning of this experience, it presumably qualifies as phenomenological geography". Talarchek (1977, 18) distinguishes between phenomenology and positive science arguing that "[phenomenologists] seem to view phenomenology as an alternative to positive science". Johnston (1978, 195) is much more definite, viewing phenomenology as 'anti-science'. Even Entrikin's (1976, 616) much lauded paper describes phenomenology in contradistinction to "scientific geography [which] can be quite broadly defined as an approach based upon empirical observation, public verifiability of conclusions, and the importance of isolating fact from value". The approach of existential phenomenology "does not offer a viable approach to, nor a presuppositionless basis for, scientific geography", but instead is best understood as a form of criticism to counter the "overly objective and abstractive tendencies of some scientific geographers" (616).

Tuan (1971a, 182) has exacerbated this tendency towards polarization of geographical conceptions of phenomenology and empirical science by introducing into the debate a neo-Kantian distinction between nomothetic and idiographic concerns. Environmentalism is implied to be largely nomothetic, and operates in a world of objects, seeking to establish lawful relationships between physical nature and man, and more recently in the form of spatial and economic constraints on human action (182–3). Existentialism is generally idiographic, operating in a world of purposeful beings, and its appropriate method is phenomenological. Under environmentalism the geographer seeks meaning in order and the general; under existentialism he seeks meaning in the landscape, as he would in literature, because it is "a repository of human striving" (184) – that is, he seeks meaning in the particular. Such an approach either builds 'critically' on scientific knowledge (Tuan, 1976, 274) or seeks to "re-emphasize the importance of studying unique events rather than the spuriously general" (Johnston, 1979, 129). Moriarty (1981, 484) combines the claims of Relph (1970), Tuan (1971a) and Johnston (1979), claiming that geographic research adheres "either to the phenomenological or positivist approach" and that the phenomenological approach is based "upon the study of problems as unique entities", while the positivist approach is "concerned with hypothesis testing and theory development or application" (Moriarty, 1981, 484; see Pickles, 1982).

16c *The foundational role of phenomenology*

The view of phenomenology as 'anti-science' – though commonly held – has been strongly criticized. Smith (1979, 360) argues that phenomenology has been rigorously anti-positivist without at all being anti-science, and Gregory (1981b) has pointed to the foundational role of phenomenology for empirical science. Relph (1970, 195), as we have seen, argued that phenomenology is not opposed to science. For Tuan (1976, 274) phenomenology in geography seems to have operated fundamentally as building "critically on scientific knowledge", and for Entrikin (1976, 629) it operates as "a form of criticism rather than an alternative to scientific method". Yet such claims in no way clarify in what relation phenomenology and science *do stand* with regard to each other. The details of such relations are only sketchily and ambiguously treated.

Buttimer (1976, 291) sees phenomenology as questioning the "assumptions and ideological foundation of conventional scientific models", while Entrikin (1976, 621) argues that phenomenology sees "empirical science as overly abstract, without firm foundation within the lifeworld or the world of experience". In this way phenomenology is to provide the 'essential' basis for the abstractions of science. It does not replace science, although in the humanistic perspective phenomenology remains a rejection of the abstraction and objectivity of science (621–5). Gregory (1981a, 15) understands this relationship better when he argues that "there is nothing in the humanist project that is necessarily incompatible with a scientific method", but it is only in the new *Dictionary of human geography* (1981b) that he explicitly recognizes the foundational project of phenomenology for the sciences.

Prior to Gregory's explicit claims the foundational role of phenomenology was seen only in terms of its aim of regaining the pre-scientific world or primordial awareness of environment (Entrikin, 1976, 625).

The concept of life-world is important in considering the relationship of phenomenology and science in that the phenomenologist's chief criticism of empirical science is that the latter uses abstractions which are not firmly based upon the grounds of experience. The phenomenologist's study of the structure of the life-world is an attempt to 'ground' science in the world of experience. (620)

We have still to determine precisely what such a grounding may entail, how it is to take place, and what sort of an enterprise this might be. For the moment, we can turn to conceptions of lifeworld in geography and ask in what ways these are 'grounding'.

16d Phenomena of lived experience

It is now a relatively simple matter to show how phenomenology has
come to be seen as the study of the pre-scientific, and how the lifeworld
has been seen as the subject-matter of a phenomenological geography,
rather than as the ground for the possibility of science or, expressed
another way, the universal horizon of all thematization. Entrikin
(1976, 627) saw the former as the task of phenomenological geography
(as humanism): "Humanist geographers argue that everyday experience and the models of it created by the social scientists constitute two
separate worlds. The humanist geographers view their role as
providing the experiential and, hence, existential base for the models
of geographers." Here we have arrived at a 'two cultures' view of
geography, encompassing the scientific and the pre-scientific. The
phenomenologist in geography is concerned to describe this pre-
scientific world. He ignores the scientific, as another realm, and hence
fails to appreciate the possibility of the world of science as a
phenomenon in its givenness; that is, fails to appreciate the possibility
of a phenomenology of science, a lifeworld which contains science, or
indeed the possibility for phenomenology to deal with any 'higher
level' social abstractions such as society, institutions, power relations,
etc. The pre-scientific is interpreted instead in an historical manner as
refering to the pre-technological experiences of individual and
community – a project foreseen in the earlier pre-industrial geographical writings of Vidal de la Blanche, to which humanism and
geographical phenomenology have been drawn (see, for example,
Buttimer, 1971; Ley and Samuels, 1978; Gregory, 1981a).

As "the natural sciences could never ultimately explain the world as
we experience it" we need to "suspend, as far as possible, the
presuppositions and conceptual structures of science and examine the
phenomena as they are" (Buttimer, 1974, 37). That is, a reconstituted
humanistic geography, from a phenomenological perspective, should
seek to explicate the whole of lived experience.

The perspectives and goals of the empirical social scientist, thus, are quite
different from those of the existential phenomenologist. But they are not
really separable: every scientific fact is seen as an abstract facet of some world
fact; the scientific perspective could be regarded as one abstract horizon
within the life-world. Whereas the positivist scientist attempts to deal with the
straight logical problems of the internal structure of scientific systems, the
existential phenomenologist deals with man-in-the-world, with the issues of
crisis, freedom, and integrity. The former demands detachment and the clear
separation of subject and object; the latter rejects such dualism and creates an
existential subjectivism. (38)

The danger of science is one of disengagement and growing distance from "the immediate data of experience and the intimate needs of human beings" (Tuan, 1974, 55). Phenomenological description seeks to get behind such scientific explanations in order to describe human behaviour as it is primordially experienced, rather than as science describes it (Buttimer, 1976, 282).

17 The turn to the lifeworld, and the ambiguity of ground and object

Geographers have generally found the term 'lifeworld' to be very congenial. Its precise meaning is not at all clear however, because it is used in at least three seemingly contradictory senses. Lifeworld is seen as the object of geographic inquiry, which may be as (1) "direct experience" (Relph, 1970, 199) or (2) as the "everyday world of immediate experience" (193), "culturally variable modes of exist-ence" (Buttimer, 1974, 37) or "routinely given facets of everyday life" (Buttimer, 1976, 280). Lifeworld is also seen as (3) the ground for the possibility of science, or the foundation for theoretical knowing (Buttimer, 1974, 37; Gregory, 1978b, 162; Ley, 1979, 222–3). Precisely how these are contradictory and why they are problematic will be taken up after I have traced their parallel development as perspectives on the lifeworld.

(1) Relph (1970, 199) claims that the method of "the contemplation of direct experience" should lead to new insights and to clarification of the foundations of sub-fields within the discipline. Such foundations are to be the elements of the everyday world. Yet such an everyday world is precisely not the world given in direct experience, if this is to mean that which is immediately given. For Husserl these were to be seen as necessarily distinct domains of experience. The situation may be different with Heidegger, but then Relph needs an interpretative phenomenology, in order to account for the pre-givenness of any world in experience.

(2) Phenomenology has been broadly interpreted as a "procedure for describing the everyday world of man's immediate experience including his actions, memories, fantasies, and perceptions" (Relph, 1970, 193), rather than as a scientific method concerned with some 'objective' or 'rational world'. On the basis of a naive (literal) interpretation of *intentionality* phenomenology is said to argue that "the world can be understood only in terms of man's *attitudes* and *intentions* towards it" (196–7, italics added). Even Gregory (1981b, 252) voluntarizes the *intentional structure* of consciousness "through which objects are made to mean something to us".

As Buttimer (1974, 38) pointed to the development of an existential subjectivism as end product of a phenomenological perspective, so Relph (1970) posits phenomenology as an alternative to objective appraisals of environments and perceptions in terms of an approach which is 'man-centred' and offers a subjective insider's view as supplementary to the "objective map of social patterns" (Buttimer, 1969). In these terms Zimmerman's concept of resource as context dependent, Lowenthal's treatment of geographical experience, Merrens's emphasis on the contexts of agents and their own accounts of their experiences in historical geography, environmental perception studies, indeed any study insofar as it refers to the actors' intentions and attitudes, are all seen to be using phenomenological ideas (Relph, 1970, 196–7; Walmsley, 1974, 103). Phenomenological concepts are "experiential rather than factual" (Walmsley, 1974, 103) and phenomenology's 'intentionality principle' is taken to be concerned with the perceived environment. This has fostered a widely held misconception that a phenomenological geography takes the lifeworld as its object of study and that phenomenology has limited appeal only to certain branches of geography. This appeal is seen to be primarily in the area of historical, cultural, and behavioural research, at the micro-behavioural level, not at the macro-spatial level (Walmsley, 1974, 106). The emphasis is said to be on the cognitive states of the people involved, which should make the approach immediately attractive to social and cultural geography as a source of "new and important insights", while it may provide clarification of the foundations of location theory and spatial analysis (Relph, 1970, 199). (We will have to return to these claims in more detail later.)

Talarchek (1977, 22) reflects the ambiguity in these claims when he is unsure as to whether a "phenomenological geography would study all phenomena (according to Relph) or the lifeworld (according to Buttimer)". Such ambiguity is compounded when Buttimer (1976, 281) defines *Lebenswelt* as the "all encompassing horizon of our individual and collective lives". It seems that her phenomenology is also to be taken as all-encompassing.

(3) Relph and Buttimer are in clear agreement that the objects of phenomenological inquiry are the intentions and attitudes of agents or actors in and toward their world. Ley (1979, 225) also accepts this voluntaristic conception of intentionality. The lifeworld can be seen as a "group-centred world of events, relations and places infused with meaning and often with ambiguity, which – following Schütz and Merleau-Ponty – as the realm of mundane experience can become the focus of study". But he also claims that the lifeworld is the ground for the possibility of such study itself, or the universal horizon of all thematization:

at the root of an empirical science, there are necessary taken-for-granted assumptions, the same subjective naivete as occurs within our own private life-worlds . . . A phenomenological examination of social science thus begins with an analysis of presuppositions, with the exposure of assumptions which are unselfconsciously taken-for-granted. (Ley, 1979, 222–3)

It is necessary to ask, with Tuan (1975b, 246), what this sense of place is that functions as basis for a spatial geography and at the same time as lifeworld origin of our decisions and actions in everyday life. More directly, what is this sense of lifeworld that functions as the focus for humanistic geography and at the same time as the ground in terms of which the thematizations of science have meaning? Thus, we need to ask: (a) How do individuals "constitute the lifeworld in general and places in particular"? (b) How do "geographers typically constitute these constructions and incorporate them into their own accounts"? (Gregory, 1978a, 137).

Buttimer fails to understand this second claim when, in suggesting that phenomenological geography study social space, she states that "[the] key message for the student of social space is that much of our social experience is prereflective: it is accepted as given, reinforced through language and routine, and *rarely if ever has to be examined or changed*" (Buttimer, 1976, 286, italics added). She fails to see that the phenomenologist's task is to bring this pre-reflective world into transparency precisely in order to allow it to be examined and, where necessary, changed. It is the task of phenomenology, as Husserl remarked in conversation with Dorian Cairns (1976, 4), "to make understandable that which presents itself as brute fact, by making evident its constitution. This in the end will give man a life he can live honestly and fully accept in a world he can accept in spite of brute facts like wars and death." While the contribution of phenomenological reflection *may* lie in "unmasking preconscious, preplanned, involuntary dimensions of experience", Buttimer (1976, 286) finds it hard to see "how the phenomenological method could yield much insight into the problems which people face in their everyday lives".

Gregory (1978b) is able to clarify this misunderstanding partly in terms of the foundational role of lifeworld in science. Generally the scientist takes the world as given without reflecting upon the foundational role of the environing world of life for all his questions, and in terms of which his methodology makes sense.

The major task of rigorous philosophy, therefore, has to be the interrogation of the connections between the constitution of meaning which takes place within the life-world and the process of objectification which takes place within contemporary science, so as to reveal the limitations of the naturalist enterprise, to establish the validity of other forms of cognition and finally to reclaim for man an awareness of the total life-world which the strictures of contemporary science had denied to him. (162)

In other words, as Buttimer (1974, 37) herself had already pointed out but misunderstood, "[theoretical] knowledge . . . should begin with experience in the everyday world, and return to it always for verification and significance".

We are left with a view of lifeworld as the pre-theoretical domain, as the ground of science *and* as the object of study of 'geographical phenomenology'. But if phenomenology's claim to be a first philosophy and presuppositionless method is to hold – and while many geographers have denied this, none have shown how phenomenology in the mundane realm avoids contradiction or avoids the paradox of subjectivity in the transcendental realm – then geographers must give an account of how lifeworld can function as *both* ground *and* object of science. The phenomenologist must therefore face Husserl's 'paradoxical question' (see "The lifeworld and the world of science" (Husserl 1954, 363)): the full universal being of the lifeworld is pre-given and unconsidered by the scientist within the horizon of his theoretical end. The lifeworld is the pre-given horizon for the conditions of possibility for the scientist to know at all and hence to engage in science. The paradoxical question (which Husserl leaves unanswered) is then "can one not [turn to] the lifeworld, the world of which we are all conscious in life as the world of us all?" Can we do this without making it into a subject of universal investigation? And, further, can we do this from the viewpoint of science? In other words, can we study the lifeworld scientifically when it is presupposed as the necessary condition for science itself? And, if this is possible, what kind of enterprise is required?

18 The phenomenological method

When we turn to the question of the phenomenological method, the geographic literature contains few details of what such a method would be. Relph (1970, 193) is correct to insist that the "most characteristic core of phenomenology is its method, and an examination of the main elements and assumptions of this method will help to provide some insights into the nature of phenomenology". More common is Buttimer's (1976, 280) view that "[it] is in the spirit of the phenomenological purpose . . . rather than in the practice of phenomenological procedures, that one finds direction". In one notable case phenomenology's concern for method is almost completely (and incorrectly) denied:

Above all phenomenology is concerned with *ends* rather than *means*.
   Husserl, himself, clearly thought essentially in terms of the ultimate *truth* for which he was searching, laying down vague guidelines as to how it might be attained. (Billinge, 1977, 62)

Thus, too few geographers have really used the phenomenological method as such to be able to evaluate it fully (Hay, 1979, 16). Precisely why the phenomenological method should be ignored and diluted, as seems to be the case, is a complex question and goes to the heart of the issue at hand. Yet a full determination of this ambiguity in geographers' approaches to the phenomenological method cannot be completed here without remaining superficial. It will require the broader reflections which will be developed in Chapter 4, and in the final analysis the presentation of the phenomenological project itself in Part III.[19] For the present I will point to the treatment geographers have given to the issue, and discuss their mishandling of the central concept of 'intentionality'.

   For geographers phenomenology is non-empirical (Walmsley, 1974, 102; Entrikin, 1976, 625), and this may have made the approach unattractive to certain geographers whose own goal has been "to derive sets of empirically and theoretically sound statements about individual, small group, or mass behaviour". The phenomenological method, as it has developed in geography, begins with the phenomena of the lived world of immediate experience, including actions, memories, fantasies and perceptions, and seeks to clarify these in a rigorous way by careful observation and description (Relph, 1976a, preface). This entails suspending, as far as possible, the presuppositions and methods of official science (Tuan, 1971a, 181), and allowing the lifeworld "to reveal itself in its own terms" (Buttimer, 1976, 277). In seeking to describe the phenomenon "the researcher works to free himself from prejudices, preconceptions and other constraints that might distort or discolour [sic] his understanding" (Seamon, 1979a, 41). Through openness, unprejudiced seeing and 'phenomenological intuiting' "the student hopes eventually to experience a moment of sudden insight in which he comes to understand the phenomenon and its various aspects in a clearer light" (Seamon, 1979a, 43). Phenomenology is seen as a method which seeks to describe "the essential nature of things and experiences as they are in their own terms" (Seamon, 1979a, 40). Guelke (1978, 54) wonders what criteria of verification such a descriptive approach could have. And despite Ley's rejection of such questions as coming from within a positivist framework, the criticism is a pertinent one, not for all descriptive methods, but certainly for a methodology whose only explicit content requires openness, calmness and waiting. Furthermore, Seamon's claim is quite specific: phenomenology is not concerned with the how of the givenness of objects, or even how entities show themselves from themselves, but with the "essential nature of things and experiences *as they are in their own terms*". It is not surprising then to find in Seamon's next step the possibility of a seeing that is "reasonably correct" (see the example of the gestalt diagram in Seamon, 1979a): that is, correct in terms of the pre-existent and independent character-istics of the things as they are in their own terms (more accurately in terms of his own prior and unreflected determination of their 'proper' character). Here most clearly Seamon fails to transcend the underlying objectivism of *all* geographic discourse and the "prehensile grip" of the natural attitude (Aitchison, 1980, 86). To pursue this point it will be necessary to consider the interpretation geographers have given to the concept of *intentionality*.

18a Intentionality

The recognition of the intentional structure of consciousness and experience becomes, in geographers' hands, the principle of return to the 'forgotten man' of the social sciences (Ley, 1979, 228), where phenomenology is seen as that part of philosophy dealing with intentions, feelings and encounters (Sack, 1979, 447). One of the primary principles of phenomenology is intentionality, where every object is an object for a subject (Ley, 1979, 216), or as Seamon (1982, 3) argues where "all human impulses and actions do not exist unto themselves but are directed toward something and have an object". In this sense geographers see the phenomenological task as identifying "the modes and range of human intentionality" (3), or where

[each] place should equally be seen phenomenologically, in its relational context, as an object for a subject. To speak of a place is not to speak of an object alone, but of an image and an intent, of a landscape . . . Thus place always has meaning, it is always 'for' its subject, and this meaning carries back not only to the intent of the subject, but also forward as a separate variable prompting the behaviour of a new generation. (Ley, 1979, 228)

Ambiguity of language modifies these positions in two ways in geographical claims: (a) through an intentional structure "objects are made to mean something to us" (Gregory, 1981b, 252). Voluntarist and idealist implications are easily drawn from such claims, and indeed earlier Entrikin (1976, 617) had argued for just such a voluntarist position when he thought that by "radical doubt or isolation from the world of science and naturalistic common sense [sic] one can identify and *hence eliminate* the preconceptions prohibiting one from attaining essential insight or necessary knowledge of the world" (italics added). (b) Meaning is seen to be inherent in the object of reflection. "Humans, therefore, have nothing to do with creating meaning and can only apprehend it by the suspension of judgement and an act of faith which is mystical in nature" (Hugill, 1979, 3). Both positions imply a naive objectivism, Gregory suggesting an idealism, and both misconstruing the idea of intentionality.

Aitchison (1980, 86) has pointed out how even the minimal reductions Seamon admits in his method of phenomenological intuiting must be approached with care; the natural attitude is left behind only with difficulty and "the 'quietistic' encounters with pure streams of intentional experience are not readily arranged". Despite the invocation of pedagogic licence and the heuristic value of simplification in his reply, Seamon (1980a) proposes only a partial method, not for phenomenology, but for a descriptive activity in the natural attitude. The things of concern are the simple everyday events which are usually taken for granted – the walk to the mailbox, the experience of being lost, the sadness of leaving a place for which one has come to care (Seamon, 1979a, 41); these involve "a set of *qualitative* descriptions of *individual experiences*" (42, italics added).

Consequently, for Seamon as well as for Buttimer before him, "phenomenological descriptions remain opaque to the functional dynamism of spatial systems" (Buttimer, 1976, 277); an opacity which constitutes "two disciplines" – descriptions of lifeworld and geographical descriptions of space – between which dialogue is needed (277; also sée Seamon's (1982) ready embrace of Gregory's triad of approaches, and his attempt to create a dialogue between 'geographical phenomenology' and positivist approaches). Buttimer (1976, 278) goes so far as to claim that phenomenology does not offer "clear operational procedures to guide the empirical investigator", and should not, therefore, be understood as a method, but as a perspective which will help in the discovery of new aspects for geographical inquiry. "Fatigue" over the "act of consciousness itself" and the unexamined need "to move beyond the letter of the phenomenological law" permit *engagement* with existential issues of survival, anxiety, alienation and hope. Entrikin (1976, 625) similarly argues that phenomenology lacks a clearly defined methodology for ascertaining the structures or form of man's experience. But as we shall see this is to misunderstand phenomenology completely, and in its own terms to take for granted that which is at issue.

In turning to Schütz, Smith (1979, 365–6) points to abstraction and objectivation as important elements of the phenomenological method. Geographers have avoided this issue, and Seamon in particular has sought to reject it in his calls to allow the things to be as they are in themselves in their own terms. Buttimer also rejects abstraction and objectivation in favour of immediacy in approaching and studying the lifeworld (a contradiction that Wood (1982) has recently pointed to in a somewhat polemical way): "Scientific procedures which separate 'subjects' and 'objects', thought and action, people and environments are inadequate to investigate this lifeworld. The phenomenological approach ideally should allow lifeworld to reveal itself in its own terms" (Buttimer, 1976, 277).

Smith's concern, in contrast to Seamon's, is to ensure that the method of science abstracts from everyday experience and yet remains rooted in that experience. This entails a careful working out of the intentional structure of knowing. In particular, the scientist must ask "[how] is it possible to form objective concepts and an objectively verifiable theory of subjective-meaning structures?" (Schütz, in Smith, 1979, 366). Geographers have sought to criticize Husserl precisely on these grounds; that he cannot account for 'intersubjectivity' in the way that Schütz manages to do. The argument is made: (1) The lifeworld comprises 'intersubjective' meaning structures because we share that world with others. (2) Social scientific accounts employ constructs which already presuppose intersubjective meaning. (3) The possibility of objectivity arises from this intersubjectivity. "Moreover, it is an objectivity capable of conveying the emotion, feeling and meaning of everyday life" (Smith, 1979, 366; see also Ley, 1979, 232).

Ley (1980a, 3), in characterizing Husserl's method of transcendental reductions as "now little more than a curiosity", illustrates the failure of 'geographical phenomenology' to appreciate how central the methodological issue is to Husserlian phenomenology and phenomenology generally, and how carefully its difficulties must be resolved if phenomenology is to be a coherent enterprise, and is not to lapse into subjectivity and relativism. The issue of reduction, and the intentional structure of experience will be raised in more detail, in answer to these questions, in Chapter 5. They remain important if phenomenology is to succeed in clarifying preconceptions (Gregory, 1981b, 252) and analysing presuppositions, exposing assumptions and uncovering the hidden structures of the lifeworld which are unselfconsciously taken-for-granted (Ley, 1979, 223; 1980a, 3). If phenomenology is ever to understand the relationship between the "abstract conceptualizations" of science and the lived experience which founds and grounds it (Smith, 1979, 363) the issue of method, reduction and abstraction must be treated more carefully. It is significant in this context that Ley and Samuels (1978, 11) include phenomenology under epistemological considerations rather than methodological. Phenomenology is clearly seen as an anthropocentric perspective, of importance for the philosophical anthropology it is presumed to provide.

4

Geographical phenomenology: a critique of its foundations

19 The metaphysics of geographical phenomenology

It cannot be denied that the founding and guiding intuitions of a phenomenological approach in geography as it exists at the moment are in the main sound and well intentioned. Such a claim is justified alone in terms of the re-thinking of the positivist emphasis in geographical science it has occasioned, a point already made by Gregory (1978a). Yet, as the previous chapter sought to show, there must be a question as to whether this enterprise is at all phenomenological in the ways it claims to be. Furthermore it should be fairly apparent by now that while these intuitions may have been sound and the results significant, we cannot claim that 'geographical phenomenology' has *in any way* moved towards a resolution of how human science is to reconstitute its scientific conceptions away from positivism and towards some positive scientific perspective on man's world. The waters have been stirred, but visibility – as a result – remains poor. In one crucial way the situation has not improved at all; the radical critique of objectivism and naturalism occasioned by 'geographical phenomenology' in its denial of the tenets of positivism and logical empiricism has been transcended in the direction of an equally radical and naive subjectivism, accepting multiple world-views, unable to develop rigorous methods or intersubjectively acceptable criteria for evaluation, and in which the taken-for-granted world of the subject is to be examined, but not that of the researcher:

It is the very essence of the failure of humanistic geography: Its adherents want to get inside others but will not let others get inside them; they want to share the outsider's world, but not let the outsiders share theirs; they want to pry and prick at the life of the housing project resident, to listen to the stories of the elderly, to crawl beneath the skin of the alcoholic, but express no interest whatsoever in exposing to the excruciating scrutiny of the wondering world the ways of the graduate student and the college professor. (Wood, 1982, 506)

In one sense such a situation is a retrograde step; for the exaggerated claims of objectivism and naturalism it is a relatively straightforward matter to show the ways in which they fail, how they are self-contradictory, and how they can be corrected. In the case of subjectivism and the usually attendant historicism this is not the case; it is much more difficult to clarify their internal fallacies, and they are therefore much more easily accepted as viable perspectives. Thus, the one-sidedly false claims of naturalism have not been improved by this one-sidedly voluntaristic and individualist turn to subjectivity. Both operate within a framework that treats the world as subjects and objects; both fail to recognize accurately the nature of experience and distinguish it from the structure of science. In this section these claims have to be developed, and the issue of the paradox of subjectivity must be raised. In order to reach this point it will be necessary to describe the metaphysical or teleological principles which have, broadly, guided the geographer's interpretation of phenomenology.

20 Humanism and the confusion of the 'objective' and the 'subjective'

We have already seen how strongly humanism has influenced geographical interpretations of phenomenology. It will be useful to recap some of the main influences. Phenomenology, from the beginning, was to contribute to the development of a philosophical underpinning for humanistic approaches in geography (Relph, 1970, 193; Buttimer, 1976, 278). The world and man were inextricably linked, the former being known only through the intentions and attitudes of the latter (Relph, 1970, 195). Phenomenology's most important contribution in this area was the development of an experientially grounded humanism (Buttimer, 1976), and its focus of concern, or primary subject-matter, was the pre-scientific awareness of our environment (Entrikin, 1976, 625). Such 'humanist' interpretations characterize the entire spectrum of geographic writings on phenomenology, even the recent sophisticated approaches to philosophical issues typified by Eyles (1981, 1381), who sees phenomenology as a means to "humanize structuralism".

Such a position is "an extreme anthropocentric view of the world in which man and nature are brought into a single system unified in its reference to man and his attitudes" (Relph, 1970, 195; see also 178; Mercer and Powell, 1972, 8). The objectivities of professional geographers, including 'superorganic' concepts such as culture and social relations are denied any privileged status, and are instead placed alongside the shared world of experience and supplemented by the subjective or inside view (Relph, 1970, 196; Buttimer, 1969, 417–26).[1]

Science thus becomes problematical, and geographers have undertaken varied contortions seeking to unify these claims within a consistent position on objectification *and* science. Two arguments are common:

(i) Scientific geography "is no more real than any other personal geography" because both are derived from shared experience (Relph, 1970, 196). That is, scientific knowing is one form of knowing alongside others. But Relph is mistaken when he implies that personal geographies are as objectifying as science, and that, in terms of the criterion of objectivity, scientific and personal geographies are of equal validity, just because they stem from the same root. It is not enough to place science and personal geographies side by side, as if the situation were one of different and separate cultural systems. Science and the everyday are inextricably linked and, for the claims Relph wishes to make, it is necessary to understand this interrelation.

(ii) Buttimer (1974, 38) argues somewhat differently:

Intentionality is man's striking toward a structuring of his world through caring, hoping, conceiving, feeling and meaning. The 'subjective' striving takes place within an 'objective' set of conditions. Insofar as these conditions assume routinized or relatively stable shape in the typified meanings of the everyday world, they could be described within the conceptual grasp of social science. But values and meanings underlying a particular society's thrust towards its own future cannot be embraced within the framework of individual scientific disciplines.

The structure of intentionality – fundamental to the phenomenological argument – is here situated within a subjectivist framework, over against 'objective' conditions.[2] Buttimer claims that only some of these subjective conditions can be described in social science; the a priori frameworks of meaning which underpin a particular society's understanding cannot be elucidated within individual scientific disciplines. Buttimer seeks to transcend the subjective/objective dualism by recognizing the validity of both modes. The approach she adopts – claimed to be phenomenological, at least in spirit – causes progressively greater methodological difficulties as we move from these early claims to their application and development in subsequent work, particularly in the work of David Seamon. Buttimer psychologizes the phenomenological method, interpreting it naively in the natural attitude. Thus the "initial criterion is the creation of a climate which makes it psychologically safe for the other person, event, or phenomenon to reveal its internal frame of reference" (Buttimer, 1976, 282).

In fact both Relph's and Buttimer's positions are in danger of falling into a relativism: Relph because he sets up a multiple-world perspective, yet provides no explication of how these worlds are related;[3] Buttimer because in psychologizing the phenomenological concept of intentionality (and in drawing the conclusions she does) she ignores the hermeneutic component to all understanding on the one hand and the necessary rigorous methodology that phenomenology entails on the other. The result is ungrounded method, unfounded claims, and the actual imposition of unexamined presuppositions.

From this basis, and from the emphasis on secondary phenomenological literature, 'geographical phenomenology' has developed a certain independent momentum. These initial premises and basic concepts have been accepted unexamined, and the project fleshed out in terms of them. The imposition of humanist and anthropocentric a priori concepts on to the phenomenological project has encouraged a voluntarist and subjectivist interpretation of intentionality. Here relativism is a constant possibility; but also here the question of the nature of science is lost. Everyday and unreflected meanings of terms – in particular of the meaning of 'objective' – form the basis for 'philosophical' discussion in terms of which particular positions are defined. Discourse becomes difficult as terminology and forms of argument become confused. Thus, in order to continue this argument in a substantive manner we will have to consider the treatment of (a) subjectivity and intentionality, (b) individualism, and (c) the things themselves, consciousness, and the problem of the 'objective world'.

20a Subjectivity and intentionality

The intentional structure of experience forms the core of the phenomenological project. When filtered through humanist lenses "man is understood as the source of acts of intention, and it is only through the study of man's intentions that we can comprehend the world, for it is these that give meaning to man's behaviour" (Relph, 1970, 194). The structure of intentionality is one-sidedly founded in the human subject, and thus Relph here, Buttimer (1974, 37) and Walmsley (1974, 101) can claim that the world is understood as being subjective. This is not far from claiming, as Billinge (1977, 57) does, that in phenomenology facts and objects exist outside of man's consciousness; that "it is what phenomena mean that define their reality, not what they are". Thus, step by step 'geographical phenomenology' moves towards radical subjectivism (see, for example, Hay, 1979, 13). From such a voluntarist view of intentionality, and a view of phenomenology as "far more concerned with an individual's *intentions* towards phenomena than with the definition of phenomena as such", Billinge (1977, 57–61) argues that presuppositional inquiry seeks to eradicate a priori assumptions, and thus seeks to "reveal to what extent reality is an individual's own construction of it" (57). It follows that precise criteria of evaluation do not exist, and that "experience and events are often obscure, ill-defined, ephemeral and, above all, by their very nature unquantifiable" (57). For Mercer and Powell (1972, 198) it is not possible to prove anything by the phenomenological method because it is a subjective enterprise. Jackson (1981, 300–1) accepts this subjective nature of experience in phenomenology, arguing from it to the need to consider the social nature of that experience through the work of Durkheim, while Cosgrove (1978) sees marxist humanism as a way of tempering the subjectivity and idealism of phenomenological approaches.

20b Individualism

While 'geographical phenomenology' seeks to counter the objectivism of exaggerated claims in spatial analysis, it has sought to do so partially in terms of a swing to subjectivism, subjectivist philosophies (Hay, 1979) and so-called philosophies of meaning (Ley, 1981). Hay (1979, 15) sees this trend as a second form of reductionism, where phenomenological accounts concentrate on the individual, denying the possible ontological status of aggregate social structures such as communities and nations. Certainly, geographers such as Johnston (1979, 140–1), Hufferd (1980, 18), and Jackson (1981, 299) see phenomenology as essentially individualistic, and call for complementary usage of 'group approaches' to offset this emphasis. Here phenomenology is thought of as restricted to a "perspective on the contextual specificity of individual meanings" (Jackson, 1981, 303), and thus fails to account for the great range in the scale of behaviour along a continuum of aggregation from individual to societal behaviour. For Hufferd (1980, 18) the phenomenological method "is appropriate for explaining human actions on an individual scale, but is not applicable as it stands to the group or regional scale investigated by geography". Indeed "the spirit of phenomenology abhors the collective – or generic-level view" (21). Certainly, if we accept Billinge's (1977, 57) definition above, of the phenomenological concern with phenomena, this conclusion is inescapable, and 'geographical phenomenology' then requires some broader perspective to lift "the phenomenological insight out of its unfruitful idiographic repose and make[s] it scientific" (Hufferd, 1980, 22).

Ley (1979, 216) points towards resolution of this confusion when he re-thinks the intentionality of experience, and Eyles (1981, 1381) most clearly transcends subjectivist and individualist interpretations when he argues:

Society is not merely a hierarchy of structures nor a collection of monadic individuals, but a fundamental structure of experience, a permanent and ever-present horizon to all subjectivity and action. Individuality and sociality are implicated in each other. 'My relation to myself is already generality,' as I am born into a world of speech, customs, institutions, and cultural objects.

Gregory (1978a, 130) is more direct: "the importance of Husserl's transcendental phenomenology is *not* that it provides for a subtle return to uniqueness, as has so often been claimed in the past. It was certainly *not* Husserl's intention to uphold the validity of a multiplicity of different frames of reference".

Nevertheless the acceptance of phenomenology's subject-matter as social meaning, individually internalized as specific and personal intentions has given rise to a multiple-world perspective, and to an emphasis on personal geographies. This view has been a difficult one to accept for those geographers whose own perspectives emphasize aggregate analysis or materialist explanation. How is Relph to distinguish fundamental from secondary world-views? How are typified social meanings to account for the hidden social and economic forces and relations of modern society? These are questions which arise from such a subjectivist and individualist interpretation of phenomenology, and must be answered if the phenomenological project is to be retrieved in a meaningful way.

20c The 'things themselves', 'consciousness' and 'the problem of the objective world'

The confusion of the 'things themselves', 'objective world' and the role of consciousness (or more broadly intentionality) underpins all discourse about phenomenology in geography. This claim has already been made above, and its demonstration is crucial to the argument of this chapter. Such confusion is not merely a slip of the pen, a careless misreading of a text, or a personal idiosyncrasy of an author. It is fundamental to contemporary geographic discourse in general, and its acceptance can be traced throughout the history of the discipline (see

Chapter 2). It comes to a head with responses to positivism, and particularly with historicism and subjectivist rejections of positivism and positive science. Constructivist theories[4] have been rejected, and with them objectivation as a fundamental principle of science has been questioned. Idealist interpretations of world have thus clashed with realist and more recently materialist conceptions, and recently Gregory (1981a; 1982) and Ley (1982) have begun a dialogue on this state of affairs, seeking to find ways in which it is to be transcended.

Buttimer (1976, 291; 1977, 183) had cautioned earlier against subjectivist interpretations of phenomenology, arguing that "phenomenology muddies the waters for those who believe in separating 'subjective' and 'objective' modes of knowing". But, in psychologizing the method and in reducing the rigour of its principles, this 'variation' of phenomenology became merely an undisciplined exercise in description, without clarification of a priori assumptions.

In 1970 Relph had already claimed that the objects of man's experience cannot exist independently of his consciousness. His precise claim was:

In the description of the world of experience, or to use Husserl's phrase, in the return to the things themselves as the objects of man's experience, it is held that these objects cannot exist independently of man's consciousness. (Relph, 1970, 193)

Relph confuses things and objects. Objects are objects of man's experience. Thus, Relph claims, we must assume that objects cannot exist independently of consciousness. But what of things? By defining an object as that which 'stands over against' a subject – as an object of man's theoretical reflection – we necessarily claim that such objects cannot exist independently of that 'standing over against'. But do we thereby say anything about the existence of things or entities which have not yet been constituted as 'objects'? The questions are the very ones that Berkeley addressed in his *Principles of human knowledge*, and constitute the basis for a radical idealism and, naively interpreted, solipsism.

20d Idealism

For Mercer and Powell (1972, 34–5) idealism in historical thought is closely allied with phenomenology, particularly in their opposition to positivism. Billinge (1977, 56, n. 1) draws explicitly on this claim equating "Guelke's idealism, derived from the historians Collingwood and Croce, with a firm phenomenological outlook". Thus the appearance of Guelke's (1975) work affords an opportunity to examine several aspects of the "standard pheneomenological mythology" (Billinge, 1977, 56). Similarly Hay (1979, 9) sees the two main strands of subjective thought as idealism and phenomenology, but does not distinguish between them (14–15). By 1979 Johnston (1979, 129–41) can argue that idealism and phenomenology are hermeneutic approaches, proposed to replace the positivism of spatial science. They focus on the decision maker and his perceived world and deny the existence of an objective world. Phenomenology becomes idealism.

The identification of phenomenology with idealism in this way has unfortunate consequences for humanistic perspectives in geography which have claimed to draw upon phenomenology. Not wishing to accept the implications of this identification, Ley (1978, 44) has sought to deny the accuracy – not of the claim itself – but of the importance of Husserlian phenomenology to the humanist project:

a series of critiques of humanism in geography . . . are beginning to appear, all of which mistakenly cast the humanist perspective in an excessively idealist mold. These essays have inappropriately overassociated phenomenology with Husserl's transcendental idealism, not recognizing that contemporary phenomenologists in the social sciences draw their inspiration not from Husserl but rather from the philosophers with an eye to social science such as Schütz and Merleau-Ponty, who were not prepared to sacrifice existence for essence, for whom perceptions were always considered in context, in the concrete world of everyday life.

The result is the further identification of Husserlian phenomenology with idealism.[5]

Geographers dealing with phenomenology have found it difficult to deal with the existence of entities (as physical bodies) independent of man's existence, with objects of immediate experience and with transcendent objects. In this regard witness Buttimer's hesitant handling of the issue of environment:

Phenomenologists affirm theoretically that environments ('world') play a dynamic role in human experience, but often in practice they implicitly subsume such dynamism within a dialogue in which human agents ascribe meaning and significance. Geographers would be more inclined to ascribe a dynamism of their own to such external conditions as ecosystems, linkage patterns, and economies. (Buttimer, 1976, 285)

Such a tentative approach to environment (*not* 'world') characterizes humanistic geography generally, and can, as Ley has argued, be attributed to overly idealistic assumptions.

Attempts to transcend the subjective–objective dichotomy, within 'geographical phenomenology', have been only partially successful. Accounts of individual and cultural experience have been produced, but phenomenology will "frustrate us by its inability to convey coherently the brutal objectivity of much everyday experience. It can say little about the societal creation and manipulation of reality" (Smith, 1979, 367). Like scientific realists before, Smith's dialectical materialism sees the clear failure of 'geographical phenomenology' to deal with, and even to take seriously, the society external to the individual (367). Such criticism must be taken seriously when positions such as those described by Buttimer (1976, 284) have been uncritically accepted:

The social scientist may object to the tendency in phenomenology to universalize about human experience from individual accounts. A geographer would be justifiably skeptical about some of the generalizations which have been propounded about lived space. The ideal person described by phenomenologists appears to be rural (at least 'local') at heart; non-place-based social networks do not seriously influence his knowledge of space, or his attractions or repulsions from places.

The critique from materialist perspectives is forceful. The placelessness and destruction of place that Relph and Seamon allude to occurs because of objective social forces that such a phenomenology cannot fully apprehend (Smith, 1979, 368; Gregory, 1981a, 16). Similarly Gregory (1978b, 166) sees hermeneutic approaches (in which phenomenology is included) as insufficient to be self-grounding because they fail to account for the "constraints on social actions" in the taken-for-granted world; that is, they ignore the 'material imperatives' and the 'external constraints' which are imposed on and flow from social actions (Gregory, 1978a, 139). The taken-for-granted world, sociality and consciousness, as the focus of phenomenology's concern, must be grounded in material existence. The "social and historical framework, therefore, shapes the production of sociality and consciousness" (Eyles, 1981, 1382).

From this perspective phenomenology is taken to be the study of the social world and lived experience. It is – as Billinge (1977) claims – concerned not with phenomena as such, but with the meaning of phenomena. This world of meaning and the structural–material exigencies of society are taken together as dialectically related, each able to curtail the excesses and deficiencies of the other (Eyles, 1981), or they are functionally related in such a way that a coherent unity of perspectives can be constructed (Gregory, 1978a; 1978b).

Geographers' failure to understand fully the claims about intentionality, their universal focus on lifeworld as ontical realm and subject-matter, and their subjectivizing and idealizing of it, have led to a stubborn refusal to admit the universality of meaning to which Husserl referred. Meaning itself is subjectivized, and consequently claims are made to justify the retention of materialist or naturalist conceptions of objective structures and forces. Gregory (1978b, 163) typifies this attitude when, after describing Husserl's position he quickly limits it to one concerned with subjective meaning, claiming that the approaches he wishes to advocate "retain Husserl's commitment to structures of social meaning, but they re-introduce elements of the naturalism which he repudiated". A problematic concept of determination underlies this thinking, and its resolution will depend "on a considered recognition of the ways in which both the social constitution of a 'science' and the structuration of society can be shown to depend on a prior *materialism*" (Gregory, 1981a, 15).

As the debate between Habermas and Gadamer has shown, the claims of phenomenology and philosophical hermeneutics *cannot* be reduced to operational conceptions within a system of interests (see Pickles, 1981). Their concern is with the very conditions of possibility and the universal structures which those interests and scientific approaches presuppose. Gregory cannot simply 'paste' together a pastiche of Husserlian phenomenology and the naturalism he repudiated, unless he can show, from some metaposition, the ways in which that repudiation is flawed. This he does not do, but instead continues to err in his delimitation of the reach of phenomenology, whose limits critical science will extend. There are, he argues, constraints on social actions which are taken for granted to such an extent that the actors "are either unable to verbalize them or would consider it irrelevant to do so" (Gregory, 1978a, 125). It is the task of critical science to disclose the constitution of these structures. (In the next chapter we will have to ask to what extent this is not *also* the task of a phenomenology whose reach is not arbitrarily and falsely delimited to the study of social meaning in its literal and immediate sense.) Consequently the issue of action versus structure has become the focus for current discussion of phenomenology, interpreted as a philosophy of meaning, notably in the work of Ley (1980a; 1981) and Gregory (1981a). Questions of constraints and power pose, for 'geographical phenomenology', insurmountable barriers, producing an "aspired for but as yet absent synthesis between intentionality and bounding conditions" (Ley, 1981, 1).

How are *we* to transcend such barriers or provide the "as yet absent synthesis"? First, by a return to the internal critique of the phenomenological project developed by geographers themselves. Second, by a retrieval of the essential arguments by which the path to these insurmountable barriers developed. The incompossibility of the unity that Ley seeks will have to be demonstrated, and the untenable nature of a conception of social reality as something of the order of a Necker cube, requiring one or another perspective to reveal one or the other condition (intentionality *or* bounding conditions), will have to be explained. The demonstration of this untenable, and in the final analysis arbitrary, juxtaposition of perspectives will be the final goal of this chapter.

21 Geographical phenomenology: its internal critique

Despite the growing and substantial criticisms of the initial steps toward a 'geographical phenomenology', early critiques of the position were often supportive of the enterprise, at least of its 'spirit'. In these critiques some important claims were clarified in a preliminary fashion; specifically the method, the attitude and the suspension of prior constructions, subjectivism, and the possibility of intersubjective validation of claims. Misconceptions have also been exacerbated by this internal critique.

Gibson (1974, 48), in particular, was able to bring a clear understanding of some of the *actual* claims of Husserl to bear: "For Husserl phenomenology was a science: its methods as he devised them were to objectify man's consciousness of objects, and to do so by cutting through the 'givens' of idealism and positivism." These methods are not subjective, nor unverifiable, insofar as they yield evidence available to all who follow the rules and who accept not only sense observation but also the evidence from consciousness: intuition, remembering, imagining. Criteria of validity entail comparison between the description contained in a phenomenological account and our first-hand experience of the phenomena described. Buttimer (and the profession generally) have not accepted Gibson's insightful comments; instead they have been attracted to the literature dealing with phenomenology (and existentialism) in seeking a path through values and subjectivity. In this literature, particularly that of Buttimer: "They will read about some value suppositions that bear stronger marks of self-gratification and deep subjectivity than of social empathy and intersubjectivity" (Gibson, 1974, 48).

The loss of rigour in approaching the phenomenological method creates certain problems of interpretation of the broader project. In referring to Buttimer's claims, Relph (1977, 179) notes that:

it is inconsistent with the major tenets of phenomenology to accept existing concepts and explanations of phenomena, on the contrary the aim is to suspend belief in such explanations and to elucidate the variety of our direct pre-scientific experiences of the lifeworld. It could be that phenomenological approaches will lead to the identification of time–space rhythms of some form, but these cannot be assumed beforehand, nor if they are discovered will they have the same ontological status as those discussed by Hägerstrand.

Relph is correct in claiming that phenomenology does not permit straightforward combinations with existing geographical concepts, yet the concepts of space, place, distance, home, travel, etc., which his own work uses are not seen to be problematical, nor does he see that it is a phenomenological requirement that they be conceived in this way. Making the basic concepts of science problematic is a necessary procedure for any science. Phenomenology is one method which seeks to clarify those basic concepts. Place is accepted as an unquestioned given, and its loss in everydayness – placelessness – is the focus of concern. But insofar as that which is missing – place – is never fully clarified, immediately and apodictically, placelessness can only be investigated unreflectively in the natural attitude; the argument constitutes itself not ontologically, but as a particular ontical world-view. In this sense, the argument is not phenomenological.

A phenomenology that sought to question and ground basic concepts – in the taken-for-granted of the everyday world *or* in the world of science – would not be open to the dismissive criticism that 'geographical phenomenology' has drawn. Entrikin's (1977, 214) claim that phenomenology is inadequate for providing a philosophical framework which can incorporate the concepts of the spatial perspective and scientific geography is thus, itself, inadequate as a description of the domain of objects with which phenomenology is legitimately (and necessarily) concerned. The essence, if not the substance, of Billinge's (1977, 63) claim holds true:

It is important to appreciate that the revised phenomenology . . . in no way retains the most important elements of the Husserlian philosophy. There is, for example, no emphasis on presuppositionless inquiry, nor on the dialectical relationship between parts; . . . little that is recognizable as phenomenology at its hardest core remains at all.[6]

21a Phenomenology and criteria of validity

Geographical phenomenology soon lost any pretence at interest in this 'hardest core', and in fact was widely criticized for being 'soft', 'loose' and too much concerned with emotive issues instead of with good science. Yet geographers (and particularly the critics of phenomenology) did not understand 'science' nor philosophy sufficiently well to defeat its claims directly, nor were they sufficiently confident as to the actual nature of geography as a science to pursue the argument to its full conclusion. Thus Guelke (1978, 59), for example, rejects phenomenology as a viable foundation for geography as such a "*scientific-type discipline*" (italics added). Critics argued that phenomenology could be dismissed because it was too subjective:

I do not doubt that emotions are an important part of life but only doubt whether phenomenological analysis can help us answer questions about man's use of the earth. Unless phenomenologists provide some objective criteria for measuring meaning, phenomenological geography becomes indistinguishable from landscape painting or poetry. It has power to touch our emotions but it does not give us the tools to understand or explain human behaviour in an intersubjective or objective way. (Guelke, 1978, 54)

Guelke continues:

The phenomenologists might, for example, provide evocative descriptions of the lives of Appalachian mountain folk, but in geography we must seek verifiable, communicable knowledge rather than evocative descriptions of doubtful empirical status.

Prior to Guelke's description of phenomenology as loosely grounded and emotionally stimulated poetic description, Billinge (1977, 64) had raised the issue of rigour in the phenomenological method used by geographers. It seemed to him that this use of phenomenology encouraged us to "justify our partially formulated hypotheses, exploit the atypicality of our data, cease worrying about the validity of our reconstruction, and within some weakly articulated framework label the whole exercise phenomenological". The issue of verification needed to be raised (Hay, 1979, 15–16). It had been ignored by geographers, and pure description of the world was inevitably guided by interpretation, and was therefore subjective (15). How then was the geographer to prove anything using the phenomenological method; verification and replicability, two necessary components of science, seemed to be missing. Indeed, since it appeals ultimately to intuition and not to the logic of language, even argument itself was said to be impossible (Mercer and Powell, 1972, 14).

Without criteria of validity and verification, and because it rejected objectification and distanciation from the lived world, some geographers wondered how science was possible at all. A phenomenological geography of this sort "would seem hard pressed to deal with large aggregations of people or objects and its adoption would necessitate the abandonment of any pretense of prediction" (Talarchek, 1977, 22). Furthermore, such a geography seemed to move in the opposing direction to a great deal of social science which served as the role models for many areas of the discipline. "If geography were to adopt a phenomenological paradigm it would surely find itself isolated from other social sciences which are either more quantitative and scientific, like economics, or rapidly becoming so, like urban history" (22).

22 The turn to Schütz's constitutive phenomenology and justifying a return to Husserl

> All of phenomenology is not Husserl, even though he is more or less its center. (Ricoeur, 1967, 3)

It is ironic that in order to explicate the nature of phenomenology it is necessary to *justify* why one should return to the writings of Husserl. It is, however, necessary to do so, and for a variety of reasons. It is necessary for the obvious but important reason that all subsequent phenomenological thinking is predicated on Husserl's own work, whether it seeks to extend or amend it. It is necessary because, and in spite of claims to the contrary (Smith, 1979, 365), Husserl more than any other phenomenologist lays out the precise and formal relationships between phenomenology and empirical science, and between philosophy and science in the context of phenomenology. In more restricted vein, it is necessary because in recent writings geographers have tended to dismiss Husserl as mistaken, or as in some way dispensable, in order to allow the work of another to be focussed upon – notably to allow for a wholesale shift of emphasis to Schütz's constitutive phenomenology (Tuan, 1971a; Entrikin, 1976; Gregory, 1978a; 1978b; 1981a; Ley, 1977; 1980a; Hay, 1979; Smith, 1979; Eyles, 1981; Jackson, 1981).[7]

The most extreme attempt to re-write the role of Husserlian phenomenology in, and its relevance for, 'geographical phenomenology' is given by Ley (1980a). He seeks to deny claims that humanism errs toward voluntarism and idealism, arguing that it *can* provide an "as yet absent synthesis between intentionality and bounding conditions" (1980a, 1), by breaking away from the Husserlian connection with phenomenology. This connection has become an 'embarrassment' to humanistic geography for the reasons given.

Geographers, much like philosophers, have made a good deal of Schütz's links with Husserl, and of the limitations of Husserl's transcendent [sic] philosophy (Entrikin, 1976). And this has indeed justified the charges of idealism, voluntarism, abstraction from context, and a sometimes metaphysical search for essences. The Husserlian connection is a distraction, and indeed it is incongruous that it has received such attention. (9)

Gregory (1978a, 125) and Billinge (1977, 66) agree when they question the extent to which any of the earlier discussions dealing with phenomenology "really have – *or can ever be* – 'informed' by Husserl's phenomenology" (Gregory, 1978a, 125).

It is not my intention to deny the importance of Schütz: far from it. Rather I wish to suggest that if Husserlian phenomenology has not yet *really been* considered in geography, as Gregory (1978a) and Billinge (1977) assert (setting aside their unsupported assertions that it can never inform geographic concerns) and as the previous chapter sought to demonstrate, Husserl may still remain important: probably for an understanding of Schütz, Merleau-Ponty and Heidegger; almost certainly if geographers are to understand precisely and clearly the formal relationships between phenomenology and science. However, it is not my intention to suggest that criticism of transcendental phenomenology is unfounded, and that it should be ignored. Yet the position itself cannot be dismissed, in the manner geographers have sought to do, on the basis of slogan and authority, nor can it be replaced fully by work that presupposes Husserl's own foundational claims, as is most clearly the case with Alfred Schütz.

Smith finds it more fruitful to examine phenomenology through the eyes of Alfred Schütz, whose analyses "are a useful antidote to the confusion of humanistic geography with phenomenology" (Smith, 1979, 365–7). Ley points to Schütz and Merleau-Ponty in particular, whose interest in social science led them 'beyond' pure philosophy and Husserlian phenomenology. Gregory (1978a, 134) and more recently Ley (1980a) argue that the price of retaining Weber's commitment to empirical validation was the rejection of Husserl's transcendental *epoche*. Geographers have thus sought to build a phenomenological approach which is "genuinely social" (Jackson, 1981, 302), which when related to the "forgotten link with Weber . . . draws Schützian phenomenology in a historical context where intents counter constraints and thus reveal the distribution of power, and where multiple realities create discrete interest groups whose values may well conflict" (Ley, 1980a, 9).

Gregory (1978a, 125–6) also rejects the limits of Husserlian philosophy and the Husserlian project as he understands it, claiming that it does not go far enough.[8] In effect he accepts Entrikin's (1976) claim that phenomenology operates as criticism, rather than as an alternative to science (Gregory, 1978a, 131). Through Schütz's constitutive phenomenology he articulates a perspective independent of Husserl's phenomenology – "to investigate the way in which they [underlying essences] were concealed by skeins of intersubjectively woven social meanings" (126). According to Gregory, Schütz was here not simply adopting Husserl's transcendental phenomenology, but also incorporating certain propositions which permit "the explicit formulation of determinate relations between a set of variables, [which are] capable of being verified by anyone who is prepared to make the effort to do so through observation [so that] a fairly extensive class of empirically ascertainable regularities can be explained" (126).

If we are to comprehend the broader implications of these somewhat complex claims, we might trace Gregory's argument step by step:

1. Husserlian phenomenology is divorced from the practical concerns of social science.

2. It operates as criticism, rather than directly informing any particular science.

3. It is obsessively concerned with uncovering 'essences' of social phenomena.[9]

4. This prevents Husserl from understanding the *social meaning* of those phenomena.

5. Schütz *is* concerned with this.

6. Schütz incorporates certain propositions concerning relations, variables and empirical determination, and in this way conjoins "humanistic and scientific enquiry" (126).

7. By implication Husserl's phenomenology has no connection with empirical science, and does not achieve what Schütz in (6) does.

8. Husserl's phenomenology is not practical, it operates as criticism, it is unable to account for social meaning, indeed it discards it as "bric a brac" (126), and it is unable to inform the practice and philosophy of empirical science.

9. Gregory uses "Schütz's work to link Husserl's treatment of the crisis of the European sciences in general to a geography of the life-world in particular" (127).

Yet Gregory (1978a, 127; 1978b, 162) chooses to treat Husserl's work only since 1935, specifically *The crisis of European sciences and transcendental phenomenology* (hereafter referred to as *Crisis*). This work is unfinished and is the cornerpiece of Husserl's historico-critical path to phenomenology. He thereby ignores Husserl's Cartesian path, which he laid out in, for example, *Ideas*, *Cartesian meditations* and *Phenomenological psychology* where he develops the necessary relationship between eidetic science and empirical science, *and* his path through the sciences, which he laid out briefly in *First Philosophy*.

Misrepresentation continues when Gregory emphasizes the significance of Schütz's going beyond Husserl "because he believed that the
propositions of social science ought to be capable of empirical
validation" (Gregory, 1978a, 142), and when Ley (1980a, 1) claims that
"Schütz is a central figure if only because of his attempt to act as a
broker between the philosophies of meaning and the empirical social
sciences." This is to remove the very aim of a rational and prejudice-
free science towards which Husserlian phenomenology was directed,
and to ignore totally the importance Husserl gave to phenomenologically grounded human sciences in the process of cultural 'renewal'
(Husserl, 1923).

In a broader context this argument seeks ultimately to justify the
limitation of phenomenological concerns to the phenomenon of social
meaning. Schütz is used instrumentally in this regard because of his
development of a phenomenology of the social world. Thus, Ley
(1980a, 1) points to Schütz as "a key figure in other important attempts
at the integration of meaning and structure, including Berger and
Luckmann (1967) and Giddens (1976), who begin with Schütz *even if
they later find his work incomplete.* Within human geography, too, his
strategic role has been identified (Ley, 1977; Gregory, 1978a)" (italics
added). To justify the turn to critical theory, Gregory (1978b, 167)
claims that "for all their [Husserl and Schütz] concern with the way in
which discourse was bound to the life-world they were unable to
account for the way in which its structures were reproduced and
transformed". Such criticism is pertinent only provided we understand
more carefully the ways in which the Husserlian project fails to situate
man within a world, although recognition of this fact does not
necessarily result in the rejection of phenomenology, as we shall see.
Gregory's argument in favour of a turn to critical theory can be
appropriated to justify our own later turning to Heidegger's treatment
of the facticity of worldhood.

Limiting phenomenology – as reflexive explanation – to the domain
of social meaning is necessary if Gregory is to substantiate his claims
for critical theory. His own project is clearly evident, and his
delimitation of phenomenology explicitly developed when he claims
that "[once] the concern for reflexive explanation is translated into
this operationally more tractable context, the limitations of a
phenomenological geography ought to emerge more clearly" (Gregory, 1978a, 126). Husserlian phenomenology is seen to have been
important in its rejection of positivism, but it "fails to provide an
alternative which is congruent with more practical interests" (130).
The structure of intentionality makes objects mean something to us,

and thus Husserlian phenomenology in seeking "to disengage from the objects and withdraw into the intentional structures" (129) left the transition from the empirical to the transcendental vague, and failed to explain "precisely how the world was to be reconstituted once it had been put in brackets" (130). It follows that this phenomenology is easily taken "to provide the philosophical props necessary to support an excavation of purely individual 'geographies of the mind'" (130). Husserlian phenomenology is then readily transposed into idealism, and, with Ley, is easily rejected.

The sophisticated manner of Gregory's presentation of important phenomenological ideas, and his support for selected *elements* of Husserlian and Schützian phenomenologies, should not blind us to the distorted conception of the fundamental project and the meaning of intentionality on which his argument is based. Intentionality and meaning for Gregory remain elements of a subjective stance taken voluntarily, to be studied in terms of a materialist framework of objective structures: "a major deficiency of the programme [of phenomenology] as it stands is its restricted conception of social structure: in particular, it ignores the material imperatives and consequences of social actions and the external constraints which are imposed on and flow from them" (139). Consequently Gregory (142) insists, with Scott (1976, 635), on "an interplay between subjective intentionality and the universe of external objective social relations". The fundamental principle of phenomenology – to transcend the dualism of subjectivism and objectivism – for which the structure of intentionality is crucial, is here posited in terms of the very framework it seeks to transcend. The claims of Husserl are denied. Phenomenology – distorted into a naive subjectivism concerned with internal meaning – is with Schütz seen to be concerned with social meaning. The '*external* constraints' of 'external objective social relations', interpreted in this manner, are co-constitutive of social reality. Social science seeks to unify or to seek some convergence between the realms of social meaning and objective social relations. David Ley (1980a, 1) agrees with this position, seeking "convergence of system and lifeworld [by] simultaneously examining the interaction of constraint and choice, structure and meaning. This rules out of court not only deterministic structuralisms which have been so popular in the 1970's, but also the excessive voluntarism of some humanistic philosophies." In particular, it rules out Husserlian phenomenology, diverting attention away from its role as foundational for the sciences, *and* it exacerbates the objectivism and subjectivism of geographic discourse through its unquestioned entrenchment of these traditional categories.

PART III

Phenomenology and the question of human science

To be sure, scientific communication between positive scientists and philosophers cannot be tied down to definite rules, especially since the clarity, certainty, and originality of critiques by scientists of the foundations of their own positive sciences change as often and are as varied as the stage reached and maintained by philosophy in clarifying its own essence. This communication stays genuine, lively, and fruitful only when the respective positive–ontic and transcendental–ontological inquiries are guided by an instinct for the issues and by the certainty of scientific good sense, and when all the questions about dominance, pre-eminence and vitality recede behind the inner necessities of the scientific problem itself. (Heidegger, 1976, 21)

5

Husserlian phenomenology: the foundational project

Philosophers, as things now stand, are all too fond of offering criticism from on high instead of studying and understanding things from within. They often behave toward phenomenology as Berkeley – otherwise a brilliant philosopher and psychologist – behaved two centuries ago toward the then newly established infinitesimal calculus. He thought he could prove, by his logically sharp but superficial criticism, this sort of mathematical analysis to be completely groundless extravagance, a vacuous game played with empty abstractions. It is utterly beyond doubt that phenomenology, new and most fertile, will overcome all resistance and stupidity and will enjoy enormous development, just as the infinitesimal mathematics that was so alien to its contemporaries did, and just as exact physics, in opposition to the brilliantly obscure nature philosophy of the Renaissance, has done since the time of Galileo. (Husserl, 1917, 17)

23 What is phenomenology?

In juxtaposing 'geographical phenomenology' to phenomenology, and in moving from the former to the latter, the claim that the two are *not* the same is implicit. Thus, we now need to move *from* what passes for phenomenology in the geographical literature, *towards* what is actually the case in phenomenology itself. In other words, and with all due respect to those geographers who have gone before us in this area, we need to allow phenomenology to show itself from itself once again. It is by no means our intention to suggest that phenomenology as such has gone unrecognized in geography (although with regard to its essential relationship with empirical science this is largely the case). Nor is it the intention of this work to be seen as a criticism of any of the research programmes that have developed from these interpretations of phenomenology. Science forges its own understanding, and is not to be constantly bound to first clarifying its fundamental premises. Nonetheless, these premises *are* to be clarified, and, in this process, false claims and misinterpretations are to be corrected. When science turns to philosophical reflection to clarify its basic concepts, those reflections themselves must be treated rigorously. Thus, we have sought to show how, in turning to phenomenology from established geographical perspectives, the traditional categories of such discourse have been presupposed and have to a greater or lesser degree influenced the understanding of the phenomenological project. It is now our task to show how a clearer understanding of phenomenology *is* important for the practice of empirical science itself. It is for this reason that the following chapters remain close to published *phenomenological* texts, drawing upon only carefully selected secondary works, and interpolating external claims only when these seem to be absolutely necessary. In what follows it is our purpose to allow Husserl and Heidegger another opportunity to present their ideas fairly and accurately to a geographic audience. This is particularly important in this *initial* transition from the claims of geographers to those of phenomenology itself. In asking 'what is phenomenology?' we seek to permit, as carefully as possible, Husserl to present his arguments, rather than present just another geographer's interpretation. At the very least such an interpretation will be closely aligned to the textual claims of Husserl (and later Heidegger), and will, we hope, present an intelligible and useful picture of phenomenology (particularly in its necessary relation to empirical science) for geography generally, and one which will not easily be brushed aside within the discipline.

In the development of the various positions referred to as 'geographical phenomenology' well-used concepts have been taken for granted, and in the process their meaning has been changed. In this process geographers have attributed to words meanings they formerly never had. Consequently we will almost certainly misunderstand unless we seek to re-vitalize our basic vocabulary through fundamental analysis. 'Object', 'objective', 'abstraction', and 'reduction' are such concepts. In reacting to what these and other terms have come to mean 'geographical phenomenologists' and others have turned strongly away from them, and have espoused what they take to be their obverse sides – 'subject', 'subjective', 'description' and 'lifeworld'.[1] On the one side are the claims of 'science' and, insofar as it is misunderstood, 'scientism'; on the other, claims of humanism and its interpretation of phenomenology. We have already seen how this dual-world conception has affected discourse generally within geography, and how it has framed an individualist and subjectivist conception of a mundane, descriptive enterprise that has sought to affiliate itself with phenomenology.

The corresponding claims of 'geographical phenomenology' to overcome empiricism and the positing, objectifying character of empirical science are only partially accurate. An unreflective empiricism of the type that burgeoned in geography during the 1950s and 1960s has, as geographers have since shown, to be grounded philosophically. This is not an overcoming of empiricism, however, but a return to its fundamental principles, that "continual self-reflection belongs to every science" (Heidegger, 1967, 177), and that scientific perspectives on which empirical investigation is based are a priori. If there is any tradition with which Husserl was affiliated in the beginning, it was classical and nineteenth-century British empiricism of Locke, Hume, Berkeley and Mill, as well as Mach and others.[2] If he criticizes them, it is not because their work lacks descriptive content in principle, but because their descriptions are flawed through the introduction of naturalistic causal explanation and in not being fully apodictic.[3]

23a Phenomenology: its origins and foundations

When we ask what phenomenology is, we can perhaps begin with Husserl's own reply: "Phenomenology – that is me and Heidegger." And, indeed, the reply answers our question, at least as to the beginnings of phenomenology. While the term 'phenomenology' is used by Lambert, Kant, and Mach, and is a vital and fully developed part of Hegel's philosophy (see his *Phenomenology of Spirit*), when we speak today of phenomenology we refer to the project of Edmund Husserl and its subsequent development (see Kockelmans, 1967b, 24–5).[4] Phenomenology, in this modern sense, begins with Husserl, and his work influenced to a greater or lesser degree all subsequent phenomenologists, including, for example, Becker, Conrad-Martius, Hartmann, Heidegger, Ingarden, Jaspers, Marcel, Merleau-Ponty, Pfänder, Sartre, Scheler, and Schütz.

Husserl provided many introductions to phenomenology, following one or other of the several ways to transcendental phenomenology (see Kockelmans, 1967b, 194–5).[5] Each of these is in some way an appropriate guide to phenomenology. For our present purposes we will initially be guided by his 1907 lectures on *The idea of phenomenology*, and his 1927 *Encyclopaedia Britannica* article,[6] to which other works will later be added. Both are introductory texts – the first for lectures delivered at Göttingen, the second intended for a wider audience. By 1927 Husserl had incorporated and clarified the important distinction between mundane, descriptive or eidetic phenomenology and eidetic reduction on the one hand *and* transcendental phenomenology and the phenomenological reductions on the other.

Heidegger had read and partly re-written the article (over which the two disagreed – see Biemel, 1977, 299–303). It provides a succinct and brief, though at times difficult, overview of what Husserl thought was important for the general audience of the Encyclopaedia. "It is", Spiegelberg (1971, 20) claims, "certainly the concisest introduction to phenomenology he ever prepared and the one on which he worked hardest. It is also the first piece he wrote for publication in the Anglo-American world."

23b The natural attitude

Husserl begins *The idea of phenomenology* (1907, 1) with the distinction between *natural* and *philosophical* thinking: "*Natural thinking* in science and everyday life is untroubled by the difficulties concerning the possibility of cognition. *Philosophical thinking is circumscribed* by one's position toward the problems concerning the possibility of cognition." From the beginning, then, we must distinguish between the sciences appropriate to each attitude; between philosophy and the non-philosophical sciences.

The non-philosophical sciences flow from the natural attitude, where our thinking is turned towards things, given as unquestionably obvious, appearing in this or that way depending on our standpoint (Husserl, 1907, 13; Kockelmans, 1967b, 27). In the natural attitude one assumes that the world can be considered in any part without its objective nature being changed. "According to this view, the object-pole of our knowing is an objectively existing, fully explainable world that can be expressed in exact, objective laws. This 'objective' world exists wholly in itself and possesses a rationality that can be fully understood" (Kockelmans, 1967b, 28). On this basis the objective sciences have been developed.

In the exact sciences of the natural attitude, then, everything is clear and comprehensible. To the extent that sound and reliable methods have been accepted and used, some objective truth about the external reality can be achieved with certainty. However, reflection on this process and on the theory of knowledge which seeks to explain it, rapidly leads to difficulties and even contradictions, with the attendant dangers of scepticism (Husserl, 1907, 17).

Through the theory of knowledge, as the critique of this natural attitude, we are able to interpret accurately and definitively the ways in which these sciences decide about what exists, and to clarify the mistakes which ordinary reflection makes about the relation of cognition, its meaning and its object. This does not mean that the theory of knowledge clarifies only how each science talks about things in the world. It also permits us to clarify the "fundamentally misleading *interpretations*" of the entities with which the sciences of the natural sort deal: where "one and the same science is interpreted in materialistic, spiritualistic, dualistic, psychomonistic, positivistic and many other ways" (Husserl, 1907, 17–18).

This critique of the natural attitude, and its corresponding misleading interpretations, seeks to show from what perspective things in the world are taken by the sciences, and how the objects of each science are constituted. This is the task of *phenomenology* in the natural attitude. It denotes a system of mundane scientific disciplines, or regional ontologies, corresponding to each domain of empirical science (Husserl, 1907, 18–19). To this end a new science is to be developed – eidetic or descriptive phenomenology – which will provide the methodological foundation for the empirical sciences.

Heidegger (1927, 27–28) also sees descriptive phenomenology as necessary to preclude "all abstract constructions and formulations, accidental findings, acceptance of only apparently demonstrated concepts, and adoption of pseudo-questions which often present themselves as real problems". Metaphysical speculation and epistemological constructions which focus upon mental and cognitive processes to the neglect of the phenomena themselves are to be rejected (Schrag, 1958, 278). The goal of phenomenological ontology "is to return to the original data of man's experience, and to provide a conceptual clarification of these data by delineating the constitutive structures which make them what they are" (278).

Besides denoting a descriptive science corresponding to the empirical sciences, phenomenology also denotes a method and a different attitude of mind; the philosophical method and the philosophical attitude. Traditionally philosophy and the positive sciences have not made this radical distinction. Instead, the idea of a single, objective, autonomous and real world implied in the natural attitude also implied that each of the different sciences had to deal with one part of that reality. If this were not the case there would be no reason to defend the differences between the sciences, differences in method having been rejected from the beginning. In this way of thinking, philosophy and the empirical sciences were on a par. Philosophy was not only related to the other sciences, but could be grounded upon the conclusions of those sciences.

This position is untenable for Husserl. That the theory of knowledge should be based on the psychology of cognition and on biology is an unacceptable prejudice, whereby philosophical thinking is treated as if it were natural thinking (Husserl, 1907, 19; see also 1). Whereas it is true that the sciences in the natural attitude can build upon one another, often interchanging methods, "*philosophy lies in a wholly new dimension*" to the positive sciences, and requires "an *entirely new point of departure* and an entirely new method" distinguishing it in principle from any empirical, positive science (19).

Thus, the term 'phenomenology' designates three things: (1) a new kind of descriptive method; (2) a set of a priori or pure descriptive sciences or regional ontologies, corresponding to, and providing the methodological foundation for, each of the domains of the empirical sciences, on the basis of which scientifically rigorous empirical methods can be established; and (3) an a priori science – philosophical or transcendental phenomenology – intended to found a rigorously scientific philosophy, and consequently to permit methodical reform of all the sciences.

23c Empirical science and pure science

Modern science deals with concrete, spatio-temporal realities, including that which belongs inseparably to them, such as the psychic processes of experiencing, thinking, etc. For the realm of physical nature (as we have already seen in Chapter 2) a universal theme or ontology of a pure natural science has been developed or formalized, where all extra-physical predications have been excluded. That is, a pure science or ontology of physical nature has been developed to found the empirical natural sciences (Husserl, 1927, 22). In our concern with the human sciences, we must ask, what is the equivalent pure science corresponding to the psychical and cultural domains of empirical sciences? As we have seen, there is no such pure science of the human realm. Consequently these sciences have primarily been seen as sciences of human and animal behaviour founded in physical realities, and hence in the corresponding physical ontology of nature. Husserl (1927, 22) responds to this situation, claiming that: "if the psychic aspect of the animal world is to become the topic of investigation, the first thing we have to ask is how far, in parallel with the pure science of nature, a pure psychology is possible".[7]

23d Original intuition

In order to establish this 'guiding idea' it is necessary to clarify what is peculiar to the particular form of experience with which we are concerned, and this means that precedence will be given to the most immediate types of experience. This original intuition of the things themselves – the basis of Husserl's call 'back to the things themselves' – is, in this way, a return to the immediate, original data of our consciousness. That which manifests itself through original intuition is apodictically evident; it is true and certain, and requires no further foundation (Husserl, 1907, 22–5; 1927, 22; Kockelmans, 1967b, 29).

Husserl does not see the ultimate root, the radical and absolute starting point of philosophy, in any single basic concept, in any single fundamental principle, in one simple *cogito*, but in an entire field of original experiences. His philosophy is a phenomenology precisely because it has as its starting point a field of primordial phenomena. Within this field Husserl does not want any induction or deduction but solely intuition on the basis of a very exact analysis and description. None of the methods used by the other sciences can be of value here, because they have to presuppose something in addition to what is actually given, while in the field of primordial phenomena presuppositions are simply inconceivable. (Kockelmans, 1967b, 29)

23e Phenomena and intentionality

If a pure science of human and psychical nature is to be developed we must reflect not upon the objects of our perception, but on the way in which they are originally given. Through reflection we turn our attention away from our everyday living into the world, and focus upon the way in which we grasp the corresponding experiences. These experiences are what Husserl (1927, 23) called 'phenomena', and the objects to which they correspond are any objects of man's attention. Thus, the world and all its parts, to the extent that there can be any awareness of them whatsoever, are 'phenomena', and can become the theme of reflection (Jordan, 1981, 6):

every kind of theoretical, valuational, practical consciousness can be made in the same manner a theme for inquiry; and all the Objectivities constituted in it can be investigated. The investigation will take these Objectivities simply as correlates of consciousness and will inquire solely into the what and the how of the phenomena that can be drawn from the conscious processes and coherencies in question. Things in Nature, persons and personal communities, social forms and formations, poetic and plastic formations, every kind of cultural work – all become in this way headings for phenomenological investigations, not as actualities, the way they are treated in the corresponding Objective sciences, but rather with regard to the consciousness that constitutes – through the intermediary of an initially bewildering wealth of structures of consciousness – these objectivities for the conscious subject in question. (Husserl, 1917, 15–16)[8]

The expression *intentionality* refers to this basic character of consciousness, of always directing itself to that which it is not. Thus, every experience is an experience of something, and is correctly said to be "intentionally related" to this something. This is not, however, a passive adapting of consciousness to whatever it encounters in the world, nor is it a relating of an external object to an internal consciousness. Rather, in "unreflective holding of some object or other in consciousness, we are turned or directed towards it: our *'intentio'* goes out towards it. The phenomenological reversal of our gaze shows that this 'being directed' is really an immanent essential feature of the respective experiences involved; they are 'intentional' experiences" (Husserl, 1927, 23).

For Husserl, then, it is characteristic of every phenomenon that it has its own form of intentionality; that the object of any act is inseparable from the meaning phenomenon itself. The structure of intentionality is one where the "object appears as essentially determined by the structure of thinking itself; this thinking itself first gives meaning to the object and then continues to orient itself to the pole of identity which it itself has already created" (Kockelmans, 1967b, 34). Intentionality is, for Husserl, the basic structure of consciousness, where every act of consciousness is directed towards its intentional object. For Heidegger, the intentional structure is present not only as this cognitive or theoretical relation between man and his world, but in man's everyday world of practical concerns. In this everyday world, which is pre-reflective, man already understands himself as fundamentally related to his world (Schrag, 1958, 280–1).

When we seek, in this way, to understand intentionality and consciousness more broadly, we may ask how we are given to ourselves and to things and the world. Here it becomes clear that in every concrete, conscious act the world is already present as constituted before it is posited in that act; thus, I perceive not an elongated compound possessing certain characteristics, but my green pen. Here "the cognitive relationship to the world is . . . no longer, in the proper sense of the term, the most primary relationship between man and world; knowledge itself is then a founded relationship and its necessary orientation to the other-than-itself then appears to be a datum no longer characteristic of knowledge alone" (Kockelmans, 1967b, 34). Consciousness is, thus, not an interiorizing transformation of an external world, but a going-out-of-itself, in the sense of the *Ur-*meaning of *ek-sistence*. In this context, explicit acts of cognition are intentional modes of ek-sisting towards this world.

24 The need for phenomenology

In developing philosophy as a rigorous science Husserl provided several introductions to his phenomenology. Each attempt to fulfil the programme which he laid out in *Philosophy as rigorous science* (1911) was a response to particular concerns he had at the time: among them the concern to counter the exaggerated claims of positive science and naturalistic misconceptions in *Ideas* (1913), and psychologism and historicism in *Philosophy as rigorous science*. His phenomenology itself changed over this period, so that later, particularly in the *Crisis* lectures (1954), Husserl realized more clearly the foundational role of the lifeworld for the sciences, and its position in explaining how positive science, independent of transcendental reflection, could have achieved the results it had. Thus, two distinct trends give rise to differences in Husserl's position over time; his argument develops in opposition to different trends in science, and the role of the lifeworld becomes more important over the same period. In what follows here, these trends are not always made explicit.

In his early works – *Philosophie der Arithmetik* (1891), and *Logical investigations* (1900–1) – Husserl dealt with the phenomenological basis of logic and mathematics; with that part which is concerned with the relationship of man with the formal objects of mathematics. Later, phenomenology (as that science which concerns itself not primarily with objects, but with how objects are primordially given) set itself the task of providing the foundations for all the sciences. Phenomenology as a rigorous science aimed also to be the science of science through explicating the science of beginnings – it sought to be the grounding philosophy. Husserl realized that the foundations of the empirical sciences cannot be clarified empirically. The positivist mistake was to treat philosophy and science as the same. However, philosophy as Husserl understands it here does need to be rigorous.

24a *The crisis of distance between science and life*

The programme Husserl set himself in *Philosophy as rigorous science*, and in all his later works, was nothing less than "saving human reason" (1911, 7), by refuting trends towards naturalism, psychologism and historicism, and laying the groundwork for a strictly scientific philosophy on a basis of unimpeachable rationality.[9] That basis was to be phenomenology, which alone could be truly scientific.

Only philosophy as rigorous science could guarantee the scientific character of any particular science. This was the Cartesian goal of a universal philosophy providing a universal science grounded in an absolute foundation (Husserl, 1911, 78; 1930, 7).

By contrast, the positive sciences, which are naive like daily and practical existence, are unable to explain the intentional acts from which their constructions originate. Phenomenology responded to the crisis of distance that opened up between the sciences and life, and which made it difficult to found the significance of scientific abstractions in and for concrete life (Kisiel, 1973, 218). "It is in the long way through the objectivity of the positive sciences that phenomenology is best seen as the endeavor to be the science of science" (Kisiel, 1970, 5), from the critique of the existing a priori sciences (mathematics and logic), to the a priori but still positive ontologies, both formal and material, culminating in the ontology of lifeworld, all of which receive their full grounding in the transcendental ontology. For the most part, this is the path we will take to clarify the nature and significance of Husserlian phenomenology for a science of geography, including empirical geographic science.

As laid out in *Ideas*, the new science of phenomenology was to be founded on an independent realm of direct experiences hitherto inaccessible (Husserl, 1913, 5). In this phenomenology empirical facts were to serve only as examples of essential generalities, much as sketches of triangles to the mathematician represent the essential character of 'triangleness'. The essential generalities were to be obtained by means of the phenomenological reductions, leading to an eidetic phenomenology – the realm of pure eidetic 'description' or the realm of essential structures immediately transparent to consciousness. Such a science would establish a science of pure possibilities, the foundation for the sciences of fact – the genuinely rational science.

Husserl responded very strongly to the ungrounded positive sciences, which were seen to perpetuate the distancing of science and life, to pose a serious threat to philosophy, and to deny the possibility of any science other than those dealing with phenomena as indications of physical phenomena (1913, 73). Empiricistic naturalism, as Husserl called it, stems from praiseworthy motives; to establish Reason as the authority concerning truth, and to oppose tradition, superstition and prejudice. To achieve this it claims to be guided by the facts themselves, not opinions or prejudices. Such a science was to concern itself with the real fact-world of experience, in order to counter false claims and imaginary science. But this approach now equates a grounding in immediate experience with the source of facts in their self-givenness. Thus, genuine empiricist science and the sciences of experience have come to mean the same thing. Consequently 'essences' and 'ideas', as opposed to 'facts', are looked upon as metaphysical ghosts – the eliminating of which was the task natural science set itself in the first place. What is not part of the 'fact-world' easily becomes part of the domain of 'imagination'; and a science based upon imagination – for empiricistic naturalism – is simply imaginary science (74).

In equating the requirement that we must return to the 'facts themselves' with the requirement that all knowledge shall be grounded in *experience*, naturalism faces the problem that the world of facts is seen as the only proper domain of science. This is a very constrained interpretation of experience and fact, and it contains within it several problems for the scientist.

(1) It is unable to justify its own position on the basis of experience alone.

(2) The theory of experience it proposes is atomistic, and cannot account for how general ideas or universals arise.

(3) The theory of experience is highly selective, consistently refusing to accept the entire phenomenal field at face value. Thus, sense impressions of physical entities are emphasized as privileged forms of experience; dreams, memories, fantasies and general intuition are disregarded as derivative (Heffner, 1974, 159–62).

Accepting the intelligible naturalistic limitation of the

field of knowable 'facts', he [the naturalistic empiricist] takes for granted without further question that experience is the only act through which facts themselves are given. But *facts are not* necessarily *facts of nature*, the fact-world in the ordinary sense, not necessarily the fact-world in general, and it is *only with the fact-world of nature that the primordial* dator act which we call *experience* is concerned. (Husserl, 1913, 75)

For Husserl the separation of fact and essence which this implies must eventually have a negative effect on the empirical sciences themselves, since the incomplete eidetic grounding of these sciences and the need to develop new sciences dealing with essences for the further advance of the empirical sciences must eventually prove inhibiting (Husserl, 1913, 73).

24b *The critique of the positive sciences*

The positive sciences and the 'prosperity' they have generated have influenced the world-view of modern man, producing a lack of concern for important questions of genuine humanity. These questions are universal and necessary for all men; they concern man as a free, self-determining being in his behaviour towards the human and extra-human surrounding world, and in shaping that world. Because it abstracts everything 'subjective' the science of the physical has nothing to say about these matters, nor do the human sciences which seek to exclude valuative positions, questions of reason, and cultural patterns in attaining a rigorous scientific character (Husserl, 1954, 6). Furthermore, as we have already seen, the empirical sciences, starting in a naive fashion, have problems with their own foundations and resultant internal paradoxes. They are theoretically ungrounded, and cannot therefore substitute for philosophy as the basis of a fully grounded science (Husserl, 1913, 19).

Such an ungrounded naturalism is essentially the same as positivism, where physical nature is sensualistically broken up into complexes of sensations (colours, sounds, pressures, etc.) and so-called 'psychical' objects are broken up into complementary complexes of the same or of still other 'sensations' (Husserl, 1911, 79–80). To the naturalist, whatever is is either physical (belonging to a unified totality of physical nature) or it is psychical, but then merely as a variable dependent on the physical and, in belonging to the psycho-physical realm of nature, determined by rigid, and ultimately the same, laws of nature. Consciousness is understood as a product of, as well as a part of, the same nature interrogated by scientists. The focus of interrogation is the causal conditions that account for the state of affairs. Consciousness may then be traced to other states of consciousness such as motivations, intentions, reasons, or the individual occasions and conditions which embody it, and to consciousness as the actualization of nature. The mental is embedded in the physical (Natanson, 1973a, 48). In this view man is a qualitatively continuous part of nature, and it follows that the natural sciences provide the proper instruments for exploring the reality which human beings share; that is, the social world with its manifold cultural and historical horizons is reduced to and founded in the world of physical nature.

To point this out as the state of affairs to be remedied by phenomenology is not to deny that there are psycho-physical mechanisms which affect consciousness. The attempt to ground the cultural world in its physical foundation is justifiable if the goal of cognitive or behavioural science is to give causal explanations, where predictions can be checked experimentally. But the idealizations required for such procedures are possible only under specific abstractive reductions, which in the final analysis give us the object of pure physics. Psychological phenomena are then reformulated in terms of observable surrogate physical phenomena. The reduction to physics is thus a necessary methodological ideal, which the behaviourists themselves must seek, and even then such attempts to connect the two realms fail unless carefully restricted within their proper limits.

In reducing psychological phenomena to surrogate physical observations, naturalistic psychology no longer speaks of psychological phenomena. It loses contact with lived experience, although in order to know which physical phenomena are appropriate surrogates for psychical phenomena it must presuppose such lived experience in the first place. Furthermore, while the methods of physical science presuppose the ideal of exact causal connections, the experience of psychic life does not imply such an ideal. Even setting the question of freedom to one side, it is self-evident on the one hand that we are unpredictable even to ourselves in lived experience, and on the other hand that something may happen in the future, of which we know nothing now, but which may change us considerably. The question of freedom further raises the issue of the possibility of wilful adjustment of the subject to the findings and claims about him or her. Reflection on lived experience shows immediately that exact causal laws do not fit the phenomena as such, a fact admitted implicitly by the naturalistic psychologist when he tries to reformulate the contents of lived experience in terms of accompanying physical phenomena. Whether this goal is in principle impossible must be left an open question for the moment. Even if such a goal were possible, it must still be remembered that the formation of such naturalistic concepts does not explain what it is to be a conscious being as such.

The same state of affairs applies when we turn to attempts by behavioural science to explain experience and behaviour *in terms of* psychological attitudes. Psychologism is another such form of reductionism. It seeks to understand logic, for example, in psychological terms, and thereby seeks to substitute extra-logical criteria of validity. By making logic a part of psychology, psychologism in turn makes psychology the foundation of philosophy. Although questions of how one thinks and why one thinks are legitimate areas of study, they are outside the realm of logic; they presuppose logic and they are fundamentally irrelevant to the question – what is the formal structure of logic? This applies to all forms of reduction of lived experience to psychic phenomena and psychological explanation.

24c The structure of the world and 'objects' of science

Not all objects in our lived intersubjective experience are objects of science. We must ask what constitutes scientific objects. In lived experience we have (a) cultural objects, (b) animated objects, and (c) physical objects (Husserl, 1913, 46; see also, Heidegger, 1927, 37, n. ii). These are related one to another in a particular manner. We can conceive of a cultural object only insofar as the two other forms of object are implied in it. We can abstract from any such cultural object gradually up to a point where animated objects and natural objects alone remain.[10] Correspondingly we cannot have a cultural object which is not at the same time also a simple object. This is not to say that cultural objects are always *first* given as not cultural objects, but that we can abstract from the cultural object to the concrete non-cultural object. That is, we may abstract all factors which make cultural objects into cultural objects; we may perform a universal abstractive reduction.[11]

We are left with physical objects and animated objects. Biology and botany characterize the sciences where such universal abstractive reductions have been fully or partially performed. The abstractive reductions can be pushed further, such that we abstract all factors which constitute animated objects until we are left with physical objects pure and simple. Physics and astronomy exemplify this reduction, where the scientific object remaining is merely Cartesian nature or the nature of Newtonian physics (and also where the gradual abstraction of elements of animated being or spirit from the physical and astronomical worlds is clearly evident in the historical development of these sciences. See Chapters 6 and 7). A third abstractive reduction may also be performed where we abstract from concrete objects themselves such that only purely formal objects remain. The sciences of purely formal objects include geometry and elements of modern theoretical physics, as well as the formal sciences of mathematics and logic. Such abstractive reductions give us the objects of the sciences. To every science there belongs an abstractive reduction which determines the objects of the field and the form of idealization which allows that field to give precise definitions of its basic concepts. Thus, physical objects are determined as individual, concrete objects through the framework of extension, space, and time, and these can be idealized as Newtonian space and time. In this way objects are constituted in the scientific attitude.

But what of the attitude of naturalistic empiricism? The scientist thematizes the idealizations which become possible as a result of performing the abstractive reductions, and these thematizations are strictly limited to the realm uncovered by the reductions insofar as they are susceptible to the scientific method. The naturalist fails to recognize these inherent limits to the abstractive reductions. In principle an acceptable behaviourist research programme might be developed *if* the behaviourist argues that exact causal explanation will be possible only if the phenomena can be redefined in terms of physical objects, this being a necessary prerequisite for the required idealizations. But the naturalist substitutes the 'in-itself'/appearance schema for the methodical steps of the abstractive reductions. The physical object or the animated and physical object is the 'in-itself', the real object, while cultural phenomena are epiphenomena, mere appearances. In the case of physical objects, naturalistic mechanism is seen to be grounding for animated and cultural objects – a claim made by such approaches to science as those of social physics, and logical atomism – and, in the case of animated objects, biological mechanism is taken to be grounding for cultural objects – exemplified fully or in part by socio-biology, behaviourism and social Darwinism.

The naturalist's error is to take the abstraction to be grounding for each of the domains of entities. It is an error to claim that "an animal *is* a machine" or that "man only abides by the laws of physics". However, it is, in principle, acceptable for the scientist to argue that research will consider animals only insofar as they can be considered as if they were machines, or that these claims will remain valid only insofar as man is affected by physical laws. In practice, and later, we will argue against even these more carefully formulated research programmes (see Husserl, 1917), since they seek to establish an analogical rather than a phenomenological basis for a scientific perspective. In other words, they impose constructions on the phenomena, without the careful and necessary prior clarification, through descriptive phenomenology, of the domain of phenomena under consideration. Furthermore, in these cases the ad hominem argument applies. If cultural phenomena are to be reduced to socio-psychic and then to physiological phenomena in order to be explained scientifically, what then is the status of the explanations themselves, and the scientist's own endeavour? Relativism and the paradox of subjectivity arise.

In fact the claims of naturalism are not the most dangerous ones for Husserl. It is a relatively easy matter to show how the abstractive reductions operate, and in what instances naturalist claims develop. In historicism, when logical laws are encompassed in the *Weltanschauungen* and so reduced to historical trends, this is not the case. Husserl agrees with Dilthey that *Weltanschauungen* are cultural formations that come and go in the stream of human development, with the consequence that their content is motivated in the given historical relationships (Husserl, 1911, 124). But, he argues, the same is also true of the strict sciences. Does this mean that, in view of the constant change in scientific views, we would have no right to speak of sciences as objectively valid unities instead of merely cultural formations? Carried through to its conclusion, this argument leads to a situation in which the ideas of truth, theory and science lose their objective validity. Instead, historical reasons can only produce historical explanations; that is, the explanation of the genesis and the history of an idea does not fully explain the meaning of the idea itself. The mathematician, for example, is not concerned with the history of mathematics when seeking to evaluate the truth of a mathematical theory or claim.

Just as we must distinguish between natural science and naturalism, a distinction has to be made between history and historicism. In historicism, where the sciences and their claims are considered as historical phenomena, the abstractive reductions of physical science are not evident. These sciences are concerned specifically with the cultural realm, which takes into account animated and physical objects only insofar as they are related to cultural objects. If naturalism, biologism and psychologism are avoided, then only a particular form of abstractive reduction occurs.

For Husserl historicism leads inevitably to relativism. Since the historian as well as the objects of history belong to history, the truth claims of historical science are of equal value. The historicist is therefore inclined to accept all kinds of different world-views as context- and time-dependent. Philosophy becomes merely another world-view. Validational criteria have equal weight; they are all true. Consequently science has *no effective* validational criteria, and has no recourse to such a world-view philosophy to help it solve its foundational questions. Such a path from history to historicism and relativism parallels the path to naturalism and psychologism, and could be constructed for other 'isms' such as sociologism, even 'spatialism' in the context of geographic science. It is essentially a problem that rationalism has continually to face, what Husserl called 'the paradox of subjectivity', where the sciences presuming an objective world as their correlate recognize that their particular method determines what is actually the case in the world. The world and the scientist's world are seen in terms of this methodological perspective. But since there are other such perspectives, the world is seen only through methodical world-views. In the case of historicism the self-reflexivity of this situation forces the historian to recognize the historical nature of his perspective and his findings. For Husserl, as Seebohm (1982) has argued, this is the testing point of descriptive phenomenology. Only if the 'paradox of subjectivity' can be solved do the claims for phenomenology as rational foundational philosophy stand. For our purposes it will be Heidegger, and not Husserl, whose ontology of facticity extricates phenomenology and the foundational project for the sciences from the paradox, and does so in such a way that the claims made about descriptive phenomenology as eidetic science stand.[12]

24d Phenomenology and the guiding idea of science

In Husserl's view ungrounded science poses important problems of relativism. The development of a full grounding for science is only possible through a rigorously critical and systematic investigation, where everything is reduced to primary 'presuppositions', which are immediately evident. It is in this sense that "the science of ultimate grounds" is a rigorous science (Kockelmans, 1966, 32). Phenomenology cannot start naively, as the positive sciences do, based on the previously given experiences of the world presupposed as something that exists as a matter of course (Husserl, 1913, 19). A distinction must be made between philosophy and the non-philosophical sciences; between the philosophical and the natural attitude. This is the problem of the transfer from the natural attitude to that proper to transcendental phenomenology – the philosophical attitude.[13] But, it must be asked, can a fully grounded science be developed independently of any established scientific conceptions? Clearly not, for how would we begin if we did not presuppose, for example, logic? (Husserl, 1930, 7).

Husserl's use of radical doubt in the form of the phenomenological *epoche* has often been criticized as denying the very thing in which the human sciences are interested. It has been said that once bracketed the world cannot be reconstituted. But, as we hinted earlier, this is to misunderstand Husserl's aim and the notion of bracketing. We will deal only with the former here, and by way of an example. In the Fifth Cartesian Meditation Husserl shows how the general aim of grounding science is not to be renounced, but shall continually motivate not only the course of his own meditations but implicitly also those of the sciences themselves (Husserl, 1930, 8). The general idea of science can be taken from the sciences as we have them as a "precursory presumption, which we allow ourselves tentatively, by which we tentatively allow ourselves to be guided in our meditations" (9). This genuine concept of science is not, however, derived by abstraction from the de facto sciences.[14] Science as facts of objective culture, and sciences "in the true and genuine sense", need not be identical. It is the task of phenomenology to disclose the latter out of the former.

This general idea of science grounded in an absolute foundation, and apodictically justified, guides all the sciences as they strive for universality, whatever may be their actual situation. Similarly, although relative evidences and truths suffice in the everyday, pre-scientific life,

science looks for truths that are valid, and remain so, *once and for all and for everyone*; accordingly it seeks verifications of a new kind, verifications carried to the end. Though de facto, as science itself must ultimately see, it does not attain actualization of a system of absolute truths, but rather is obliged to modify its 'truths' again and again, it nevertheless follows the idea of absolute or scientifically genuine truth; and accordingly it reconciles itself to an infinite horizon of approximations, tending toward that idea. (Husserl, 1930, 12)

Science does, therefore, involve a movement from earlier to later cognitions that is not arbitrary, but has its basis "in the nature of the things themselves" in the manner of their givenness. This 'idea of science' guides the meditations of all the sciences whatever may be the situation of any particular science with respect to the de facto actualization of that idea. Consequently, reflections on the scientific endeavour may permit us to discover elements of the genuine idea of science which guides the striving of the naive sciences (Husserl, 1930, 12–13).

While the crisis of the sciences (and of European man and rationalism) is real, Husserl still retains admiration for the sciences, especially those which are models of rigorous and highly successful scientific discipline (Husserl, 1954, 3–4). Phenomenology itself is dependent upon them for its development. The practising scientist, like the artist or craftsman, possesses a certain 'technical rationality' which permits important discoveries in science despite its lack of grounding (Husserl, 1911, 100). But if the ideal of science is to be actualized, especially in the domain of cultural objects, and if the crisis is to be overcome, the sciences (as well as European man) would need phenomenology, whose function was "to provide transcendental rationality to all sciences, to give them a new and ultimate rationality, the totally different rationality of all-sided clarity and intelligibility and thereby to transform them into branches of a single absolute science" (Husserl, in Kisiel, 1973, 218).

6

Phenomenology, science and phenomenological geography

25 Descriptive phenomenology and science

25a Sciences of fact and sciences of essence

Husserl asks whether science can be 'exact' if it leaves its concepts without scientific fixation and without methodical elaboration. He answers: surely it would be no more so than a physics that would be content with the everyday concepts of heavy, warm, etc. But how can everyday experience become scientific experience? How does one arrive at the determination of objectively valid empirical judgements? Historically this occurred as the pioneers of empirical science intuitively grasped the necessary method, and, by pursuing it faithfully in an accessible sphere of experience, achieved some objectively valid insights thus getting science started (Husserl, 1911, 99–100). By contrast, Husserl's guiding idea "of a science that shall be established as radically genuine, ultimately an all-embracing science" (Husserl, 1930, 7), "a science covering a new field of experience, exclusively its own, that of 'Transcendental Subjectivity'" (Husserl, 1913, 5), and a science to counter the growing dominance of "sciences of fact" (Husserl, 1907, 33), requires explicit methods and a framework in which empirical, formal and transcendental aspects of the science of science can be developed.

In the natural standpoint the world is the totality of objects that can be known through experience. The sciences of the world, including the natural sciences (the sciences of material nature), biological sciences (the sciences of psycho-physical nature) and the human sciences (the cultural and sociological disciplines), each corresponds to its own object-domain in that world (Husserl, 1913, 46). At the same time:

An individual object is not simply and quite generally an individual, a 'this-there' something unique; but being constituted thus and thus '*in itself*' it has *its own proper mode of being*, its own supply of *essential* predicables which must qualify it.

Whatever belongs to the essence of the individual can also belong to another individual, and the *broadest* generalities of essential being, of the kind we have been indicating through the help of examples, delimit '*regions*' or '*categories of individuals.*' (47)

Thus the mathematician working with geometrical figures such as a triangle, line or point, recognizes that the geometrical eide (the essential figures) with which he is concerned are given *through instances* of those figures – the blackboard sketch, the plastic facsimile – but never *in* those sensible objects and never perfectly represented by them.

In this way we can distinguish different types of eide: formal eide are ideal objects, and we are most familiar with them in terms of logico-mathematical entities, to which logic, set theory and formal mathematics refer; exact material eide are the objects to which geometry and traditional mathematics (i.e., not formalized) refer; and material eide refer to qualities of material entities. Since cultural objects are given in many instances yet never fully in any one, they can be said to be 'ideal objects' also, in the sense that sketches of triangles are ideal objects of the formal eide 'triangleness'. Thus we can also distinguish a region of cultural eide.

For any entity to be an object for eidetic description it is necessary that it be represented by some actually given, imagined or remembered symbols or material objects in sensual intuition. Through abstraction from the concrete instances of these symbols or objects – 'eidetic reduction' – the essence (*eidos*) is given. But it is not, as geographers such as Billinge have argued, a negation of the object or of the world. The reality of object and world occurs anyhow. What is inhibited is what the world is presupposed to be in certain cogitative types, in which it appears as this or that kind of world. In the case of the geometer working with the hexagon, he merely abstracts from the chalk marks, the blackboard on which they occur, and the inaccurate form by which he represents 'hexagon' to arrive at the ideal object – the hexagon, with eidos 'hexagonality'. The geometer is not interested in the particular instances of the chalk diagrams on the board, only with the spatial structure they represent.[1]

In an example where the geographer claims that reciprocal daily migration occurs between the inner city and the suburbs, or where differences in emotional attachment to place are fundamental in explaining local planning issues, we start with symbols, signs, or material objects. Eidetic reduction gives us the object, not in its factual existence – people moving between places, or emotional arguments for or against development proposals – but the object as a general type.

That is, we have not just factical collections of individual emotions, but what it is to feel attachment to community or place in general. We are concerned not with what makes this particular place special, here and now, nor with aggregate collections of facts about those individual or collective views, but with, in this case, what place and attachment to place are, such that we readily recognize the force of genius loci regardless of who or where we are.

Further abstractive reductions fix properties of the essence-object giving basic structures of the phenomena; in the case of geometry or spatial analysis this is the structure of spatial extension. The resultant general structures, about which descriptive phenomenology speaks, are not grasped in experience, based on induction, but in eidetic intuition. In this way eidetic phenomenology as it deals with psychological phenomena, for example, does not refer to factual consciousness, but to an eidos consciousness, or to the formal, universal structures of psychic objects. Similarly, a phenomenological geography, insofar as it is a descriptive, eidetic phenomenology, will not refer to actual experiences, factual places and worlds, but to the formal and universal structures of environmental experience, placehood and worldhood.

Such formal objects remain part of complex wholes whose structures are always of a relatively abstract character. Through phenomenological description we arrive at *sets* of such eidetic structures – always partial ones – which illuminate experience, place or world from different perspectives.

What we do not arrive at are descriptions of the world naively given in its immediacy in the natural attitude, as Seamon argues. We do not arrive at 'phenomenological descriptions' of everyday activities such as going to the mailbox. Descriptive phenomenology provides us with formal and abstract universal structures through methodically conscious performance of the eidetic reduction, a series of necessary abstractions, and the method of guided free variation. These have to be reconstructed if the concreta Seamon seeks are to be regained, because reflection can never grasp the whole as a concretum, but can only give it through perspectives.

Seamon and Buttimer fail to show how their own perspectives are constituted, or how they are able to reconstruct the concretum in such a manner that it has been shown as it is in itself. In any case, such concreta do not require the rigour of the phenomenological method, or even of the scientific method. The capturing of immediacy or the things as they are in themselves has little to do with phenomenology or science. Both involve abstractive reduction, both work on the world, both require rigour. Seamon's phenomenological geography involves none of these.

Epoche and reduction imply neither negation nor doubt, nor do they imply the founding of a particular phenomenon in another realm of phenomena, as in naturalism. Instead they lead to a focus of attention on the cogitative type. To a greater or lesser extent, and with varying degrees of methodical clarity, such reductions are common even in the natural attitude and on a pre-scientific (as well as of course on a scientific) level. For the sciences they have the character of reflections on method and on the meaning basic concepts have. In phenomenology these are phenomenological reductions, and are characteristic for eidetic phenomenology. *Only by this turning of attention away from the world as it appears in particular sciences, perspectives or cogitative types to the analysis of the cogitative types themselves and how they constitute their basic concepts can we critically show what the limits and meaning of claims in each perspective are.* Furthermore, because the world is revealed differently through each pespective, what passes for adequate evidence also varies with the perspective. For every perspective, what is positive and negative evidence has to be specified through an eidetic phenomenology.

By taking his starting point in the general eidetic science of the world of our immediate experience, Husserl aimed to reveal the general structures of the world and all the worldly objects manifest therein. The 'regions' (or domains of objects) so determined would be examined for their most general and necessary structures, through the subject-matter of the different sciences, by their regional ontologies (Kockelmans, 1978a, 177–8). To the pure regional essence belongs a *regional eidetic science*, or *a regional ontology*, in which the basic concepts of a particular region become clarified. Every empirical science is comprised of regions and will be essentially related to the corresponding regional ontologies. A regional ontology seeks the essence of a particular object; it seeks the essential structures of the subject-matter of a particular science, and therefore can be developed only by a reflection upon the corresponding empirical sciences. The regional ontologies do, nonetheless, precede the empirical material ontology *de jure* (179–80).

The formal 'region' or formal ontology is not something co-ordinate with the material regions; it is properly no region at all, but the pure form of region in general. Its subject-matter does not constitute the class of essences, but mere essence-form. The formal ontology conceals in itself the forms of all possible ontologies in general, prescribing to the material ontologies a formal constitution common to all of them (Husserl, 1913, 60). That is, formal ontology abstracts from all the regional distinctions of the different objects, dealing with the formal idea of 'object in general'. These are *pure sciences of essential being*, comprising the whole *mathesis universalis* (formal logic, arithmetic, pure analysis, set theory, etc.). They are free throughout from factual considerations, dealing with 'ideal possibilities', not actual but essential relationships, the ultimate ground being essential insight and not experience. Formal ontology, therefore, investigates a new dimension of being – the necessary conditions of 'being-object'.

While the formal ontologies are intrinsically independent of all science of fact, the opposite is true of the sciences of fact themselves. "*No fully developed science of fact could subsist unmixed* with eidetic knowledge, and in consequent *independence of eidetic sciences formal or material*" (Husserl, 1913, 57). Every empirical science is essentially related to the formal as well as to the regional ontological disciplines. In other words, all empirical sciences are grounded in their regional ontologies, as well as in the pure logic common to all sciences and the formal ontology specific to a particular science (Kockelmans, 1978a, 181).

The problem of a radical 'classification' of the sciences is in the main the problem of the separating of the regions, and for this again we need, as a preliminary, pure logical studies of the kind we have been briefly outlining. But, of course, we need also, on the other hand, Phenomenology. (Husserl, 1913, 71)

It was through phenomenology, particularly the reductions, that the legitimizing ground for science was to be attained.

25b Descriptive phenomenology

The essential relation between an individual object and its essence – such that to each object there corresponds its essential structure, and to each essential structure there corresponds a series of possible individuals as its factual instances – necessarily leads to a corresponding relationship between sciences of fact and sciences of essence. That is, every empirical science of fact has a corresponding eidetic science or science of essence (Husserl, 1913, 55–7). Concrete, empirical objects and their material essence belong to 'regions' of empirical objects, and since every empirical object has its own essence, each region must have a corresponding regional essence; a corresponding *regional eidetic science* or *regional ontology*. Just as there is a regional empirical science or set of sciences corresponding to the 'region' of empirical objects so there is a regional ontology corresponding to the 'region' of essences.[2]

This usually implicit domain of investigation – the region or domain of concern and its regional ontological structure – can be made explicit by essentially descriptive methods, and it is this to which we refer when we call for a *descriptive science* or a *descriptive phenomenology*. Accordingly, "every empirical science which deals with entities belonging to a given region will be essentially related to a corresponding regional ontology in such a way that it has its essential counterpart and theoretical basis in that eidetic ontology" (Kockelmans, 1973, 233–4). Each factual science must have such a corresponding eidetic science, at least implicitly, in order for facts as such to be selected as relevant and meaningful. Facts do not speak for themselves, but appear only within a pre-given context of meaning. It is the role of regional and material ontologies to articulate this pre-given context of meaning, as an a priori understanding of the essential structures of phenomena which is usually implicit. Not surprisingly, as the context of meaning changes so does the character of a fact and the evidence by which it is given.

The task of the regional ontology is that of exploring the different ways in which objects are given for the sciences. The different modes in which an object is given, each requiring its own categories, can then be explicated and made transparent. Such transparency of the basic concepts is the primary aim of phenomenology and provides clear foundations for the empirical sciences. Thus there are different regional ontologies seeking to describe the various regions of phenomena and the manner in which objects are constituted because there are different types of evidence. Each scientific perspective must pursue the ideal of science in its own way. Each perspective is different because its corresponding objects are different. This suggests a methodological pluralism; insofar as the objects differ between logico-mathematical objects, physical objects, animated objects and cultural objects, the methodological structure of each scientific perspective will differ, as will the nature of appropriate evidence, verification and scientific rigour.

By 1925 in *Phenomenological psychology* Husserl argued that all material ontologies were also founded in a "general material ontology of the world of immediate experience as such" (quoted in Kockelmans, 1978a). The subject-matter of the different regional ontologies could no longer be determined by beginning in the empirical sciences themselves as he had previously suggested (in *Ideas*). Instead they must be drawn from this general material ontology of the world of immediate experience. This realm of immediate experience was now to serve as the foundation for the individual regional ontologies (Kockelmans, 1967a, 104–5). Descriptive phenomenology as eidetic science was to provide a firm basis for the empirical sciences by grounding them in this general ontology of immediate experience. This in turn was to be radically grounded in *transcendental phenomenology*.

Transcendental phenomenology was the apodictic ground, self-founding and founding for all the sciences. The relationship between descriptive phenomenology and empirical science on the one hand, and descriptive phenomenology and transcendental phenomenology on the other, can thus be made clear. Empirical science deals with facts, while descriptive science or descriptive phenomenology deals with the essential structures underlying and governing these facts; that is, with the a priori framework of meaning adopted by a particular empirical science. On the other hand, while the subject-matter of descriptive science is the eidetic structures or regional ontologies of the phenomena, including the empirical sciences, transcendental phenomenology deals with the eidetic structures of the realm of intentional consciousness: with that realm which gives rise to the possibility of scientific reflection in the first place. Descriptive phenomenology occurs within the natural standpoint, and is correctly seen as a science. Transcendental phenomenology, through the transcendental reduction, seeks a transcendental and thus apodictic and fully grounded point of view in the philosophical attitude (Kockelmans, 1973, 234–5).

Regional ontologies are the necessary bridge between empirical science and transcendental phenomenology. Since they cannot be determined a priori nor be delineated by the empirical sciences empirically (for they presuppose this delineation), regional ontologies must take their starting point either in reflections on the sciences themselves (which Husserl later rejected, in part) or in the general material ontology of the world of our immediate experience. But such an eidetic grounding is not sufficient for the sciences. If such a foundational project should stop with the ontology of the lifeworld (as the general ontology of our immediate experience later became in the *Crisis*) "we should have invariant structures which are simply there, as an eidetic facticity. But what of their origin?" (Kisiel, 1970, 41). The question of origin is crucial in the *Crisis* where Husserl realized most clearly that the sciences are in crisis because they are unable to account for the meaning of their own activity. "By becoming merely the means of transforming the world technically, the sciences have undergone a radical 'emptying of sense'. Thus, *the crisis of European sciences* is none other than *the crisis of the modern technical world*" (Landgrebe, 1981, 178). In this sense the essence of phenomenology itself is, for Heidegger, the clarification of methodological conceptions to avoid 'technical devices'.

> The more genuinely a methodological concept is worked out and the more comprehensively it determines the principles on which a science is to be conducted, all the more primordially is it rooted in the way we come to terms with the things themselves, and the farther is it removed from what we call 'technical devices', though there are many of such devices even in the theoretical disciplines. (Heidegger, 1927, 27)

26 Phenomenology, science and lifeworld

If geographers and social scientists generally have taken any single concept from phenomenology then it must be the concept of "lifeworld". This term, as Gadamer (1963; 1969) emphasizes, "has found astonishing resonance in the contemporary mind" (1963, 151) and remains one of the few new words coined by a philosopher and adopted by a much larger audience. If it stands for anything in particular in this popular view it is as a counter-concept to the world of science, and it is in this guise that lifeworld has been emphasized by geographers. If, as Gadamer suggests, a word is always an answer, then what is the question to which 'lifeworld' presents an answer?

26a The lifeworld ontology

In *Ideas* Husserl had not yet developed a general material ontology of the world of our immediate experience as such. The subject-matter of the regional ontologies was to be derived from the empirical sciences themselves. But in *Phenomenological psychology* he introduced a new science: the general ontology of the world of our immediate experience. The result was to transform radically the relationship between the regional ontologies and the corresponding empirical sciences, and to lay the ground for his foundational lifeworld ontology to be developed in *Crisis* (Kockelmans, 1978a, 181).

It will be useful to distinguish between Husserl's conception of the 'original' lifeworld and the lifeworld of our everyday life, even though this distinction was not initially made so explicit by Husserl himself. In his *Phenomenological psychology* Husserl used both the 'world of our immediate experience' and 'lifeworld'. Whereas in *Crisis* the two seem to be the same.[3] The original lifeworld – the world immediately given in experience – is that immediately given in consciousness. "It includes only what is immediately perceived, that which we passively find present in its bodily selfhood and is to be taken, therefore, as completely deprived of any layer of meaning which refers to our active apperception and understanding" (Kockelmans, 1978a, 182–3). Such an experience of the world would be difficult, if not impossible, to materialize, and could only have been realizable by the very first human beings in the very beginning of their life as human beings. It is a world that presumably remains the same, insofar as it remains for all people. But, as Landgrebe (1940, 55) and Kockelmans (1978a, 182–3) point out, such a world – the horizon of every possible experience, in no way formed by men but ready given as a basis for all their deeds – is precisely *not* what lies most immediately at hand in experience. In the natural attitude no "world" is an immediate object of experience, for experience is both mediated and complicated.

The world, as Husserl came to see it in *Crisis*, is the total horizon of possible experience; something that is pre-given as the basis for every communal accomplishment, and yet is itself formed through communal accomplishments (Landgrebe, 1940, 55). The lifeworld is thus the cultural world surrounding us, and differs from the lifeworld of other cultural groups. It is the world which we constantly 'live in', and in which we find, not 'objects' or 'things' as such, but houses, fields, gardens, etc. "Above all", Husserl (1954, 125) says, "one must not go straight back to the supposedly immediately given 'sense-data', as if *they* were immediately characteristic of the purely intuitive data of the life-world. What is actually first is the 'merely subjective–relative' intuition of pre-scientific world-life."

26b The sciences and the lifeworld

Objective science has distanced itself from its roots in the lifeworld, a lifeworld that is not the same as the world of science. Yet the sciences themselves belong to the lifeworld; they arise from and flow into it, add themselves to its own composition, and enrich its content (Husserl, 1954, 104, 113, 131). "The sciences build upon the life-world as taken-for-granted in that they make use of whatever in it happens to be necessary for their particular ends. But to use the life-world in this way is not to know it scientifically in its own manner of being" (Husserl, 1954, 125). Thus the lifeworld with science is one-sidedly founded in the lifeworld without science – the pre-scientific lifeworld. Social scientists have sought to make such a claim an evaluative one, suggesting that the ontologically primordial lifeworld (without science) is preferable or the one we should seek to understand. But such an ontological primordiality cannot be translated into a factual primordiality. The lifeworld of the modern world is a lifeworld suffused with the thinking and products of science. It is a scientific lifeworld. In turning to the lifeworld we turn to a lifeworld influenced through and through with science, not to a pre-scientific lifeworld.

Husserl himself seeks merely to describe the state of affairs and does not judge between the two. However, it is clear from what has gone before that, were he to make such a judgement, far from agreeing with the interpretation of 'evaluative primordiality', he would seek to demonstrate the validity of the lifeworld form of higher complexity and its importance for cultural renewal: the truly scientific, in the sense of rational, lifeworld. Instead of seeking a return to the pre-scientific lifeworld, which would be a judgement about relative cultural positions, Husserl argues for the foundational role of lifeworld as such for all cogitative types, including scientific perspectives.

Objective science has a tendency not to concern itself with the familiar, but to divorce itself from its roots in the lifeworld as the immediately experienced reality (Husserl, 1954, 124). Yet science, as a human enterprise, presupposes, both historically and in every new teaching experience, this pre-given world of life which exists in common for all. Scientific research addresses issues and questions found in this pre-given world, and pre-scientific knowledge and its goals play a constant role in the direction such inquiry takes (Husserl, 1954, 121).

When science poses and answers questions, these are from the start, and hence from then on, questions resting upon the ground of, and addressed to, the elements of this pregiven world in which science and every other life-praxis is engaged.

. . .

It is pregiven to us all quite naturally, as persons within the horizon of our fellow men, i.e., in every actual connection with others, as 'the' world common to us all. Thus it is, as we have explained in detail, the constant ground of validity, an ever available source of what is taken for granted, to which we, whether as practical men or as scientists, lay claim as a matter of course. (Husserl, 1954, 121–2)

The lifeworld was, thus, an antidote to the exaggerated claims that science presents the objective world as it is in itself.

26c *The science of the lifeworld*

For Husserl every theoretical activity presupposes the structures of the lifeworld. The pre-theoretical character of the lifeworld and its pre-givenness in relation to all the sciences is stressed by him. Into this lifeworld flow the theories of the sciences, as we become familiar with them, accept them, and begin to see the world in terms of them.

But, in what sense, then, is the lifeworld pre-theoretical or the foundation for all theoretical interpretations? Further, is it possible to describe the lifeworld when, as Husserl admits, such a description is itself a theoretical activity – indeed, one of the highest order: phenomenology (Carr, 1970, xli)?

For Husserl, the lifeworld is not the deepest layer to which phenomenological analysis can penetrate, but itself requires a foundation in transcendental phenomenology in order to demonstrate in what ways the lifeworld is constituted. For the scientist turning to the lifeworld as foundational for the theoretical structures of the sciences, but denying the need for any transcendental foundation, the question above becomes a problem. We must then ask, with Husserl (1954, section 36) how the lifeworld can become the ontic and explicit subject-matter of a science?

The lifeworld is the universal horizon for establishable facts, which we experience or know to be experienceable pre-scientifically and extra-scientifically as the spatio-temporal world of things, including plants, animals and human beings (Husserl, 1954, 138). Each such lifeworld is a relative one, as we rapidly discover when visiting 'foreign' lands. If we ask about what is true for all people "beginning with that which normal Europeans, normal Hindus, Chinese, etc., agree on in spite of all relativity" (139), then, Husserl claims, we are on the way to positive science. In this way we enter the domain of positive science and the pure lifeworld is surpassed. A science of the lifeworld cannot begin with ontical descriptions and the commonalities of different factual lifeworlds, for this becomes either empirical science or unscientific description. In both cases phenomenology and lifeworld have not been grasped.

Despite its relativities the lifeworld does have a general structure, however. Although all relativities of a particular world are bound to this structure, the general structure itself is not relative (Husserl, 1954, 139). The task of phenomenology is to clarify this *universal a priori of the lifeworld*, and to show how the positive sciences are grounded in it. This task cannot, however, and contrary to the claims of much 'geographical phenomenology', be a capturing of the everyday lifeworld as it is lived. This lived world is life *within* a universal horizon – the lifeworld. In the natural attitude this horizon is precisely the world always pre-given as that which exists. Here the world is a constant actuality; its pre-given nature is not at issue, and questions about it refer to something within it. This world means "the universe of the 'actually' existing actualities" (146).

The task of phenomenology from the beginning has been to step out of this 'straightforwardly living into the world', and to focus upon the mode of givenness or on the pre-givenness of the world. Thus, "[in] opposition to all previously designed objective sciences, which are sciences on the ground of the world, this would be a science of the universal *how* of the pregivenness of the world, i.e., of what makes it a universal ground for any sort of objectivity" (146).

26d Lifeworld and transcendental phenomenology

In order to clarify the nature of the sciences Husserl goes back to the everyday lifeworld from which they are constituted. But is, then, the lifeworld the ultimate ground for experience? Gadamer (1975b, 309) claims that this is not the case:

The authentic Husserl would have rejected the contention (begun by Merleau-Ponty and carried on by many other so-called phenomenologists who isolate that single dimension in the framework of phenomenology connected with the very popular expression 'lifeworld') that the lifeworld is a new foundation of phenomenology that can be helpful for the social sciences.

Kockelmans (1967a, 259; 1978a, 275) has shown that the view, held by many phenomenologists including Merleau-Ponty and Landgrebe, that Husserl sought to replace transcendental phenomenology with studies of the lifeworld, is mistaken. The path through the lifeworld remains only one of four ways in which the constitutive nature of transcendental subjectivity can be shown. The lifeworld is not the final foundation of phenomenological investigation, but is itself also constituted, and that this is so is clearly shown in Part III (A) of the *Crisis*, which is entitled 'The way into phenomenological transcendental philosophy by inquiring back from the pregiven lifeworld' (Husserl, 1954, 103). The lifeworld thus has a very definite place within Husserl's broader transcendental phenomenology. Furthermore, the idea of the lifeworld derives from his earlier work, in which the pregiven world was implicit. For Kockelmans (1967a, 260–1) the view of the lifeworld in *Crisis* "appears as an harmonious synthesis of his view on the phenomenological reduction found in *First philosophy* and *Cartesian meditations* on the one hand, and his mundane phenomenology of the world, which was briefly outlined for the first time in *Phenomenological psychology*, on the other."

A formal or universal structure of the a priori of the lifeworld can be disclosed in the way we have shown for any domain of phenomenon. It is in this way that the lifeworld ontology remains, for Husserl, within the realm of the natural attitude. It does not then become a new fundament, a final grounding for truth claims, as geographers have sought to argue, but is itself constituted. And, if this is so, it does not displace the transcendental ego. But in so arguing, a careful distinction has to be made between the science of the lifeworld and the objective sciences that have developed since the time of the Greeks. The objective sciences are part of our own lifeworld. The science of the lifeworld, as developed by Husserl, cannot then be taken as "a new foundation of phenomenology that can be helpful for the social sciences", because they at one and the same time presuppose that lifeworld as pre-given and are themselves a part of it. The lifeworld ontology cannot be introduced as an ontical lifeworld in the natural attitude, and still retain its foundational and grounding role, as social scientists, including geographers, have argued.

We can say that the empirical sciences and the descriptive sciences of essence are situated in, and partially comprise, a lifeworld. That is, the scientific discovery of intramundane things depends, initially and in principle, upon the original attitude of man towards these beings. Thus, the scientific world-view is the consequence of a change in man's attitude to the world, a change which fundamentally modifies the primordially given world – the lifeworld – and feeds back into that world. Phenomenology of science seeks to understand the relationship between this primordially given world and the world of science, and such a phenomenology can disclose the universal structure of the lifeworld that underlies scientific conceptions. The development of such an ontology of the pre-given lifeworld is one of the tasks of Husserlian transcendental phenomenology.

As far as a phenomenology of the world of science goes, such a phenomenology would seek to lay bare the domain of the everyday world from which a particular science develops. In other words, such a phenomenology of science asks: What is science? How does each scientific perspective constitute its objects? And, what are the basic concepts with which each perspective is constituted?

For Husserl then, acceptance of these claims about the lifeworld requires that lifeworld be situated within the broader context of descriptive and transcendental phenomenology, in which it functions as an integral component. If the foundational roles of descriptive phenomenology and lifeworld are to be accepted while Husserlian transcendental phenomenology is rejected, some attempt must be made to show in what ways lifeworld itself is constituted. If this fails or the attempt is not made, the possibility remains either that lifeworld is incorporated into science as naively-given, objective world, or that scientific world-views remain merely relative, unfounded in any common world. A transcendental grounding of some sort is required.

7

Towards a fundamental ontology of science

The transformation of science is accomplished always only through itself. But science itself thereby has a two-fold foundation: (1) work experiences, i.e., the direction and the mode of mastering and using what is; (2) metaphysics, i.e., the projection of the fundamental knowledge of being, out of which what is knowledgeably develops. Work experiences and the projection of being are reciprocally related to one another and always meet in a basic feature of attitude and of humanly being there (*Dasein*). (Heidegger, 1967, 65–6)

27 Phenomenology and a fundamental ontology of science

The phenomenological aim of returning 'to the things themselves' permits Husserl and Husserlian phenomenology to seek a foundational ontology for the empirical sciences and the creation of new a priori formal sciences in the formal and material regional ontologies, in a lifeworld ontology, and ultimately in transcendental phenomenology. Grounding the sciences in this way was a task for phenomenology as rigorous philosophy and method, alone capable of clarifying the basic concepts of the sciences. Thus, geographers can clarify their empirical investigations through their own regional ontologies, to secure the foundations of a geographical perspective in the phenomena themselves, and in dealing with the human realm this requires an interpretative component to ensure that their concepts are relevant and meaningful, and not mere constructions. In this way:

[the] totality of entities can, in accordance with its various domains, become a field for laying bare and delimiting certain definite areas of subject matter. These areas, on their part (for instance, history, Nature, space, life, Dasein, language, and the like), can serve as objects which corresponding scientific investigations may take as their respective themes. (Heidegger, 1927, 9)

Scientific research thus arrives, in a preliminary fashion, at the delimitation of its subject-matter and the basic concepts to be used. These permit us to disclose this area of concern concretely for the first time. It is, phenomenology argues, through inquiring into the ways in which each particular area is basically constituted, rather than the collecting and storing of information, that the real progress of science derives (9).

The basic aim of phenomenology as it deals with the sciences, then, is for such clarification and revision of the basic concepts to be transparent to the sciences themselves. One such basic and necessary transparency is the origin and nature of science itself. It is one of the tenets of phenomenology, demonstrated convincingly by Husserl and Heidegger, that the basic structures of any subject area of science have already been worked out after a fashion in our everyday ways of experiencing and interpreting. It is to this that geographers' arguments regarding the phenomenological basis of geography should point, and only in this way that we can say that the concepts of 'formal' geography are pre-given in the world.

It is thus true to maintain that geology teaches us what a mountain, a valley and a river [really are]. But if we have never been on a journey or to the countryside, then we do not exactly know what it is that geology is explaining. The conclusion we draw from this example is that every scientific thesis or explanation refers back, possibly by a series of intermediate steps that are susceptible to analysis, to an experience of the lived world . . . This does not mean that the thesis in question cannot maintain something different from what this original experience puts forward, but scientific knowledge is still necessarily the explanation of an aspect of the experience of the life-world. (de Waelhens, 1958, 166)

Heidegger agrees with the Husserlian foundational project to ground the sciences in the everyday ways of experiencing and interpreting, through laying out their basic structures and concepts (Heidegger, 1927, 9–11). But he points to a further aspect of this project which allows us to penetrate deeper into the question about the nature of the scientific enterprise, showing how the Husserlian project presumes the primacy of the theoretical attitude. Man's fundamental and primordial relation to the world is not one of awareness of "manifold and shifting *spontaneities* of consciousness" (Husserl, 1913, 103), but one of involvement in, alongside and towards the world (Heidegger, 1927, 11–15, 67; see also Kockelmans and Kisiel, 1970, 152).

With Heidegger, then, we can question more radically the origin and constitution of science through (a) an *existential* conception of science, where the character of science is seen as a mode of man's being-in-the-world, and (b) the projective character of science, which has the character of an a priori constitution of the realms of being within which we are able to encounter entities as the ones they are. Such an approach will answer several of our initial questions concerning the nature of science and its relationship to man's mode of being; it allows us to radicalize the claims of Husserl concerning the lifeworld basis to all scientific understanding; and it will permit us to raise questions regarding the possibility and nature of human science as such, and its relation to man's mode of being. This will lead us away from Heidegger's explicit claims, since he only occasionally and then only briefly addressed the social and human sciences, and towards work dealing explicitly with these sciences (see, for example, Kockelmans, 1975; 1978b; 1979; 1980; 1982). Finally, it will permit us to raise the question of the possibility of a non-objectifying thinking and speaking in geographic discourse.

In this regard we seek to deal with something fundamental and important. While we approach this issue from the point of view of Heidegger's claims about it, this is not intended to suggest that this is the sole or the necessary means of access to the problem. It is chosen here as an appropriate means of access because Heidegger has important things to say about the issue. Nonetheless, the issues themselves are at stake here, and only secondarily Heidegger's claims about them. While we seek to understand Heidegger's claims as accurately as possible, we do not want to suggest that these concerns cannot be discussed in many ways from different perspectives.

28 Science and objectivation in geography

Our treatment of phenomenology in the context of certain geographical problematics has begun to clarify some crucial issues regarding the nature of science, and its relation to reflection and philosophy. Yet we have refused to follow Husserlian phenomenology to its ultimate foundation in transcendental subjectivity. In the first place the question of such a transcendental foundational project is a philosophical question and not directly an issue of science (although it will already be evident that the relationship between science and philosophy is more closely drawn in this work than has traditionally been accepted by geographers). More importantly Husserlian transcendental phenomenology as absolute science ultimately leaves us worldless; it is a philosophy compiled on an ontology of the 'present-at-hand', presuming the primacy of the theoretical attitude. Consequently the explanation of science in terms of abstractive reductions and the explication of the lifeworld ontology falls short of our goal of giving an account of science as a human enterprise, which can be carried out in the human realm without falling into traditional metaphysical positions and their attendant problems. For Husserl every empirical science of fact has a corresponding descriptive science of essence: an eidetic science or a descriptive, eidetic phenomenology. Such corresponding regional essences occur in all research, whether one knows it or not, whether one wants them or not. Eidetic descriptive phenomenology seeks to lay out this realm of essential structures; to make the basic concepts and a priori frameworks of meaning intelligible and transparent.

The immediacy of the lived world is the fundament from which all perspectives and domains of inquiry derive. All science must formalize and thematize, and 'reduce' this lived world to its domain of study in order to obtain the stable objects of purely theoretical reflection. Science is thus reductive and *thematizing*. This is not to argue that science should engage in reductionism in the sense of naturalism, historicism or psychologism. This much we have established already. Yet how does science obtain its stable objects of purely theoretical reflection? This question and its implications are the subject of this chapter.

This is particularly important for geographers at the present time because it has been argued in the recent literature of humanistic geography that non-objectification *must* be the goal of a truly human science: that a humanistic geography seeks to understand the world of man as a whole, without reducing that phenomenon; to grasp the dynamism of the lifeworld; to stand open to the flux of the taken-for-granted and everyday worlds. Thus, it is claimed that geography should seek to deal with the lived world as it is actually lived by real men and women, and should not adopt the objectifying myths of natural science methodology. These claims result from the strong and widespread rejection of positivist perspectives and the attendant reductive naturalism within the discipline. Phenomenology has been seen as a movement running counter to the approaches which are overly abstract, objectifying and divorced from the worlds lived by men and women. Here positivism and naturalism are taken as the paradigm and defining cases of empirical science. But the two are not synonymous, and the fallacies of the former perspective are not necessarily visited upon the latter method. While positivism is to be criticized, we must be careful not also to reject empirical science.

So-called 'scientific' approaches reply that humanistic geography misunderstands the necessity for rigour and definition in scientific inquiry, and, in a romantic rebellion against the attendant and necessary abstraction has turned to what amounts to little more than 'bad poetry', drawing upon 'existence' as if immediacy and involvement can somehow produce intellectual insight which avoids the need for distancing, abstracting and objectifying from which the scientist begins. Such positions have brought about the recognition of the broader issue facing the philosophy of science, that between alienating distanciation and participation. On the one hand distancing makes possible the objectivation which occurs in the human sciences, on the other hand this distancing breaks the fundamental relation by which we belong to and participate in that which we study as object. It seems that we either accept the methodological attitude and lose involvement in the reality under study *or* we retain the immediacy of experiencing such reality and give up the objectivity of the human sciences (Ricoeur, 1973b, 129). But before we accept such an antinomy as a stalemate we should ask again what constitutes science, and how does science relate to the extra-scientific domains of life or to the everyday, because in the unfolding of this debate in geography and the human sciences generally the nature of science and its relationship to the world of the everyday has been presupposed or ignored. In particular: (1) The origin of scientific constructs in the everyday world has been forgotten. (2) Analogy and metaphor, rather than sound description of phenomena, have, in part, provided the foundation for scientific perspectives and claims. (3) Rigour has been presumed to involve tight control over the phenomena through mathematics and experimental design, rather than the accurate understanding of the nature of the phenomenon as it shows itself, and the adopting of methodologies to specific realms of phenomena. (4) The rejection of the constraining exactitude of mathematical physical science, and its attendant 'thingification' (Olsson, 1980, 5e) when applied to human phenomena, has also been a rejection of the scientific as a mode of being in and understanding the world. (5) The abstracting and thematizing, and therefore objectifying nature of humanistic inquiry itself has been overlooked.

We need to consider what science is, and to explain to what extent and in what way all science is an objectifying activity. Only in this way can we assess the seemingly opposed claims of so-called 'humanists' on the one hand and 'scientists' on the other. Only in this way will we be able to raise the questions: Must science objectify man as its main theme of study? If so, what does this mean? Does it mean that man is necessarily to be treated as a thing? Is there a non-objectifying mode of thinking and speaking appropriate to geographic discourse and inquiry?

About these questions logicians, historians, and sociologists could all give excellent answers. The logic, history and sociology of science illuminate the questions, but they cannot be taken as grounding. In all of these sciences that which is most at issue is presupposed in their discussion (Heidegger, 1927, 356–7). With Feyerabend (1979, 106) we are "prepared to take a lot for granted – except the point at issue in our debate". If that which we seek is not to be already presupposed in our talk about it we need to ask some fundamental questions about the nature of science and geographic inquiry, corresponding to the regional ontological structure of science we have described earlier. We must ask: (a) How does science, as we have laid it out thus far, relate to the world of the everyday? What are its limits, and how does it influence that world? (b) In what does the essence of modern science lie? (c) Must science abstract and objectify? Must distanciation from the object of concern take place for scientific inquiry? Can science exist without such distancing and objectifying? (d) What do we mean when we say that science must be rigorous? Must this involve quantification? Does this presume a natural science methodology? (e) Can a non-objectifying thinking occur?

But to answer these questions correctly, we must carefully clarify the way in which science understands the world. In other words we must ask, how we are to understand the ontological genesis of the theoretical attitude, which is a necessary condition for scientific research? That is, we seek to understand science as a mode of being-in-the-world, which discloses or discovers either entities or being.

In seeking the *ontological genesis* of the theoretical attitude, we are asking which of these conditions implied in Dasein's state of Being are existentially necessary for the possibility of Dasein's existing in the way of scientific research. This formulation of the question is aimed at an *existential conception* of science. (Heidegger, 1927, 357)

But why, it might be asked, do we raise the question, 'what is science?' Is it not true that we know what science is, how it develops, and what it means? To live in the modern world and not to understand what science is and what it offers is equivalent to not being part of that world. Science is a part of us, it surrounds us, and goes along with our every project. To be in the world is to be alongside the scientific. Indeed do we not find science everywhere we go, even in places we would prefer it not to be – in politics, in ethics, in war, in planning a family or a community. Surely we know science all too well.

Yet even with this daily familiarity do we really know what the essence of science is, or has its essential meaning slipped away as we have become increasingly familiar with it? Do we comprehend its precise nature as we deal with it daily, and on the basis of which dealings we proffer advice and guide the lives of others? Or do we instead fall into 'a science' ready packaged, predetermined, passed on to us through our textbooks, our methods and our examples as already given? Do not the sciences constantly tend to overlook and forget their own origins and founding intuitions as they become buried under the sedimentations of on-going activity and acquisitions? And do not the sciences themselves constantly seek to become themselves foundational for experience itself, and thus tend constantly towards naturalism, biologism, historicism or spatialism? Do we as scientists not concentrate on the more immediate tasks at hand, while presuming that we understand the meaning of science that has given rise to these tasks?

28a How does theoretical discovery arise?

Science, as we have seen, has a variety of characteristics; it is an affair of groups of technically trained individuals, its procedures are agreed upon through institutionalized means that constantly hold open the possibility of error correction, and it has a particular sociology and history. Moreover it has an internal character of being methodical, logical, and formal. But in our present investigation we are not concerned with the factual (or ontical) history and development of science, its sociological dimension, or its own immediate claims. All of these views of science presuppose that with which we are here concerned. We seek instead to understand the ontological genesis of the theoretical attitude as the precondition for the possibility of conducting scientific research at all. In other words, we seek an *existential* conception of science: understanding science as a mode of man's being-in-the-world; a mode of being which discovers or discloses either entities or their being as *objects* of theoretical concern.[1]

This question must be raised carefully if we are to reach beyond the traditional arguments of metaphysics. The question is already prejudged in this traditional understanding, where 'knowing the world' is interpreted as a relation between a subject and its object. Here knowing is presupposed to be a theoretical knowing in a world of subjects and objects. But such a world does not coincide with man's everyday conception of the world. Such a world is constituted by an inner world of perception and knowing, set over against an outer world of things and physical nature (Heidegger, 1927, 59–62). Eventually the epistemological question must be asked of how the former is related to the latter. The knowing subject as a theoretical subject, divorced from involved concern with the world is presumed to be 'proto-scientist' or 'problem-solver'. Still the question of the kind of being which belongs to this knowing subject is left entirely unasked (see 59–62; 1929, 87–91).

What, then, can we say about knowing which allows us to pass beyond this presumption of a universal theoretical attitude in a world of subjects and objects? The structure of intentionality provides a necessary starting point. With Heidegger we can add that we must now bear in mind that knowing is grounded beforehand in a being-already-alongside-and-toward-the-world; that the world is essentially co-constitutive for man's being. "The kind of dealing which is closest to us is, as we have shown, not a bare perceptual cognition, but rather that kind of concern which manipulates things and puts them to use; and this has its own kind of 'knowledge'" (Heidegger, 1927, 66–7). It is through this essential dialogue with the world that man lets things and the world be what they are, uncovers them, brings their meaning to light. "There is nothing in man which escapes this being toward the world. No matter how deeply one penetrates man's subjectivity, one always will find the world already there" (Kockelmans, 1969, 156). Thus man is situated (placed) in the midst of the world, relating to it in such a way that being (or world) is always already manifest as a whole (Heidegger, 1929, 83).

Man's relation with the world is therefore originally and primordially not a cognitive or theoretical relation, but is one of *Dasein* – of 'being-there'. Theoretical knowledge and science are only special modes of man's orientation toward the world, in which this primordial relation has been made manifest beforehand. The primordial relation of man and world is thus one of fascination (or concernful involvement) with the world, whereas theoretical knowing is a standing back, observing something. In this way entities are encountered purely in the way they look, as merely there.

It is this changeover from the circumspective concern with the world of involvement to an exploration of what we come across as just-there within the world, divorced from concernful involvement, that is central to understanding the development of the theoretical mode of being from the everyday mode of being.

28b The everyday world and the theoretical attitude

But how is this changeover to be understood? Does it occur with the *disappearance of praxis*, when concern holds back from any kind of manipulation so that involvement changes over to merely looking at entities? Is this a matter of a changeover from practical concern to theory (as the absence of praxis)? Were this to be so we would be left with a pure reflection, a just looking around. Such a 'just looking around' is not the theoretical attitude of science, although it may be a way of inspecting and checking things (Heidegger, 1927, 357–8). To see the development of the scientific attitude as a changeover from practical concern (or praxis) to theory is to misunderstand the nature of praxis *and* of theory. Praxis has its own kind of seeing (theory), and theoretical research has its own kind of praxis. The praxis of theoretical research is well known and, in popular culture, typifies the activity itself; the careful setting up and carrying out of experiments, tests, questionnaires, interviews, and evaluating the results through mathematical manipulation using sophisticated machinery and electronics. Even in the most abstract work problems can only be solved with the aid of some equipment, even if only for writing or to 'sketch out' examples of the form 'triangle', a schematic map of relations, or a complex notation. Empirical science involves experimental design, *measurement*, the production of samples for *observation*, the uncovering, sifting and sorting of data, and the manipulation of materials in the *explication* of findings (357–8). While these are obvious parts of scientific research, they do show how scientific behaviour remains *a mode of being-in-the-world*, and not just a 'purely theoretical activity'. It is not obvious where the line is to be drawn between the 'theoretical' and 'practical'. Another way of characterizing the emergence of the scientific attitude must be found (358).

We seek to understand how some entity within our everyday, cultural world can become an *object* for theoretical reflection, and how this is constituted in scientific research; that is, how some thing first constituted in an horizon of concernful involvement can become an object – a just there – in the theoretical attitude. How the hammer of the craftsman becomes a mere point with mass, or how the mountain and brook of the hiker become the landform and the stream of the geomorphologist. As a result of this changeover, objects are no longer presented in an horizon of concernful involvement. Instead we now look – in the case of the heavy hammer – at what is *suitable* for an entity with 'mass' "as a corporeal Thing subject to the law of gravity" (361); in the case of the mountain and brook, at what is suitable for an entity with 'form' and 'process', as a 'physical system', or as a 'stochastic relationship', in a framework of relationships and causal dependencies. Thus, what was initially seen as a tool or a landscape is now seen differently, as a thing subject to the laws of gravity, with key properties, such as mass, volume and location (360–1).

The hammer or the landscape does not show itself differently because we have ceased to manipulate it, nor because we are just looking away from the everyday character of the entity. Instead we are looking at the hammer or the landscape in a new way; as a thing and object of our theoretical concern, from a particular perspective. Nature is here projected in such a way that mass, force and location are meaningful for the world of mechanics; or stream flow, erosion and sediment transport, as well as the world of mechanics, are meaningful for the world of fluvial geomorphology (361).

In this way we can begin to show how theoretical knowing involves a change of attitude or a modification of our understanding about how entities are grasped within the world. In the theoretical mode of being entities are grasped as part of physical nature, whose limits and meaning we have determined beforehand. In asserting that 'the hammer is heavy' and that 'the flood stage of a river carries x amount of sediment' we *overlook* the everyday character of the entity we encounter, as something that has its place in a broader context of concernful involvement, whether it be a workbench and carpentry or Sunday afternoon strolls along the Susquehanna. Its place within this context of everyday use becomes a matter of indifference. The location of the entity is not lost, but its place becomes a spatio-temporal position, a 'world-point', which is in no way distinguished from any other (361–2). "This implies not only that the multiplicity of places of equipment ready-to-hand within the confines of the environment becomes modified to a pure multiplicity of positions, but that the entities of the environment are altogether *released from such confinement*" (361–2).

Perhaps now we have arrived at the characteristic necessary for the changeover to the theoretical attitude, at least for physical nature; the characteristic that the place of equipment within the confines of the environment becomes a pure multiplicity of positions, or world-points, released from their environmental confinement. In more formal terms we can say that the constitution of the theoretical attitude in the sciences requires that the world be in some sense *demundanized*, that it be abstracted from, and that the particular characteristics relevant to each scientific perspective be formalized. In the case of physical nature the world has been released to a pure multiplicity of positions in a systematic way. The multiplicity of positions has been situated within the context of formal mathematical structures; the world has been mathematically projected. Precisely how any particular science develops depends on how this changeover and the multiplicity of world-points are constituted; that is, on how the world is projected.

29 The development of science and the concept of 'progress'

What is it that allows science to deal so effectively with the world it seeks to understand? Is it simply that modern science is factual, experimental, measuring? And does this, then, distinguish modern science from earlier medieval and ancient science?

It has been argued that modern science differs from previous science in that modern science starts from facts while medieval science started from general speculative propositions and concepts. But it is interesting that in looking back on previous scientific arguments, from which we are now divorced by time and change of perspective, we can often argue that unfounded speculative propositions were introduced, which, since we have clarified or changed them, no longer influence our own science. Does this then make our own science free from speculative propositions and unfounded concepts? Furthermore, while it is to some extent true that modern science starts from facts, while medieval science started from speculative propositions, medieval and ancient science also observed facts, and modern science works with universal propositions and concepts for which it often has no other justification than traditional or pragmatic usage, or convenient and productive assumptions. While Galilean science criticized Scholastic science for being 'abstract', proceeding with general propositions and principles, Scholastic science criticized Galileo for the same reason. The difference between ancient and modern science is not on the one side facts, on the other concepts and principles; both necessarily have to do with facts and concepts. It is in the way that these are conceived and established that is decisive.

Is it that modern science is more exact, more accurate, and in some sense closer to understanding the world than medieval science? Certainly science today means something essentially different from Greek and medieval science. The latter were never exact – they could not and need not be. Therefore there is *no sense* in arguing that modern science is *more exact* than Greek science. Nor can we say that, for example, the Galilean doctrine of freely falling bodies is true and that Aristotle's physics, where light bodies strive upward to their proper place, is false. For the Greeks the essence of body and place and of the relation between the two rests upon a different interpretation of beings, and hence a correspondingly different kind of seeing and questioning of natural events. It is not possible to claim that the modern understanding of whatever is is more accurate than that of the Greeks (Heidegger, 1977b, 117). "Therefore, if we want to grasp the essence of modern science, we must first free ourselves from the habit of comparing the new science with the old solely in terms of degree, from the point of view of progress" (117–18).

What makes modern science different is the way in which the world is understood. In the paradigm case of science – mathematical physics – what is decisive is not the high value placed on the observation of facts, nor is it the application of mathematics. Rather it is the way in which the world is uncovered as a world of physical entities that can be measured mathematically: a world of motion, force, location and time. For Edmund Husserl this is the reduction of the world to a mathematical manifold, or the reduction of the world to a set of characteristics that can be captured mathematically. For Martin Heidegger the world is thus mathematically projected. In this projection something is uncovered beforehand, and an horizon of meaning is opened up in such a way that one may be guided by looking at those constitutive items in it which are quantitatively determinable (motion, force, location, and time). Only in the light of a nature which has been projected beforehand in this way can anything like a physical 'fact' be found and an experiment set up. Only with the demundanization of an entity from its everyday context and the projection beforehand of a world of entities as just-there – as world-points in an abstract world-space – can the object of modern physical science be determined (Heidegger, 1927, 362). "The objectification of that which is, in which the positive sciences variously constitute themselves in conformity with the intrinsic content and mode of being of the specific region of being, has its center in the projection, in each case, of the ontological constitution of the beings which are to become objects" (Heidegger, 1982, 321). The mathematical as such is not decisive. What is decisive is that this projection *discloses something that is a priori.*

Thus the paradigmatic character of mathematical natural science does not lie in its exactitude or in the fact that it is binding for 'Everyman'; it consists rather in the fact that the entities which it takes as its theme are discovered in it in the only way in which entities can be discovered – by the prior projection of their state of Being. (Heidegger, 1927, 362)

The entities which any particular science takes as its theme are discovered by this prior projection of their state of being. This involves articulating how these entities are to be understood, delimiting the subject-matter guided by this understanding, and defining the way of conceiving which is appropriate to such entities. This we call *thematization*, and its aim is to free entities we encounter within-the-world from their contexts of immediate involvement in such a way that they can become objects of theoretical inquiry. Heidegger says "in such a way that they can 'throw themselves against' (i.e. project) a pure discovering – that is, they can become 'objects'" (363). Thus freed, these entities can be interrogated by the scientist and their character determined. In this way all thematizing objectifies.

30 Human science and objectification

Given this state of affairs, must the sciences of man also objectify their primary subject of inquiry? The answer depends on what we mean by 'objectify'. If by objectify we mean making into a physical thing – in other words projecting the world as a world of physical entities – then human science cannot objectify, for it would no longer be 'human'. But if we correctly take 'objectify' as making into a theme (or object) of research, then all empirical science is objectifying. "Were objectness to be surrendered," Heidegger (1977c, 169) says, "the essence of science would be denied." In the same essay Heidegger shows how: "Theory makes secure at any given time a region of the real as its object-area. The area-character of objectness is shown in the fact that it specifically maps out in advance the possibilities for the posing of questions" (169). In the case of entities in the world of physical nature, we constitute the thing as object in such a way that its place becomes a matter of indifference, and its location becomes a spatio-temporal position, a 'world-point', which is in no way distinguished from any other. In this way the places in the world of concernful involvement become modified to a pure multiplicity of positions, and the entities of the environment are released from their confinement in that world of involvement.

Yet the world of concernful involvement can also be made a theme for science, as when a geographer studies someone's environment, or milieu, in the context of a cultural or historiological biography. The lived world is then an object for the science of geography, and it becomes an object of a science without having to lose its character as a place, milieu or cultural context. Similarly, if we project a context of work, tools and equipment (in their broadest sense) as they are integrated in everyday life and as they developed with the particular world of which they are a part, we begin to constitute the objects for a science of economics, or for an economic geography or sociology (depending upon how we continue to constitute these objects). In this way the world of concernful involvement can become the 'object' of a science without losing its character as equipment (Heidegger, 1927, 361–2).[2]

31 Rigour and exactitude in science

But, one might ask, how, in this context, is human science to be treated rigorously? In fact we already have the answer, and it depends upon our understanding of phenomenology. Phenomenology seeks, methodically and carefully, "to let that which shows itself be seen from itself in the very way in which it shows itself from itself" (Heidegger, 1927, 34). Each domain or region of phenomena shows itself differently, as we have already seen, and thus requires different forms of evidence and conceptions of validity and rigour.

The rigour of mathematical physical science is exactitude. Here all events, if they are to be seen as events of nature, must be defined beforehand as spatio-temporal magnitudes, through measuring, with the help of number and calculation. Such research is not exact *because* it calculates precisely, rather it must calculate in this way if it is to adhere rigorously to its object-area, which itself has the character of exactitude. By contrast, the human sciences and all sciences concerned with life must necessarily be inexact just in order to remain rigorous. A living thing can indeed be grasped as a spatio-temporal magnitude, but then it is no longer apprehended as living. The inexactitude of the human sciences is, therefore, not a deficiency, but the fulfilment of the essential character of this type of research. The projecting and defining of the object-area of these sciences is not of a different kind to that of the physical sciences, but it is much more difficult to achieve than is the achieving of rigour in the exact sciences (Heidegger, 1977b, 119–20).

The projection sketches out in advance the manner in which the knowing procedure must bind itself and adhere to the sphere opened up. This binding adherence is the rigour of research. Through the projecting of the ground plan and the prescribing of rigour, procedure makes secure for itself its sphere of objects within the realm of Being. (118)

32 Theory and its reach and hold over nature and world

It may seem that the form of argument used to explicate the nature of science comes close to justifying the traditional claims for the universality of objective, positing science. In fact the claims made seek not to justify a universal conception of science, but to clarify precisely the limits within which science operates, and thus the domains within which its claims are fallacious, and to be denied. On the other hand it may seem that the argument regarding the projective character of all science leads to a dangerous relativism of views, whereby any perspective or projection is theoretically possible, and where new projections could completely overthrow the present scientific world-views we cherish. This is of course not the case. It is certainly the case that new projections are always a possibility, and that these might alter or, in the extreme case, completely overthrow accepted scientific views. But it is not an argument leading to relativism. Clarification of the relationship of theory and world (including the world of nature) may be helpful at this stage.

Even for a science such as physics, nature remains that which *cannot* be completely mapped out; theory always remains directed towards nature, never contiguous with it. Theory is never able to encompass the essential fullness of nature. Heidegger claims:

> Theory never outstrips nature – nature that is already presencing – and in this sense theory never makes its way around nature. Physics may well represent the most general and pervasive lawfulness of nature in terms of the identity of matter and energy; and what is represented by physics is indeed nature itself, but undeniably it is only nature as object-area, whose objectness is first defined and determined through the refining that is characteristic of physics and is expressly set forth in that refining. (1977c, 173–4)

Physics or any other science can never embrace the fullness of the coming to presence of nature, for its object-character is only one way in which nature exhibits itself. Even the totality of all possible sciences cannot exhaust the fullness of such a nature, because it always presents itself as also other than 'object' (174). The sceptic might ask, but is it not possible that the ways in which nature presents itself as other than 'object' can become the focus of some other science, and can thus be encompassed by a new scientific perspective? Such a scientific perspective is, of course, always possible, but as we have seen in Husserl's position regarding abstractive reduction and the impossibility of dealing with the immediate as immediate, the objectification of this new relation of man and nature, for example, says something about that relationship as object for science, but not as relationship experienced.[3] (This does not mean, however, that the findings of science will not then influence that experience through its sophisticated 'capture' of some element of it.)

33 Science and the lived world

We have seen that science is a projective enterprise, and that distanciation, objectification, abstraction and thematization (properly understood) are essential elements of it. But we have also seen that to 'objectify' in science does not necessarily mean 'to make into a thing', but to make into a theme (or object) of study. In this way, insofar as empirical science is conducted, distancing, objectifying and abstracting are necessary, if implicit, procedures. The lived world is always necessarily reduced to the theme (or object) of theoretical concern. This is not to justify anything like a neo-positivist position – far from it. But it is to recognize the essential characteristics of the scientific enterprise, and the power of the objectifying nature of empirical science.

In the projection and thematization of the natural world the objects of theoretical concern are taken as things against a background of an undifferentiated world-space, divorced from any context other than the mathematical and the purely physical. However, not all scientific inquiry requires that the human world be projected against such an undifferentiated space of indifferent spatio-temporal positions divorced from involved concern. Indeed this would be to project precisely a non-human world. The scientific projection and thematiz-ation of the human world, while it is likewise an objectifying enterprise, is one where the horizon, within which objects are projected as the objects that they are, remains their context of involved concern. Thus, the world of involved concern can become 'object' for a science without losing its character as involved (Heidegger, 1927, 361).

This process of thematization (objectivation), while it does not turn the world of man into a physical thing, does require that the observer distance himself or herself from the immediacy of the lived world under consideration. The scientist must stand back and look at the phenomenon as object of concern. In this way the lived world is projected as a theme (object) of research. Only in this way is the prior projection of the state of being of the world open to thematization as scientific project. But the working out of this thematization need not demand of itself the exactness of the mathematical physical sciences; indeed were it to do so it would be distorting the nature of its own phenomena. Instead it must demand the rigour appropriate to human sciences, which are necessarily inexact. On the other hand, such inexactitude must be obtained rigorously.

Furthermore, if we follow Heidegger's argument regarding science and the principle of identity, then it seems that we *must* admit of formalization if human science is to be sure in advance of the identity of its object. Heidegger claims that:

Everywhere, wherever and however we are related to beings of every kind, we find identity making its claim on us. If this claim were not made, beings could never appear in their Being. Accordingly, there would then also not be any science. For if science could not be sure in advance of the identity of its object in each case, it could not be what it is. By this assurance, research makes certain that its work is possible. (1969a, 26–7)

And in the human world, only formalization of the phenomena under study can carefully provide such a necessary assurance of the identity of the objects for each science. Put another way, we must question whether there can be a human science which does not idealize its object of concern in order to retain and be sure in advance of the *identity* of its object. To fail to hold the object of science stable through objectivation, formalization and thematization is to fail scientifically; to revert to a mere gathering and accumulation of facts; to engage in mere empirical inquiry devoid of possibilities for an on-going research programme. It is to seek to construct a science based on naive collections of information, without any common and explicit general framework of meaning from which beings are projected as this particular being, taken in certain specified ways, and without any common horizon within which the identity of the object in the human realm can be grasped. We need for the human realm what Heidegger describes for the realm of nature:

The 'previously projected' plan of nature in general determines in advance the constitution of the Being of the essent [being] to which it must be possible to relate all modes of questioning. This precursory projection relative to the Being of the essent [being] is inscribed in the basic concepts and axioms of the natural sciences. (1962, 15)

Thus we need to understand the human sciences in terms of prior or precursory projections of their state of being, clarified through their basic concepts. For the realm of human experience as such this prior projection must be phenomenologically grounded and rigorous; that is it must allow the phenomenon to show itself from itself in the very way it shows itself. In the case of human experience the primordial phenomenon we seek to uncover is the everyday mode of being as one of involved concern. Such experience is not, like the stone or the stream, something to which we have no prior access and of which we do not already have a coherent interpretation. Such access and such interpretations are prior to every question we ask about the human situation. For this reason we need an interpretative or hermeneutic phenomenology.

PART IV

Human science, worldhood and spatiality

He inquired about the geological structure of his landscapes, convinced that these abstract relationships, expressed, however, in terms of the visible world, should affect the act of painting. The rules of anatomy and design are present in each stroke of his brush just as the rules of the game underlie each stroke of a tennis match. But what motivates the painter's movement can never be simply perspective or geometry or the laws governing color, or, for that matter, particular knowledge. Motivating all the movements from which a picture gradually emerges there can be only one thing: the landscape in its totality and in its absolute fullness, precisely what Cezanne called a 'motif'. (Merleau-Ponty, 1964, 17)

8

Implications for the human sciences and a human science of geography

[The] scientific structure [of the human sciences] (not, indeed, the 'scientific attitude' of those who work to advance them) is today thoroughly questionable and needs to be attacked in new ways which must have their source in ontological problematics. (Heidegger, 1927, 45)

The goal is to attain a fundamental illumination – using phenomenology – of the basic problems of [geography] as human positive science by bringing out its inner systematic relations. (Adapted from Heidegger, 1982, xvii)

34 Phenomenology

Phenomenology seeks to ground the relationship between the scientific and the pre-scientific, the theoretical and the everyday, ontologically.

[It] does not subscribe to a 'standpoint' or represent any special 'direction'; for phenomenology is nothing of either sort, nor can it become so as long as it understands itself. The expression 'phenomenology' signifies primarily a *methodological conception*. The expression does not characterize the what of the objects of philosophical research as subject matter, but rather the *how* of that research. The more genuinely a methodological concept is worked out and the more comprehensively it determines the principles on which a science is to be conducted, all the more primordially is it rooted in the way we come to terms with the things themselves, and the farther is it removed from what we call 'technical devices' though there are many such devices even in the theoretical disciplines. (Heidegger, 1927, 27)

By contrast, the presumption of the primacy of the theoretical attitude in contemporary human science, where a starting point is taken in a subject who is world-less or divorced from its world, has given rise to the corresponding understanding of the world as a world of things, objectively determinable and external, over against a knowing subject and an internal subjective world. The resultant epistemological problems require clarification of the relationship between subject and object. But such a clarification cannot be given when the primacy of the theoretical attitude is presupposed from the beginning.

Phenomenological inquiry concerns itself with the mode of being which is characteristic of the knowing subject. If one interprets knowledge as a special mode of man's being-in and orientation towards the world, then it makes no sense to conceive of knowledge as a process by which the 'subject' creates 'for and in himself' a 'representation' of something that is 'outside' the knowing subject. Similarly it makes no sense to ask how these 'representations' could harmonize with 'reality outside of consciousness' (Kockelmans, 1969, 9; Heidegger, 1927, 86–7). In other words, the questions of whether there is a world at all, and whether it can be proved and known, make no sense if they are raised by a being who is not worldless, but who is in and towards the world as its basic mode of being, and for whom the theoretical attitude is not the most primordial mode of being.

The aim of phenomenology is therefore to clarify the mode of being of these original experiences, to make explicit the frameworks of meaning from which the sciences construct their particular thematizations of the world, and to examine critically the limits of their application as well as their relevance to the phenomena to be considered. Such frameworks of meaning are somehow already implicit in the world of everyday experience, to which the insights of the sciences must be capable in principle of being brought back and from which they are originally derived.

35 Phenomenology and the science of geography

Husserl's reaction against naturalism was against the claim that there was only one mode of being – that of the 'objectively' determinable object, determinable in conformity with and using the methods of exact natural science. On the contrary, Husserl argued, being must be spoken of in different ways. "Not all of that which 'is' may be considered an object conforming to the specifications of the natural sciences, that is, an object given, in the end, via the senses" (Landgrebe, 1981, 150). If naturalism continues to reject this proposition the sciences will be unable to explain the intentional acts from which their own constructions originate, the relationship between science and life would be unclear, and philosophy itself would be unnecessary (Husserl, 1931, 36). Yet, even if naturalism is to be discredited because it attempts to apply uniform methods to both nature and spirit, its ultimate aim of a scientific philosophy, providing a firm grounding for the empirical sciences was not to be discounted (Husserl, 1911, 82).

In this regard phenomenology has been greatly misunderstood and misrepresented within geography as to its essential premises and, in particular, one of its major aims. It has been suggested that phenomenology is individualistic and subjectivist, unable to deal with phenomena at the aggregate or regional level, and that as a result it is not to be considered a scientific perspective, but rather a study of unique entities. On the other hand, geographers defending a phenomenological approach have confused science, empirical science, positivism and logical empiricism, and have perpetuated a view of phenomenology as anti-scientific, non-scientific, or in some way pre-scientific.

As we have seen, phenomenology is not anti-scientific nor is it a criticism of science as such, provided we do not understand by science a caricature of its essential nature and do not equate it with positivism or logical empiricism. Phenomenology may, however, criticize the practice and claims of some scientists and some regions of science, and it does reject the possibility for empirical science to provide its own foundations as positivism and naturalist approaches claim. Husserl's critique of empiricistic naturalism was a necessary step – not in the denial of science – but in a return to the fundamental principles of science and in developing phenomenology as the 'science' of the sciences. Even Merleau-Ponty's claim that phenomenology "is from the start a rejection of science" should not be taken to mean that in the final analysis science is to be rejected (Merleau-Ponty, 1962, viii). For Merleau-Ponty, as well as for Husserl and Heidegger,

if we want to subject science itself to rigorous scrutiny and arrive at a precise assessment of its meaning and scope, we must begin by re-awakening the basic experience of the world of which science is a second-order expression. Science has not and never will have, by its nature, the same significance *qua* form of being as the world we perceive, for the simple reason that it is a rationale or explanation of that world. (viii)

Phenomenology seeks to return to the things themselves;

to that world which precedes knowledge, of which knowledge always *speaks*, and in relation to which every scientific schematization is an abstract and derivative sign-language, as is geography in relation to the countryside in which we have learnt beforehand what a forest, a prairie or a river is. (ix)

The primordial experience of the world is the world of practical or everyday involvement; a world called into meaning by the task man engages in. Only when he has some problem with this world, when he stands back from it and questions it, does he engage in theoretical speculation. The concern for empirical science begins first by adopting such a theoretical attitude. For Husserl (1913, 45) this attitude remains in the 'natural standpoint' of the world, and its development is the

sciences of the world. Every science has its own object-domain as a
field of research – a field which requires the scientist to disengage
himself from his primordial orientation towards the world in which he
lives. As scientist he now wants to 'observe' and to 'contemplate' the
world as object, not as the world he lives in. In this distancing from the
lived-world the scientist thematizes the world as experienced. We can
recognize this thematization in the sciences themselves: Newton's
world is comprised of space, time, force and mass, a productive
thematization for mechanics, but, as Pascal is reputed to have
remarked, "a frightening world in which to live". In the first few pages
of the Definitions and Scholium to the Definitions of *Mathematical
principles of natural philosophy*, Newton (1687, 81) explains "the
definitions of such words as are less well-known, and . . . the sense in
which I would have them to be understood in the following discourse".
That is, he seeks to articulate the a priori framework of meaning and
concepts on the basis of which a scientific world of mechanics can be
projected as itself a meaningful world in which space, time, mass,
point, motion, etc., can all be understood in a coherent and productive
manner. He seeks to lay out a regional ontology of physical entities. In
the same way each empirical science must determine its realms of
investigation and project a formal ontological framework from which
the entities, events and relationships to be studied are to be taken and
viewed.

In thematizing from the phenomena under consideration basic
concepts and categories are established, which provide the starting
point for formalization, functionalization, and in some cases quantification, upon which the scientific investigation of relationships
proceeds. Such procedures applied to the originally experienced
phenomena necessarily reduce the latter to more or less ideal entities,
which are abstract in comparison with the original phenomena. Which
concepts and categories are appropriate in this process derive from the
phenomena under investigation and the perspective of the tradition
brought to the phenomena, i.e., they derive from the particular form of
the projection of the world. The world of mechanics, as we have seen,
projects a world of significant and insignificant characteristics. The
moon, for example, is defined in terms of its position, mass and
relation to other similarly defined bodies. From this perspective its
colour, phases and possible inhabitants are irrelevant.

Phenomenology, then, seeks to clarify the foundations of the
positive sciences. Only in the radical clarity of its presuppositions, in
making its basic concepts transparent to itself, is it that a science is
truly a science. In regard to science it is phenomenology's task, as

method, to clarify these concepts and provide the foundations for the empirical and formal sciences. Phenomenology itself has no subject-matter as such, but is a method. In this sense, what would be the purpose of a descriptive phenomenology of geographic science, and what would such a regional ontology look like?

Such a descriptive phenomenology would first seek to make transparent the a priori framework of meaning, or the particular projection of the world adopted by a discipline in its empirical work, as thematizations of the everyday world. This would usually be implicit in the sciences themselves and thus phenomenology would seek to make it explicit and transparent. It would seek to lay bare the region of concern of the particular science, and how its objects of concern are constituted and how they relate to the world of the everyday prior to their projection or thematization in the world of science. Such a clarification of the objects of geographical concern is essential not only for the subsequent development of scientific claims, but for founding the basis of geographic inquiry in and for a world understood as a lived world. Such a descriptive science therefore seeks to ensure that the thematizations of the world as object of concern and the constructs presupposed by empirical geography are relevant and meaningful. It seeks to make explicit this meaning and the limits within which concepts and scientific thematizations are valid, and to ground accepted principles and methods in terms of these claims. This it must do by a return to the original experiences; to the things themselves. "'[Descriptive] science of man' means that regional ontology which tries to bring to light the essential and necessary structures of all the various modes of orientation toward the world which are character-istic of the entities belonging to the region of human beings" (Kockelmans, 1973, 259).

36 Towards a formal projective human science

The effect of the projection of beings as a pure discovering of entities is to set up a framework within which those entities show themselves in a particular way and in particular relationships. Put another way, things call or conjure up a framework within which they are allowed to be the things that they are; when we posit an atom, the atom itself calls up a framework of meaning within which it sits meaningfully; stream erosion calls up a world of forces, movement and resistances in space and time, within which the concept 'stream erosion' makes sense. For the non-initiate such objects conjure up no such world, and even the most basic scientific relationships may then remain meaningless. This showing is not the everyday way of their being, but is derived from it in a particular way (Chapter 6) and with a particular aim. In not being the everyday way of being these entities and relationships are projected as *problematic*, at least in principle. We can say, contrary to all humanist claims, that science is not a procedure for capturing the everyday world in its everydayness. Everydayness and understanding have their own modes of expressing that. Science is, on the contrary, the systematically and methodically bound process of making the immediately obvious and the everyday taken-for-granted world problematical, in such a way that we can explain it differently. It must be intersubjectively verifiable (or falsifiable). It must open up horizons for future and on-going research programmes.

We see implicit recognition of this in the way Galileo developed his mechanics, describing a counter-intuitive world of planes, friction-free surfaces, and free-falls. Newton formulated such a world much more carefully by projecting and defining an abstract world of space and time, and an axiomatic physical world of relations. Einstein returned to counter-intuitive arguments when he challenged the validity of Newtonian and Galilean conceptions of dimensionality, space and time, which by then had flowed into and influenced the everyday, taken-for-granted ways of looking at the world.

In the human sciences similar frameworks have been postulated, but generally within a framework of naturalism and empiricism, as we have already seen (Chapters 2 and 4). Also, in the human sciences the principle of the sciences as a means of problematizing the world has been distorted by empiricism. It has increasingly become a methodical procedure *for overcoming that which is a problem* in the everyday world. It has become a tampering and mending process, and has as a result become a technical enterprise.[1] Science as a formal, eidetic, projective, a priori enterprise has failed thus far in the human sciences.[2]

37 Husserl and human science

That Husserlian phenomenology devotes a great deal of attention to the human sciences should by now, contrary to the claims of geographers (Ley (1980a) in particular), be self-evident. Husserl specifically addressed the situation in psychology (in *Phenomenological psychology*, for example) and throughout his work sought to define various layers of a science of pure consciousness in its relation to an empirical science of consciousness. For the moment we will place these treatments to one side, however, and turn to Husserl's explicit claims for the human sciences whose subject-matter and manner of treating it is more immediately similar to that of geography. But it should still be remembered that these claims presuppose Husserl's work on psychology and the sciences of consciousness, and, of course, on descriptive, eidetic psychology or phenomenology.

In 'Phenomenology and anthropology' Husserl (1941) addressed the issue of philosophical anthropology, prevalent, then as now, as an argument for relating the sciences, philosophy and concrete, worldly existence. Here "true philosophy should seek its foundations exclusively in man and, more specifically, in the essence of his concrete worldly existence" (315). At first sight it might seem that at last we have reached common ground between the claims of 'geographical phenomenology' and the aims of phenomenology. In fact, philosophical anthropology, derived in particular from Dilthey's *Lebensphilosophie*, involves a reversal of phenomenological principles. "The original phenomenology, in mature transcendental form, refused to derive any part of the foundations of philosophy from any science of man and opposed, as 'anthropologism' and 'psychologism', all attempts in this direction" (315). The perennial question as to whether the sciences can be grounded scientifically or whether they must be grounded philosophically is at issue here, and Husserl argues strongly for the latter and against the claims of philosophical anthropology. If this implies a subjectivism, then the "specific meaning of subjectivity must also be determined a priori" (315). A decision between anthropologism and transcendentalism must be possible. If we are to accept the arguments of philosophical anthropology, if a rigorous and founding science of science is not available, and if we therefore have no corresponding science of essential forms of the human realm, how are we to decide between different sciences and competing theories and explanations? Is it a matter of voting on such issues, such that the commonly accepted explanation is the true, if contingent claim? Are the different sciences then merely conventional entities, each telling a different or conflicting part of a larger story? Do we judge on instinct or on inclination? Surprisingly these crucial questions have been avoided in geographic reflection.[3] Husserl's answer is instructive:

Actions like these may be perfectly justified if the day comes on which such a decision is required, and with it the action is completed. But in our own case there is a concern for the temporal infinity and for the eternal in the temporal – the future of mankind, the genesis of true humanity – for which we still feel ourselves to be responsible. (1923, 331)

Only philosophy as rigorous science can provide us with the rationality necessary for a truly rational science. In the same essay Husserl addressed the fact that we lack the science which, with respect to the *idea of man* (and consequently, also with respect to the a priori inseparable pair of ideas: the individual man and his community), would have to undertake to accomplish something similar to what the pure mathematical science of nature has undertaken for the *idea of nature* and, in its principal divisions, has actually accomplished (328).

The idea of nature in general, as a universal form, includes all the individual natural sciences. It is such an idea of a spiritual being in general, especially of man, as a universal form, that is needed to encompass and ground all the individual human sciences. The mathematical science of nature, with its basic a priori concepts of space, time, movement and force, provides the necessary a priori framework for the idea of nature in general that, when applied to the facts of observed nature, "an empirical science of nature with a rational, that is, mathematical method" is possible. "Therefore, the mathematical science of nature, with its a priori, provides the principles for the rationalization of the empirical domain." By contrast, "we now have many fruitful sciences related to the realm of the spirit, that is, humanity, but they are entirely and 'merely' empirical sciences". Such "'merely' empirical sciences" are not held together by any form of rationality equivalent to, though not necessarily the same as, the mathematical method in the science of nature: no purely rational, a priori truths that are rooted in the 'essence of man', no pure *logos* to guide the method in the domain of the human sciences. "Such an a priori system of truths . . . would make possible the rational explanation of empirical facts, just as the pure mathematical science of nature has made empirical, natural science possible as a mathematical, theoretical, and consequently, rational, mode of explanation" (Husserl, 1923, 328). An a priori science based on essential characteristics from the domain of human affairs is necessary. But such a science will not, indeed cannot, be the same as the a priori science of physical nature; physical and human realities are fundamentally different, and thus to found the latter in a priori concepts of the former is naturalism, as we have already seen. The point can be further clarified if we consider that nature as factual existence is given only in external experience, as spatio-temporal form within a causal, lawful framework. The forms of human realities are quite different. Space and time differ in this context, and each complex human reality has what Husserl refers to as "its own inwardness", by which acts stand in "motivational connection", and within which they are valued and evaluated (329). It is possible to consider the spiritual in terms of physical surrogates; "men and animals as being mere occurrences in space, 'in' nature" (329). But, unlike the case of the natural sciences, these resultant inductive regularities are not indications of exact laws, nor do they reflect the objectively true nature of these realities. The human sciences, like the natural sciences several centuries before, require a formal a priori framework, within which basic concepts and methods permit the human domain to be 'captured', and in such a way that phenomenologically sound description permits the foundation of rational, interrelated empirical human sciences. Such an a priori framework requires an investigation of practical reason (329).[4]

How is this to be achieved? Does Husserl give any practical guidelines? Clearly he does, and, as we have seen, this is the aim of his foundational project for the sciences. The first task of such a human science must be to determine the essential and formal structures of what it is to be human, and the possibilities for actualizing this idea. In the parallel case of the a priori formal structures for the idea of nature, Galileo, Descartes, and Newton characterized the formal properties of space, planes, motion and force, proceeding to actualize each formalization as a series of pure possibilities illustrated through critical experiments. Thus Galileo's experiment with falling bodies *failed* for the citizens of Pisa simply because the formal framework within which it was actualizing one possibility was not then evident to them – it was not a possibility (see Gingerich, 1982).

Which particular, normatively justified forms would then be possible and necessary within a mankind that is in accordance with this idea of genuine humanity? Which forms would be possible and necessary for the individual persons who, as members of a community, constitute this humanity, as well as for the different types of associations, social institutions, cultural activities, etc.? – All of this would belong together in a scientific, eidetic analysis of the idea of a genuine, rational mankind, and would lead to various individual investigations with numerous ramifications. (Husserl, 1923, 330)

We may be unaccustomed to practising explicitly such abstraction in the spiritual sphere, but, Husserl points out, such methodical, conscious disregard of the empirical content of specific concepts gives us, in our everyday existence, examples of such 'pure' concepts: the community in general, the state in general, the people, man, the citizen.

Thus all empirical factual distinctions of corporeality and spirituality, of concrete earthly life, are obviously circumstantial, and likewise, 'indeterminate' and 'freely variable' in the same sense that pertains to the concrete features and to the contingent, empirical magnitudes that the algebraist investigates. For fundamental considerations such as, for instance, those of pure reason, matters such as whether man's senses, eyes, ears, etc., are formed empirically in this or that way, whether he has two or more eyes, whether he has this or that organ for locomotion, be it legs or wings, etc., are entirely extraneous questions that always remain open. (330–1)

This is a somewhat different vision of human science from the one we now accept, but it is largely implicit in that science, if for no other reason than that it has developed out of natural science where such a view is more obvious. Clearly Husserl is not saying that the body, for example, is not important; it is, and he has devoted much effort to showing how, for example, the hyletic field is constituted through man's frontal, binocular vision. But in the light of these claims we can perhaps better understand Heidegger's formal ontology of man, as *Dasein*, to which we now turn again.

38 Towards a formal and a priori 'mathesis of spirit and of humanity'[5]

The human sciences require a formal a priori ontology for the realm of human nature, in the same way that Kant formalized for the physical sciences an ontology of material nature. Husserl had set Oskar Becker the task of developing a phenomenological account of such an ontology for physical nature and the physical sciences, giving to Heidegger the task of developing an ontology *appropriate* to the realm of human being and the human and historical sciences; of developing an ontology of practical reason for the historical sciences. Although Heidegger's fundamental question in *Being and time* is different – the question of the meaning of being – he nonetheless seeks to develop just such an ontology of human being and practical reason. In a lecture course of 1925–6 Heidegger (1962, 3–4) clarifies this aim: "By fundamental ontology is meant that ontological analytic of man's finite essence which should prepare the foundation for the metaphysics 'which belongs to human nature'."[6]

The question of Being aims therefore at ascertaining the *a priori* conditions not only for the possibility of the sciences which examine entities as entities of such and such a type, and, in so doing, already operate with an understanding of Being, but also for the possibility of those ontologies themselves which are prior to the ontical sciences and which provide their foundations. *Basically, all ontology, no matter how rich and firmly compacted a system of categories it has at its disposal, remains blind and perverted from its ownmost aim if it has not first clarified the meaning of Being, and conceived this clarification as its fundamental task.* (Heidegger, 1927, 11)

Man's modes of behaviour have been studied extensively by the sciences and in poetry, biography, and the writing of history. But, Heidegger asks, does the existential primordiality of these interpreta-

tions match their *existentiell* primordiality? Only through a clarification of the basic structures of *Dasein* will these interpretations be fully
justified, and therefore an analytic of *Dasein* is of the first priority if we
are to ground the human sciences in an appropriate ontology
(Heidegger, 1927, 16). But how is access to such an analytic to be
attained? It cannot be done dogmatically using theoretical constructions, no matter how obvious they may be. Nor can any of the resultant
'categories' be imposed without proper ontological consideration.

We must rather choose such a way of access and such a kind of interpretation
that this entity can show itself in itself and from itself. And this means that it is
to be shown as it is *proximally and for the most part* – in its average
everydayness. (Heidegger, 1927, 16)

To show a phenomenon as it shows itself in itself and from itself is the
task of phenomenology. Phenomenology is the method of ontology as
the being of entities. It has the character of being transcendental and
analytical in a similar manner to Kant. But, because it is dealing with
the realm of human being, this phenomenology must also be a
hermeneutic, in the sense of an interpretation (Heidegger, 1927, 37–8;
see also Schrag, 1958, 289–90).[7] It follows that hermeneutic phenomenology is the necessary foundation for any ontological investigation
whatsoever, including those of the sciences, and for which it contains,
in a derivative sense, the roots of a 'hermeneutic' or methodology
(Heidegger, 1927, 37–8).[8] As a hermeneutic phenomenology of man (as
Dasein) Heidegger's existential analytic seeks to make clear the
formal, a priori constellation of characteristics that are typical for
what it is to be human. Such an analytic is prior to and founding for any
human science, such as psychology, anthropology, biology or geography (45).

39 The existential analytic and the human sciences

Hitherto, investigations of man, despite their vast contributions, have
failed to grasp the essential problem of man as a philosophical issue,
without which the firm grounding they seek cannot be achieved. This is
possible only through an existential analytic, which is prior to and
founding for the individual human sciences. Yet, while this analytic is
to focus upon man, it cannot begin by positing an 'I' or a subject as that
which is central to the inquiry. Nor can we begin with an ontical
concern, dealing with 'personal' or 'private' concerns of individuals.
Every idea of a 'subject', 'reified consciousness', 'spirit', or 'person'
presumes the very entity that is to be questioned. We need an
ontological determination of the basic character of this entity who is

man, or *Dasein* (Heidegger, 1927, 45–6). In terms of our present concern, the scientific disciplines need an a priori determination of the ontological character of the kind of entity with which they deal.[9] This is not to pass judgement on the actual work of the positive, empirical sciences.

We must always bear in mind, however, that these ontological foundations can never be disclosed by subsequent hypotheses derived from empirical material, but that they are always 'there' already, even when that empirical material simply gets collected. If positive research fails to see these foundations and holds them to be self-evident, this by no means proves that they are not basic or that they are not problematic in a more radical sense than any thesis of positive science can ever be. (50)

Heidegger thus accepts Husserl's view that the unity of the person must have a constitution essentially different from that required for the unity of things of nature (48–9). Scheler too takes this view, and seeks to show how the specific character of acts is distinct from anything 'psychical'. A person is never to be thought of as a thing or substance, but rather as "the unity of living-through which is immediately experienced in and with our Experiences – not a Thing merely thought of behind and outside of what is immediately Experienced" (Scheler, in Heidegger, 1927, 47). The person is not a thing, nor a substance. Nor are acts things, for they are experienced only in their performance itself within a particular framework of meaning.

It is still possible to take 'body', 'soul' and 'spirit' as designating phenomenal domains as themes for definite investigations, but we cannot then reconstruct man from these 'pieces' when we ask the more fundamental question of the kinds of being of this entity. Instead, Heidegger seeks an ontology, such that for biology an ontology of life determines what must be the case if there is to be anything like mere-aliveness. Similarly for geography we need an ontology of spatiality, environmentality and worldhood that determines what must be the case if there can be anything like spatial and environmental behaviour, and the creation of different worlds. Both an ontology of life and an ontology of spatiality, as well as of the psyche, of primitive man, etc., all presuppose, and implicitly draw upon, a fundamental and hermeneutic ontology of *Dasein* (48–50).

40 The existential analytic and the 'natural conception of the world' (or lifeworld)

But in returning to man's everydayness we do not strive to describe some primitive stage, through some empirical investigation such as anthropology. "*Everydayness does not coincide with primitiveness,* but is rather a mode of Dasein's Being, even when that Dasein is active in a highly developed and differentiated culture – and precisely then" (Heidegger, 1927, 50–1). This is not to say that the study of primitive societies cannot be revealing, especially where the phenomenon of everydayness is less concealed and less complicated by the extensive self-interpretation that characterizes Western society.[10] But our information about such societies and their conceptions comes from ethnology and history, both of which, as positive disciplines, operate with definite preliminary conceptions and interpretations of man. As such they already presuppose an unclarified analytic of *Dasein* (51).[11]

Similarly when we as geographers seek to understand a 'natural conception of the world', or even the essential characteristics of a region of the world, we cannot achieve such a universal view by collecting different conceptions and seeking to synthesize them through comparison and classification. If an ordering principle is genuine it cannot be found by means of the ordering procedure, but is already presupposed by it. That which is presupposed then, should, in this case, be the primary object of study. Primordial for geographic discourse is the question of the meaning of worldhood, environmentality and human spatiality.

9

Towards an understanding of human spatiality

The space about us here is merely space, no meaner or grander than the space above the shacks and tenements and temples and offices of the capital. Space is space, life is life, everywhere the same. (Coetzee, 1982, 16)

Whatever variety of existing theory about geometric space is taken, be it Euclidean, Lobatchevsky's, Riemann's, Minkowski–Einstein's, or the 'n-dimensional' notion of G. Cantor, it cannot be used to locate sociocultural phenomena, nor their spatial relationship to one another. (Sorokin, 1962, 359)

41 Geography, world and space

The themes with which geographers have traditionally claimed to be concerned are world, environment and nature, particularly insofar as they relate to man and earth. We have seen how this relationship has recently been interpreted formally as a spatial relationship, where space is the organizing principle for geographic entities (Whittlesey, 1957). Yet this view has been challenged, notably by the schools of geography concerned less with spatial relations per se and more with the sense of place (*genius loci*), landscape, region, and man–environment and man–nature relationships; with the creation of particular worlds and their interpretation of man's relationship with the land. Here space and spatial relations are subsets of these relationships, not the organizing principle itself. Consequently the geographic tradition displays and retains a certain inherent tension and ambiguity with regard to its basic subject-matter and approaches to it.

Thus far we have brought one element of that tension into question. Geography as spatial science is predicated on a physical conception of space, inappropriate for interpreting *human* spatiality. How far phenomenological and hermeneutic methods take us in suggesting an alternative conception of spatiality for human science and ultimately a resolution of geography's own ambiguity regarding its object-domain or subject-matter, still has to be seen. This final chapter shows how place and space are related, how they derive from a fundamental spatiality, and how this requires a certain interpretation of nature, environment and world. This interpretation, which contemporary geographic use presupposes and takes for granted, must be 're-vitalized' (literally breathing life into them) if space and place are to be made transparent to geographic science, if objectivist, subjectivist and relativist positions are to be avoided, and if different conceptions of spatiality and space are to be accessible to empirical geography without, at the same time, denying their own founded nature in man's places.

To conclude this work with a section on place and space may appear to be falling back into the metaphysics of traditional geographic discourse, necessitating dialogue with spatial analysis, regional and cultural geography, with histories of places, and the varied claims these positions make about particular places and spaces. Of course, such dialogue is necessary, and is intrinsic to the process of geographic understanding and research. But, given the claims of the preceding sections, such a turn (albeit accepting the necessity of dialogue) is *not yet* appropriate. Nor, indeed, is this turning to place and space intended as a return to such a metaphysic. In the way in which we have sought to retrieve phenomenology and science for human science, it is the aim of this section to retrieve two basic concepts of geographic concern – place and space – for a viable and vital regional ontology of the geographical, on the grounds of which geographical inquiry as a human science of the world can be explicitly founded. This turning is marked by an attitude different from that which geographers have commonly adopted. We turn not to the ontical, factical places and spaces of man's existence (although in the long run these will be important to and informed by our inquiry). Rather we seek an ontological, existential understanding of the universal structures characteristic of man's spatiality as the precondition for any under-standing of places and spaces as such. That is, we seek to clarify the original experiences on the basis of which geography can articulate and develop its regional ontology if geography as a *human* science, concerned with *man's* spatiality, is to be possible at all. This necessarily also entails a hermeneutic critique of the 'geographical' and 'spatial' conceptions that have been generally accepted and have led to an understanding of the genuine meaning of space as physical space.

In thus clarifying the spatiality characteristic of man's ek-sistence, we seek to provide a phenomenological grounding on the basis of which different ontical spaces can be constructed which are neither relative nor subjective, and which remain firmly tied to the place-character of man's world. This we seek to achieve through Heidegger's insightful investigations, but it is not a project limited to these investigations (see, for example, Walter's (1980–1) 'The places of experience'). Through this fundamental ontology – whose method is phenomenology – we turn towards the general framework of meaning within which particular places and spaces, nature and worlds, have the meaning that they do.

On the one hand this is a categorical concern: to inquire into the universal structures of place and space, and to understand the horizon of our world which gives them the meaning they have for us. On the other hand, this is a transcendental concern: to remain open to being as such, as the totality of all possible worlds from which place and space enter concretely into and constitute our own particular world. Thus, we seek to re-unite empirical geographical inquiry with ontology in such a way that radical objectivism and subjectivism are overcome; to claim that science is, and must be, informed by philosophical reflection, and that human science in particular, if it is to avoid tendencies towards social physics in its broadest sense, must itself become philosophical after a fashion.

This final chapter shows what such an ontology of human spatiality might be like as an ontological foundation for human science, specifically geographical science concerned with man and earth. But this question can only be broached in a preliminary fashion. It will suffice if, having laid the theoretical foundation for an understanding of how we might approach the spatiality characteristic of man, we can show here something of what this spatiality entails. A fuller unfolding of this domain must await further investigation. The geographer's concerns – his objects of study and his subject-matter of discourse and inquiry – are varied, and, so it seems, such as to defy explicit characterization in any but the broadest terms. The previous chapters sought to lay the ground for understanding the nature of any science as rooted in particular phenomena, and the necessity for each empirical science to clarify its own essential a priori concepts. They have shown the method through which this might be achieved, without reverting to either conventionalism, an encyclopaedic approach, or an unreflective, merely technical enterprise.

42 World and worldhood

This work began with a single quotation from Jan Broek (see p. xi): the purpose and aim of geography is "to understand the earth as the world of man". Geographers seek to describe the world around them. But what is meant by 'the world' in this context? Traditionally this has been a description of 'entities' within the world: houses, vegetation, people, occupations, mountains. "We can *depict* the way such entities 'look', and we can give an *account* of occurrences in them and with them. This, however, is obviously a pre-phenomenological 'business' which cannot be at all relevant phenomenologically. Such a description is always confined to entities. It is ontical" (Heidegger, 1927, 63). With Heidegger we seek, instead, a phenomenological description of the 'world'. But 'world' itself has several different meanings, not all of which we intend at this point. (1) Used in an ontical way 'world' signifies the totality of entities which can be present-at-hand within the world. (2) As an ontological term 'world' refers to the being of entities in the world. In this sense we can have several different but related worlds: the world of the scientist, the artist, the geographer, where world signifies the realm of possible objects for each perspective. (3) In another ontical sense we may refer to the we-world, the world of people, the world of the home; in this sense world refers not to entities, but rather to the 'place' where man lives. (4) World can also be taken ontologically and existentially to mean worldhood. This sense of the term comprises structural wholes of particular worlds, but also the universal structure of worldhood in general (64–5).

We have already seen what happens when world and worldhood are passed over in traditional metaphysics, and entities and space are presumed to be of a certain kind (Chapter 2). Failing to see the fundamental mode of man's being as being-in and towards a world, the world gets interpreted in terms of entities within it that are present-at-hand, essentially in terms of the scientists' conception of nature. But we have also seen (Chapter 6) that the understanding of nature in this way is a special and limiting case of man's being-in-the-world, where the world is projected as entities just-there for theoretical attention. This is one of man's ways of being in the world, and the phenomenon of 'nature' so conceived is appropriate to this theoretical way of grasping the world. But it presupposes and is derived from a horizon of everyday involvement which is man's 'closest' way of being in the world, and this is the one which seems to be the most difficult to recognize (65–6).

The world of everyday ek-sistence which is closest to us is the *Umwelt*, the environment or the world-around. This expression itself suggests that this closest, everyday world is one where spatiality is an integral moment. But we cannot presuppose what this spatiality is like and then go on to define world and worldhood in terms of it. Traditional metaphysics begins this way, with a particular conception of spatiality with which it interprets the world as *res extensa*.[1]

43 Space

We seek to question the assumption that pure extension, as projected by technological science, is the sole genuine meaning of space; further, to show that it is a conception of space developed from material nature, not an adequate description of human spatiality. This entails that we indicate how the place-character of things is fundamental to human experience, and how the origin of pure extension lies in abstraction from the place-character of things. This chapter is, therefore, concerned with the ontological character of spatiality that is characteristic for entities present-at-hand, ready-to-hand, and for man. I seek to show how Heidegger's ontological analysis of the spatiality characteristic of man allows us to go further towards understanding how a human science of geography might ground itself anew on foundations that go beyond the present limitations of space as the *res extensa* of Descartes, or the pure intuition of Kant; further, to show how this conception does not vitiate the physical ontology of space, nor does it entail a more subjectivist conception of space. It seeks instead an ontological conception of spatiality through phenomenological reflections, which is foundational for these other conceptions.

43a *The technological view of space*

We begin by asking whether the space with which we normally deal in our everyday world is the same space which Galileo, Descartes, and Newton first characterized as a homogeneous expanse, not distinguished at any of its possible places, equivalent towards each direction, but not perceptible with the senses? If the answer is yes, then the physical space of physics is the sole genuine space. All other articulated spaces, such as those of the builder, the sculptor, of everyday practice and perception are then only "subjectively dependent prefigurations and modifications of one objective cosmic space" (Heidegger, 1969b, 4).[2] But how can we regard technological space as the sole and genuine objective space? Technologically determined space assumes a distinction between subjectivity and objectivity, yet such a distinction is historically a modern one and ontologically a derived one. How, then, can the one be the sole genuine space? And how can it be the one space against which others are compared and measured? As long as we do not experience the spatial character of space we will remain within the sort of thinking that accepts space as the kind of 'thing' that encloses volume, subsists as emptiness between volumes, and can be encountered as an object present-at-hand; that is, as physical, technological, world-space.

43b *The spatiality of the present-at-hand*

The interpretation of the world which begins with entities within-the-world, instead of with the phenomenon of world in general, is characterized by a Cartesian and Newtonian world-view. This ontology of the world, which takes extension as its definite component, underlies much subsequent and current interpretation of world, entities and spatiality. It begins by distinguishing the thinking self ('ego cogito') from the corporeal thing ('res corporea'), the latter being characterized by substantiality. Substances have the property extension – length, breadth and thickness – and this comprises their reality. Other characteristics such as hardness, weight and colour can be taken away from such an entity without changing what it is. What makes up the being of the *res corporea* is the property *extension* (Heidegger, 1927, 89–91).

Descartes takes this world of theoretical entities as his starting point, for which mathematics and physics provide the most genuine access. He is not concerned with the manner in which entities show themselves as coloured, flavoured, hard and cold, since these are of no importance as regards their real being. The being of man is to be taken in the same way as the being of the *res extensa*, namely as substance. But, Heidegger (95–7) asks, does this ontology of the world grasp the phenomenon of the world at all? And, does not the Cartesian world, to become accessible as extension, require that nature is first discovered in the world beforehand?

It can be argued that by developing an ontology of the things of nature Descartes has nonetheless provided us with the starting point from which we can construct an ontology of the world. By rounding out material thinghood in such a way that non-quantifiable qualities and values can be added to the thing-entities can we not then arrive at the world as it is given to us immediately? In other words, having determined the basic elements of material nature can we not, by accretion, build up a human world? In geography a similar question has been asked: having modelled human spatial behaviour in terms of its most simple components, as if it were a physical system, can we now broaden the parameters to include behavioural, cognitive and experiential factors to explain that behaviour (see Chapter 2)?

Heidegger's response is that by adding on value-predicates we discover nothing about the being of goods, but still assume that those goods have the same kind of being as stones, for example. To reconstruct a thing of use, let alone man, in terms of the thing of nature is a questionable undertaking (Heidegger, 1927, 99–100).[3] It is then necessary to ask about the mode of being which is characteristic for man.

44 The everyday mode of being-in-the-world

Phenomenology seeks, as we have seen, to return to the original experiences prior to their thematization by any scientific activity. Thus Heidegger seeks to disclose the being of those entities we encounter as closest to us through our everyday dealings with the world. Ontologically the closest form of such dealing is not one of perceptual cognition, "but rather that kind of concern which manipulates things and puts them to use" (Heidegger, 1927, 67). Such entities are not thereby objects for knowing the world theoretically, but what gets used, produced, and so on. Such concern is not a theoretical knowing, but it does have its own form of 'knowing'.[4] Those entities which we encounter in this concern Heidegger calls 'equipment' (68). We do not encounter a single piece of equipment unless it already belongs to a totality of equipment in which its role or function and hence its place is given, and in which it can be the equipment that it is. Equipment is 'something in-order-to', it always is in terms of its belonging to other equipment. In our everyday involvements we always encounter entities in terms of these structural wholes or constellations of relations and meaning, within which a single entity can be the one that it is in that context. Things never show themselves as they *are for themselves*, so as to fill up a room for example. We first encounter, as closest to us, the room, not in a geometrical sense of a container of certain dimensions, but as equipment for dwelling. What is first given is the totality of equipment, out of which any 'individual' item of equipment can show itself.

Equipment can genuinely show itself only in dealings cut to its own measure (hammering with a hammer, for example); . . . In dealings such as this, where something is put to use, our concern subordinates itself to the 'in-order-to' which is constitutive for the equipment we are employing at the time; the less we just stare at the hammer-Thing, and the more we seize hold of it and use it, the more primordial does our relationship to it become, and the more unveiledly is it encountered as that which it is – as equipment. (Heidegger, 1927, 69)

This kind of being, where equipment manifests itself in its own right, is its '*readiness-to-hand*'. This is not grapsed theoretically, but is the sort of being that withdraws in being ready-to-hand. Our everyday dealings are closest not to the tools which are ready-to-hand, but to the work itself; that is, with that which the equipment is used in-order-to.

It is the work that carries with it the referential totality within which equipment is encountered.

Nature is encountered in precisely the same way, through the structural unity of the 'in-order-to'. Certain entities in the environment become accessible as ready-to-hand as equipment is used; leather for making shoes, wood for the carpenter, paper for the writer. This is not yet the nature of the physicist, however.

The wood is a forest of timber, the mountain a quarry of rock; the river is water-power, the wind is wind 'in the sails'. If its kind of Being as ready-to-hand is disregarded, this 'Nature' itself can be discovered and defined simply in its pure presence-at-hand. But when this happens, the Nature which 'stirs and strives', which assails us and enthralls us as landscape, remains hidden. The botanist's plants are not the flowers of the hedgerow; the 'source' which the geographer establishes for a river is not the 'springhead in the dale'. (Heidegger, 1927, 70)

The work which gives us this world of entities ready-to-hand, also gives us the *public-we-world* for whom that work is intended and whom we encounter in its undertaking. In this way we encounter the world in which makers and users live, the world in which we live, and the environing nature which thus becomes accessible to us. This concernful involvement becomes a discovering, where the work (or the intentional structure of everyday ek-sistence) shows the world in particular ways from different perspectives (71).

45 The spatiality of the ready-to-hand: places and regions

We have referred to man's relationship with entities ready-to-hand in the world as the closest one. Indeed, the expression 'ready-to-hand' itself implies some degree of proximity.[5] Such closeness is, however, different in each concrete situation, and is not a closeness that can be measured by distances. Closeness in this sense is determined by the use we make of equipment. Each piece of equipment has its place within an equipment totality, and gains its importance (and hence its closeness) from this context. The spatial ordering of entities occurs through man's activities (Heidegger, 1927, 102; Kockelmans, 1965, 45–6).

Place here is not a mere location in geometric space. It is the proper place of an item of equipment which belongs somewhere.[6] That is, place belongs to an equipmental context necessary for the work to be done. Before such places can be assigned in terms of such equipmental contexts, however, a *region* has to be discovered in which they will appear in their necessary connection. This is not a three-dimensional manifold of possible positions, which is to be filled up with places, nor is a region the sum of its places. The region is the necessary condition for the assignment of places, and the nature of work and the equipmental context determine the relation of each place to other places within it.[7]

Consequently human spatiality, in being related to several concurrent and non-concurrent equipmental contexts, is hierarchical and worldly, and cannot be understood independently of the beings that organize it. Man does not discover space, but space is given in the form of places which equipment, in its equipmental context, creates. The places have the character of being inconspicuous and yet familiar. Only when something goes wrong, when the hammer is broken, the door is stuck, or the pen is empty, do we thematically discover the ready-to-hand and its place, and we do so through its deficiency – it no longer works as it should. Often it is only when we fail to find something in its place that the region of the place becomes noticeable (Heidegger, 1927, 103–4).[8] The spatiality of entities ready-to-hand thus always belongs to the place each entity fulfils within the equipmental context of a particular activity. The environment is not arranged in space given in advance, but a totality of places is articulated by a world of involvements. "The world at such a time always reveals the spatiality of the space which belongs to it" (104). But it must be remembered that this space is not the bare space of Newton, nor are places isolated points.

In 'Building dwelling thinking' (1971b) and again in 'The nature of language' (1971c) Heidegger returns to the theme of man, place and space.[9] Man ek-sists as dwelling, which takes the form of building and tending (1971b, 148).[10] We will see more easily how building, dwelling, spatiality and place are interrelated by following Heidegger's own example of the bridge. In geographic discourse the bridge might be thought of as merely a thing, admittedly a thing with important functions, nonetheless a thing. With its use and in the course of time the bridge may come to stand for the prosperity of the town or the capability of a local architect. It may become a symbol. But, Heidegger reminds us, if the bridge is a true bridge it is never first of all a mere bridge and then afterward a symbol. The bridge does not at first just connect the banks that are already there. But in crossing the stream the bridge allows the banks to emerge as lying across from each other. The bridge brings the stream, the banks and the surrounding landscape together into each other's neighbourhood. "The bridge *gathers* the earth as landscape around the stream." But it also gathers the landscape together with man's dwelling, and his movement to and fro. Before the bridge was built banks, stream and landscape were, of course, appropriated to each other but differently in the sense that the location was not there, but merely many spots that could be occupied. Only one such spot becomes a location, and it does so because of the bridge (152–4).

46 Space and science

This everyday space of man's concernful dealing with things normally goes unthematized. Primordially such spatiality derives from involvement with the world, and creates places and relationships between hierarchies of places. But because this spatiality is so discovered it can also become a theme for science. By giving up involvement in such places, space can be studied purely by looking at it. Through the projection of a world of entities merely there and their subsequent formalization in terms of their relationships one to another, the pure space of the sciences can be derived and spatial relations discovered. Through a series of stages of formalization, abstract spaces of different kinds and degrees of generality can be projected. What we saw earlier as 'environmental regions' are here neutralized to pure dimensions. Places and their corresponding constellations of involvements get reduced to a multiplicity of positions. The spatiality of equipment ready-to-hand within the world is deprived of its involvement character, and becomes merely present-at-hand. Places are a matter of indifference, becoming mere locations – spatio-temporal points in no way distinguished from one another (Heidegger, 1927, 361–2).[11]

The world loses its character as the world-around (*Umwelt*); the environment becomes the world of Nature. The 'world', as a totality of equipment ready-to-hand, becomes spatialized to a context of extended Things which are just present-at-hand and no more. The homogeneous space of Nature shows itself only when the entities we encounter are discovered in such a way that the worldly character of the ready-to-hand gets specifically *deprived of its worldhood*. (112)[12]

Such parametric spaces become accessible only if the environment is deprived of its worldly character. But we have already established that man's spatiality is to be found only on the basis of the world.[13]

To the calculating mind, space and time appear as parameters for the measurement of nearness and remoteness, and these in turn as static distances. But space and time do not serve only as parameters; in this role, their nature would soon be exhausted – a role whose seminal forms are discernible early in Western thinking, and which then, in the course of the modern age, become established by this way of thinking as the standard conception. (Heidegger, 1971c, 102)

47 Man's spatiality

Man is essentially not an entity just-there in the world like a stone, and his own spatiality cannot be thought of as anything like "occurrence at a position in 'world-space'" (Heidegger, 1927, 105). If closeness in human affairs was a function of metric distances then one foot would have to be taken as closer than one yard. But closeness does not have the kind of relation given by spatial–temporal measures. Closeness in human affairs does not depend on space and time conceived as parameters (Heidegger, 1971c, 102–6). Nor, however, can it be like a piece of equipment, with its place. These are two modes of being with which man is familiar in his theoretical and practical dealings with entities in the world, but they are not his own mode of being. Man's spatiality must be discovered within-the-world, not imposed a priori. It must be uncovered as that which is closest in a similar way to that uncovered for entities ready-to-hand.

In asking about the nature of space and human spatiality as foundational to a science of man's world, we have seen how Heidegger stresses the place-character of spatiality. It is perhaps to point to this place-character of spatiality that he begins his essay on 'Art and space' (1969b, 3) with an interpretation of Aristotle's '*topos*', as something overwhelming and hard to grasp; that it has the character of *space– place*. Also, we must remember that 'places' are always places for dwelling. Heidegger suggests in this essay, as he did earlier in *Being and time*, that the making room for space through clearing away is founded in the settling, situating, and dwelling of man; that dwelling always means the creation of places. Places open a region within which things are gathered and allowed to be the things they are (6). Such a place is not located in technological space. It is space that is discovered through the places of a region. Parametric spaces are the product of the very scientific projection, thematization, objectivation and formalization to which we referred in detail in Chapter 7. These formalized conceptions of space derive from and remain founded in an experience of world, which is primordially one of dwelling and the creation of places. Dwelling-places, with their horizons or regions of concernful involvement with world, things and others, through a process of distanciation and abstraction, are gradually forgotten when technological conceptions of space are projected for worldless and not-yet human things. Place is not located in a pre-given space, such as this physical, technological space. Nor is space an arbitrary and thus subjective creation of consciousness. Technological space unfolds only through the "reigning of places of a region" (6).

We see now that besides its meaning as a clearing-of-places, spatiality has an even more fundamental meaning. It means a place cleared or freed for settlement and dwelling. The clearing 'takes place' within an horizon (or boundary) within which dwelling begins; the clearing away becomes the region of dwelling. Accordingly space comes into being from the creation of 'dwelling places'. From a certain viewpoint these places can be treated as points with measurable distances separating them in a three-dimensional manifold. Through a series of abstractions spaces can be projected within which these points can be located. Ultimately the possibility exists for a purely mathematical space constructed with any chosen number of dimensions. But such formal space contains no 'spaces', places and locations, within which man dwells. It is a space of world-points, undifferentiated and undifferentiatable. By contrast, in the places gathered around locations there is always the possibility of space as interval and pure extension. The latter is one-sidedly founded in the former.

Spatium and *extensio* afford at any time the possibility of measuring things and what they make room for, according to distance, spans, and directions, and of computing these magnitudes. *But the fact that they are universally applicable to everything that has extension can in no case make numerical magnitudes the ground of the nature of spaces and locations that are measurable with the aid of mathematics.* (Heidegger, 1971b, 156)

This kind of spatiality has a particular character. It is one of giving directions or situating ('directionality') *and* one of making the remoteness of something disappear, bringing close (or 'de-severance') (Heidegger, 1927, 105; Kockelmans, 1965, 48).[14]

This spatiality, characteristic for man as worldly and ek-sistent, must then have the character of a 'situating' enterprise or of *directionality*, where the world is already oriented through man's taking a direction towards it beforehand, and out of which arise the fixed directions of left and right. These are vital for orienting the world and for finding one's way around.[15] Situating oneself in the world in this way is necessary for the world to be familiar (Heidegger, 1927, 108–10).

In 'bringing close' man makes the remoteness vanish; something once remote is brought close. This is not meant ontically, in the sense of carrying from afar across a distance, but ontologically as a description of man's mode of being. This closeness or remoteness is not the physical distance separating two entities. It refers to the de-severant character of man's being which makes possible such measuring distances. Only through bringing entities close in this way can 'remotenesses' and distances be determined, and can the spatiality characteristic of man be understood. Estimates of closeness and farness in this context have their own definiteness, albeit imprecise and variable: the library is 'close', 'down the road', 'across the way', or 'five minutes from here'. These measures have no quantifiable 'length' at all. Rather the estimated duration – 'five minutes', for example – is to be interpreted *only* in terms of well-accustomed everyday ways of behaving. Indeed they may and do differ through the day and from one day to the next. For the recreational runner, for example, the concernful and variable nature of duration and closeness is an ever present reality; the run that yesterday could hardly be completed today passes almost unnoticed. Heidegger comments that "[as] Dasein goes along its ways, it does not measure off a stretch of space as a corporeal Thing which is present-at-hand; it does not 'devour the kilometres'; bringing close or de-severance is always a kind of concernful Being towards what is brought close and de-severed" (106). The consequences are clear. Closeness of the ready-to-hand and objective distance of the present-at-hand do not coincide. It is not that the former does not agree with or match up with or is a distortion of the latter. The two refer to *different* modes of being-in-the-world. Nor can the former – closeness – be described fairly as subjective, for it uncovers "the 'Reality' of the world at its most Real" (106), and has nothing to do with any arbitrary choice.

That which is metrically the smallest distance from us is not necessarily closest. We come across this aspect of man's spatial reality daily; the search for the spectacles that have been 'lost' on the scholar's nose, the possibility of an engrossing conversation on the telephone where the receiver slips into obscurity as speakers and conversation come together; the person whose walk to the office remains totally oblivious of pavement, lamp-posts, stores and traffic – all negotiated safely – as the problem of the night before is gone over and over again. In all these situations that which is physically least distant remains environmentally remote. That which is closest is the painting on the gallery wall for which the spectacles are needed, the conversation, and the problem. It is concernful involvement that decides as to the closeness and farness of what is ready-to-hand environmentally. Where this concern dwells is what is brought close. This is not an alteration of physical distance in relation to my physical body, but is a change of relationships of entities ready-to-hand in the world and of other people in terms of my everyday concern and dealings with them. Nor does this change of relations originate from the fixed or particular position my body occupies here and now. Man's spatiality, in being de-severant, is precisely always being there alongside and with the activities in which the person is involved. For this reason man cannot be said to move from one point to another in geometric space, but only change his 'here'. Nor can distances be crossed, because these are not fixed metrics, but are projected from the place where man is concernfully involved (Heidegger, 1927, 107–8; Kockelmans, 1965, 49–50).

48 Space and man's spatiality

The space we have arrived at lacks what Heidegger calls "the pure multiplicity of the three dimensions" (1927, 110). It is a 'region' wherein a world of everyday concern belongs, is situated and is brought close. In this sense the region has been 'placed'. The place character of the region derives from the referential totality which comes from the everyday concern of a particular situational complex – the 'in-order-to' or the 'for-the-sake-of-which' of a particular activity and its context; that is, the place character of the region derives from the task man engages in. In this way, and because of such involvement, the ready-to-hand can be encountered as something having form and direction in a place and a region (110–11).

We describe this situation in everyday speech. We 'make room' for things, or we 'give space' to them. The German word for space is *Raum*, and the word *räumen* means to clear away, to free from wilderness or to bring forth into an openness. *Räumen* is thus a clearing away or a release of places, a making room for the settling and dwelling of man and things (Heidegger, 1969b, 5). The result is space. Such a distinction between place and space was unknown to the Greeks. Their *chaos* and the *void* was not space. *Topos* (or place–space) embodied both the place and the space concepts we now use. In the modern conception clearing away is a release of places. Yet what then is a place? "Place always opens a region in which it gathers the things in their belonging together" (6). Such gathering shelters things in their region and allows them to be the things that they are. Thus, making-room takes its special character from the collecting of places. Fundamental to the reigning of places of a region through which abstract spaces are created is the simple act of dwelling. Places are dwelling places; they are established and open up a region in which man and the things with which he dwells are appropriated one to the other in the form of dwelling and belonging together. Only with the forgetting of the dwelling places and the character of place as regioning dwelling can the technological concept of space as extension be seen as the sole genuine concept of space.

In this way space is discovered and becomes accessible for formalization through man's own spatiality. Space is not, as a result, subjective, nor is it objective. "Space is rather 'in' the world in so far as space has been disclosed by that Being-in-the-world which is constitutive for Dasein. Space is not to be found in the subject nor does the subject observe the world 'as if' that world were in a space; but the 'subject', if well understood ontologically, is spatial" (Heidegger, 1927, 111). Man as spatial 'spatializes', not in the sense of a worldless subject emitting a space out of itself, and not as pure subject. Rather man spatializes in the sense that it is through his mode of being in and towards the world that the discovering of space is made possible.

49 Place and space: implications for a regional ontology of spatiality for a geographical human science

To many the preceding arguments may seem a rather unpromising beginning for a reconsideration of the spatiality of human activity, on which scientific investigation and geographic theory can be based. The possibilities for exact statistical analysis seem to be limited. Traditional graphical techniques, which assume standard metrics, may not be appropriate to the representation of these places of human concern. Even the more relativistic mapping techniques, which operate by distorting Euclidean space, may themselves be distortions of the actual spaces with which we seek to deal. Above all these spaces of involvement do not seem to be conducive to the powerful aggregate analysis and predictive abilities of entropy models and the like. But it should not be forgotten that this work is only a beginning. That sophisticated formalizations seem to be lacking, for the moment, is typical for any newly developing perspective, and cannot be a criterion for the rejection of its foundational claims.

The question is not, which conception of space is most useful? The question is, to what do we refer when we talk about spatial behaviour? Insofar as we are concerned with the activity of people as atomic particles in abstract space, the assumption of space as the space of the physical world is appropriate and may be useful, and this has certainly been the case in several areas of applied geomorphology (such as in erosion studies) and in spatial analysis (such as in the study of disease). Where this perspective is adopted for the study of human spaces the important questions then become why we wish to know this, and what prior assumptions have been incorporated in the evaluative and interpretative process to make this perspective an important one.

Although non-parametric concepts of space may lack the exactitude of the physical models, they do not lack the rigour necessary for scientific investigation. If rigour is achieved through the most accurate description of the state of affairs, and if we are talking about human spatial behaviour, then conceptions of space which do not ignore or deny the human character of spatial behaviour, but seek to encompass it, can be said to be rigorous. The extent to which such rigorous description of the phenomena of human spatiality can be usefully incorporated into spatial theory and human geography depends, in large part, on the nature of the research programme that develops and is allowed to flow from it. This in turn will depend upon the leeway accepted thinking and academic structures give to such a research programme as a concrete possibility.

It has not been the intention of this work to prescribe to geography the nature of its basic concepts and theoretical perspectives. Nor, even, has it been its task to deny the appropriateness of physical conceptions of space in certain contexts; such a position, in any case, would be foolish given the obvious power of the models developed. What has been attempted has been to ask what is necessary *if* a *human* science of geography concerned with man's spatiality is sought, and how such a science is possible. Answering these questions has entailed the clarification of phenomenology, science and human spatiality.

We are thus now at the beginning of the geographical task as such, having in a preliminary fashion completed the necessary reflections on which such a science can build. This task is to clarify the regional ontological structure of the 'geographical', to provide a critique of the taken-for-granted conceptions of space and the geographical, and to explicate a place-centred regional ontology of human spatiality.

Only through the clarification of its basic concepts and perspectives (though not necessarily in the same way as presented here) can geography hope to hold together its dual concerns with world and place on the one hand, and abstract spaces on the other, in anything other than a purely artificial manner. Only through a critical, interpretative enterprise, and by grounding it in a more genuine conception of spatiality, is space to be retrieved from naturalism. For physics and for physical geography, such a grounding may be unnecessary (but, in this regard, see Heelan, 1983). For human geography it is vital.

On the basis of such a genuine conception of spatiality we are now in a position to understand the relationship between ontical places and spaces. Indeed, only when the place-character of spatiality and space is fully recognized can we avoid treating actual human places and spaces as subjective and relative distortions of some absolute space. From this position we can move to describe ontical spaces, such as the body-space and anthropological space of Merleau-Ponty (1962), the poetic-spaces of Gaston Bachelard (1969), literary spaces and places, Heelan's (1983) hyperbolic spaces of visual perception, the landscapes of Van den Berg (1961), the eccentric spaces of Harbison (1977), and the everyday places of involvement, senses of places, and activity spaces with which geographers have long been concerned.

Continual self-reflection belongs to every science. For geography, such reflections entail a radical clarification of the genuine and original experiences of geographical phenomena. We have sought to show how this is the task of a phenomenology that properly understands itself. The task is an interpretative one insofar as it deals with human phenomena. It is critical insofar as the sedimented meanings of the everyday taken-for-granted world are made transparent.

We have shown how and in what ways phenomenology and empirical science are essentially related, and how an empirical science of geography *can* be a *human* science of human spatiality. What is needed now is the working out, in detail, of what a regional ontology of the geographical would encompass, and this requires a thorough clarification of the meaning of *geo-graphus*, ontologically and histori-cally. This is not the task of any single work, but of a research programme.

Notes

1 Introduction

1 See, for example, Schrag (1980) and Kockelmans (1982). Here I want to distinguish between the human, social or anthropological sciences on the one hand, and the historical sciences on the other. I am concerned specifically with the former. The latter are important and problematic in a different way, and raise different issues when dealing with the claims of Dilthey, Husserl, and Heidegger. For my present purposes I will set them to one side.

2 For example, with regard to social theory and sociology, see Habermas (1971) and Kockelmans (1978b; 1980); to economics, see Leontieff (1982); to psychology, see Kockelmans (1978a); and to the human sciences generally, see Schrag (1980) and Kockelmans (1982).

3 In geography, this turn to philosophy and philosophical reflection is obvious. Walmsley (1974, 95) argues that geography has undergone a 'philosophical revolution', in the sense that geographical work now draws from philosophical literature. Sack (1979, 447) has gone so far, in reviewing Gregory's *Ideology, science and human geography*, to claim that "this book is more about philosophy than geography". Recent articles have appeared dealing with the importance of particular philosophers' work for geographers: Schütz (Ley, 1977), Merleau-Ponty (Seamon, 1979b), Kant (Livingstone and Harrison, 1981), and Vico (Mills, 1982); or philosophical perspectives: phenomenology (Relph, 1970), existentialism (Samuels, 1978), the interactionism of Mead (Duncan, 1978), positivism (Hay, 1979; Couclelis, 1982), logical positivism (Guelke, 1978), critical theory (Gregory, 1978a, 1978b), marxist humanism (Eyles, 1981; Gregory, 1981a), and surrealism (Olsson, 1980).

   Two volumes in particular illustrate this turn to reflections of a radical nature: *Philosophy and geography* (Gale and Olsson, 1979), and *A search for common ground* (Gould and Olsson, 1982). See also Harvey and Holly (1981).

4 While the present work deals specifically with human geography, many of the claims made regarding phenomenology and science are not specific to this domain, but are concerned with the nature of science as such. In this regard, many of the claims for phenomenology also apply directly to an empirical and a descriptive physical geography. The extent to which this is the case will be evident from the text.

5 See, for example, Guelke (1978), Johnston (1979), Hufferd (1980), Jackson (1981), Moriarty (1981).

6 The use of the term *phenomenology* in the sense of Mach or Kant is not intended here. For an example of its use in this way see Lesse (1982).

7 "We . . . do not seek that force in what has already been thought: we seek it in something that has not been thought, and from which what has been thought receives its essential space (that realm in which it can move and abide). But only what has already been thought prepares what has not yet been thought, which enters ever anew into its abundance. The criterion of what has not been thought does not lead to the inclusion of previous thought into a higher development and systematization that surpasses it. Rather, the criterion demands that traditional thinking be set free in its essential past which is still preserved" (Heidegger, 1969a, 48).

8 That Husserl was genuine in these claims is borne out by the extended 'tolerance' he seems to have shown towards Heidegger's gradually and substantially diverging project (see Kockelmans, 1967b, 273–4). Husserl had intended Heidegger to develop an ontology of the human realm, particularly the historical sciences, while Oskar Becker worked in parallel on an ontology of nature and the natural sciences. Husserl seems to have held out this hope for Heidegger's fundamental ontology until quite late. Furthermore, as Ricoeur (1967, 13) points out, a comprehensive and definitive interpretation of Husserl's work remains impossible without full access to the unpublished manuscripts in the Husserl Archives in Louvain, which amount to 56,000 handwritten pages. For recent work drawing upon or publishing from these manuscripts see Landgrebe (1981) and McCormick and Elliston (1981).

2 Geographical discourse and its central themes

1 See, for example, Blaut (1961; 1962), Haggett (1965), Tuan (1965), Nystuen (1968), Hägerstrand (1973), Gould (1981).

2 See, for example, Ley (1977), Gregory (1978a; 1978b).

3 This last issue involves an important question which has recently again come to the fore in the discipline and to which attention must be drawn early in this work. In his critique of Schaefer's (1953) work, Hartshorne (1955) found little he could recognize as correct or truthful in that work. His subsequent methodological attack on Schaefer was devastating, and was based almost entirely on the sloppy methodological investigation underpinning Schaefer's arguments. By destroying this foundation Hartshorne assumed that he had destroyed the argument as well, and thus had removed the need to comment on the substantive issues which Schaefer sought to address. So Hartshorne never fully addressed these issues, on the grounds that what Schaefer claimed to have been the case could be shown to be otherwise in the literature to which he referred.

More recently a different issue has arisen within the methodological debates in geography. Golledge (1981) corrects the misconceptions geographers have shown over the nature of behavioural geography, defines its terms, and explains again how these came to be important when they first were raised. Golledge has gone so far as to claim that many other writers could not possibly know what the case really was because what happened in the early 1960s was often a product of personal discussion and closed door meetings. In other words Golledge claims authority over the issue on the grounds of direct involvement. Clearly there is some truth to this. Those involved in a situation often know a great deal more about the actual happenings than those who come along later and piece together what happened from published records. However, this priority is no priority in so far as we are concerned with the question of the importance of or the meaning of these events.

The interpretation of the participants cannot be the sole or even the privileged criteria for judging any interpretation of this event, just as the exact specifications of a written text cannot be the sole reason for rejecting any particular argument, for what is most crucial to this 'naive' standpoint is that it takes for granted the very concepts that are at issue. That Golledge and his colleagues meant something in a particular way certainly does not bind the discipline to that particular meaning; conditions change, new horizons open up with time, and we see the past in a new light. The interpreter of an event, piecing together the picture of what happened may well come to know that event better than those involved (but in a special way only).

This argument does not seek to validate Guelke or Schaefer against the criticisms of Golledge and Hartshorne respectively, but to illustrate the need to recognize that if we did accept literally the word of those who brought ideas to light in the first place then we may as well not re-think those issues. Indeed, if we merely accept the claims of previous geographers at face value as representing the nature of the 'geographical', we run into the problem that Habermas has raised, of how we are then to avoid passively accepting the status quo, and thereby perpetuating existing ideology. In this regard, to accept the much repeated claim that 'geography is what geographers do', while superficially true, is to accept uncritically the prevailing ideology (or ideologies). In re-thinking arguments we seek precisely to see them in a new light; to problematize them, in order to move beyond them. We seek to clarify the basic concepts in such a manner that the a priori interpretations can be laid out for consideration. Textual exegesis and biographical detail are a necessity, but, on their own, an insufficient basis for ontological analysis.

In contrast to the positive sciences, concerned with things that are, ontology (or philosophy in general) is the critical science, or the science of the inverted world (Heidegger, 1982, 17). (Such a critical science of being is called *transcendental science*). This is not a denial of the claims of science, nor a negation of the tradition, but signifies a "positive appropriation" of them (23). It seeks to understand that which is not said in what is said.

4 In this way, Heidegger (1927, 10–11; see also, 1967) shows how Kant's *Critique of Pure Reason* works out the basic concepts and perspectives of what belongs to Nature: "this transcendental logic is an *a priori* logic for the subject-matter of that area of Being called 'Nature'".

5 Generally this has been translated as 'representational' thinking (see Heidegger, 1977b, 128–36). For *presentative, pro-posing* thinking, see Richardson (1967). For *pro-posing, re-presenting* (or positing) thinking, see Kockelmans (1970c).

6 Heidegger (1971a, 44–5) says of this world: "The world is not the mere collection of the countable or uncountable, familiar and unfamiliar things that are just there. But neither is it a merely imagined framework added by our representation to the sum of such given things. The *world* [holds sway], and is more fully in being than the tangible and perceptible realm in which we believe ourselves to be at home. World is never an object that stands before us and can be seen. World is the ever-nonobjective to which we are subject as long as the paths of birth and death, blessing and curse keep us transported into Being. Wherever those decisions of our history that relate to our very being are made, are taken up and abandoned by us, go unrecognized and are rediscovered by new inquiry, there the world [holds sway]."

7 All non-philosophical sciences have as their theme some being or beings, given to those sciences from a particular perspective. Such beings are *posited* by the sciences

in advance. To distinguish them from philosophy these sciences are called *positive* sciences. They deal with that which is; with beings, in their specific domains, such as nature, history, and the formal spaces of geometry. Within each domain, scientific research carves out certain spheres – physical nature, living nature, which can be further sub-divided. This sub-division takes place through the research problems of the positive sciences and grounds the division of the sciences into distinct, if interrelated, disciplines (Heidegger, 1982, 13; see also 1976, 6–9).

8 Thus, Cox and Golledge (1981, xiii) for example, claim that this new-found confidence was "subverted" in the 1970s by "periodic fits of self-consciousness at the epistemological level".

9 Even discussion of positivism is generally uncommon among positivists (Lenzer, 1975, xix), a fact that John Stuart Mill (1865, 2) noted in the nineteenth century: "though the mode of thought expressed by the terms Positive and Positivism is widely spread, the words themselves are, as usual, better known through the enemies of that mode of thinking than through its friends; and more than one thinker who never called himself or his opinions by those appelations, and carefully guarded himself against being confounded with those who did, finds himself, sometimes to his displeasure, though generally by a tolerably correct instinct, classed with Positivists, and assailed as a Positivist."

10 See Heidegger (1971a), Clark (1981).

11 See, for example, Lockean psychology.

12 See, for example, Comte (1854, 3).

13 I am grateful to Dr Joseph Kockelmans for pointing out that, for Dilthey, the philosophy of history and sociology (including all then existing social sciences) are not sciences. Dilthey's concern is with the *Geisteswissenschaften*, or the historical sciences; that is, with all products of the 'spirit', in contrast to the natural sciences whose concern is with the natural relationships between things.

14 In this regard see the very similar claims of William Morris Davis (1906, 80).

15 Dilthey's inquiries into the *human studies* concerned the question of 'life'. 'Life' taken as a whole provides the horizon within which lived experiences are studied in their structural and developmental inter-connections. Such inquiry is no longer oriented towards psychical or physical elements from which life will be constructed, but aims at the *Gestalten* and 'life as a whole' (Heidegger, 1927, 46–7).

16 Otto Liebmann (1840–1912) closed each chapter of his book *Kant und die Epigonen* (1865) with this call. See Heidegger (1967, 59, n. 15). Also Livingstone and Harrison (1981, 363).

17 According to James and Martin (1981, 163), geography as a field of formal study developed in Germany in the 1870s.

18 It is important to note that Hettner – the first professor of geography in Germany after Ritter to be trained as a geographer – also studied philosophy, and was influenced by the neo-Kantians, particularly at Heidelberg where he lectured, and where Windelband and Rickert also taught. Hartshorne (1939, 379) refers to Hettner's discussions of the work of Windelband and Rickert in Hettner (1905, 254–9; 1927, 221–4). Of course, Kant's direct influence on geography is of importance; Hartshorne (1939) and May (1970) have shown this in some detail. For discussion of the idiographic/nomothetic distinction see Hartshorne (1939, 378–9, 457; 1959, 146–72), and Livingstone and Harrison (1981, 361).

19 In this article they review more fully than is possible here some of the various influences, explicit and implicit, direct and indirect, of Kantianism and neo-Kantianism on the geographic universe of discourse.

20 Kant lectured on geography at Königsberg University from 1756 until 1796 (May, 1970, 3).

21 For the influence of the Vienna School on geographers' writings see the footnotes and references in Schaefer (1953), Harvey (1969b), Sack (1973).

22 While Ritter insisted that 'the new scientific geography' must seek to identify the causes of observed features, it was Guyot who had argued against the practice of making geography a 'compendium' discipline, and it was Guyot who most influenced William Morris Davis (James and Martin, 1978, 14). In Davis's research programme, geography, as regional physiography and ontography, was situated within a framework of material nature (see his 'Inductive study of the content of geography'). Such a geography has to do primarily with (1) the earth, (2) maps and explorations, (3) statements of relation of cause and effect, "usually between some element of inorganic control and some element of organic response" (Davis, 1906, 71) and (4) the study of location or distribution. Through physiography (dealing with inorganic elements) and ontography (dealing with organic elements) a phenomenon became geographic "in so far as it brings an organism into contact with the rest of the world and thus causes it to enter into geographical relations" (74). Biogeography dealt with relations or responses which responding organisms enter into with their inorganic controls. Ontography was not concerned with the study of organic response (for this was the geographic relation itself) but with the study of the organic act or deed or motive which results in a response or relation when a physiographic control is encountered.

The organic side of geography was not to be limited to man, but instead should be concerned with Life: "Life is a unit; if one form of life comes under the study of geography because it responds to physiographic controls, then all forms of life come under geography" (80). To this essentially physiographic conception of geographic entities, to which life as organic and ontographic was related, Davis added a biological conception based on evolutionary principles and "evolutionary philosophy" (Davis, 1924, 210).

The radicalization of these claims occurred in the work of Huntingdon and Semple. The geographic focus was precisely the geographic relation of which Davis had spoken. The conditioning influences of the physical world and the resultant organic responses, together with the relations and patterns of relations that followed, formed the framework within which an *environmental* science of geography could be developed.

Barrows (1923) recognized, however, that a geography of physical nature such as Davis had proposed, and as had subsequently developed, was an insufficient foundation for geographic inquiry. Davis's distinction between geology and regional physiography on the basis of areal differences alone, left Barrows (1923, 3) unclear as to whether a body of facts and principles could be "shifted from one science to another *merely* by giving it areal application". Instead geography should be defined as the *mutual* relations between man and his natural environment. "Geography will aim to make clear the relationships existing between natural environments and the distribution and activities of man. Geographers will, I think, be wise to view this problem in general from the standpoint of man's adjustment to environment, rather than from that of environmental influence" (3). In this way Barrows re-opens the horizon of geographic concerns, arbitrarily delimited to the ways in which the environment influences man, and once again allows for a more traditional conception of geographic inquiry as the earth as the home of man, studied in terms of the milieux, regions or cultural complexes that man creates and the meaning these have. Such a geography, for Barrows (12), deals not with human facts as such, nor with environmental facts as such, but rather with the relation which may exist between the two.

But was the focus of geography to be seen as relation or as distribution? Hartshorne's (1939) conception of geography was historically and textually founded in the more established European traditions, taking as its central principle the notion of geography as areal differentiation. His claims are complex, and certainly deal with some of the traditions running counter to this view. Thus, his views are not to be characterized superficially (see, for example, the discussion of the basis for his fundamental definition of geography as the study of areal differentiation of the world (242ff)). However, the overall impact of his work was the rationalization of a neo-Kantian ontology, premised upon a physical conception of space. Thus, the criteria for the selection of data as geographic include "the difference from place to place together with the spatial association of things situated beside each other . . . No phenomenon of the earth's surface is to be thought of for itself; it is understandable only through the conception of its location in relation to other places on the earth. The second condition is the causal connection between the different realms of nature and their different phenomena united at one place. Phenomena which lack such a connection with the other phenomena of the same place, or whose connection we do not recognize, do not belong in geographical study" (Hettner, translated in Hartshorne, 1939, 240).

The conception of Newtonian space and physical entities in Euclidean space underlying these arguments is clarified by Sack (1972, 69). Most, if not all questions are about location. "Objects of geographic inquiry are located or distributed. They can be identified by coordinate positions in a synthetic space. Most often geographers consider the synthetic space in which geographic events are located to be the physical space of Newtonian physics."

23 "The end-in-view of all geographic study, whether regional or systematic, is the analysis and description of the whole of areal differentiation for the earth's surface" (Ackerman, 1945, 133).

24 "What then gives geography, in essence, a character of its own? What distinguishes it from the other social sciences? It is its concern with the character of 'places', that is, the integrated whole of a people and its habitat, and the interrelations between people" (Broek, 1965, 3).

25 Repetition of this argument is common, for example: "the movement toward quantification should be viewed as part of the general spread and growth of scientific analysis into a world formerly dominated by a concern with individual areas or events" (Kohn, 1970, 213). More recently, see Johnston (1979).

26 "In pursuing his objectives the geographer must necessarily resort to an appropriate language. The spatial language adopted should be appropriate for (i) stating spatial distributions and the morphometric laws concerning such distributions, and (ii) examining the operation of processes and process laws in a spatial context" (Nystuen, 1968, 191).

27 Under the auspices of the Committee on Science and Public Policy of the National Academy of Science and the Problems and Policy Committee of the SSRC.

28 See also Stewart (1947; 1956), Stewart and Warntz (1958; 1959), Warntz (1957).

29 On this issue Golledge provides a valuable resource. He has continued to ask the crucial and perplexing questions raised by pushing behaviouralism to its logical limits. His several attempts to come to grips with the questions illustrate

increasingly clearly the fundamental problems that presupposing a Newtonian conception of world creates. See also Burnett (1976, 23–48).

30 See Heidegger (1927, 60). Also Burnett (1976). More recently Richardson (1981, 325) has commented on this situation in reviewing cognitive mapping methodologies: "Each method elicits spatial information from the mind and represents it in some form. None of the cognitive mapping methods, however, make any assumption about how spatial information is stored or accessed in the mind. It is a common misconception that individuals carry spatial information in their minds in the physical forms of the familiar cartographic map. The manner in which spatial information is stored is not known although a variety of hypotheses exist. What is assumed is that spatial knowledge internal to the mind can be extracted and represented by some external source."

3 The interpretation of phenomenology in geography

1 For example, Relph (1970), Mercer and Powell (1972), Buttimer (1976), Entrikin (1976), Gregory (1978a; 1978b; 1981b).

2 For example, Buttimer (1976), Ley (1977; 1980a; 1981), Gregory (1978a; 1978b; 1981b), Aitchison (1980).

3 For example, Walmsley (1974), Billinge (1977), Guelke (1978), Hay (1979), Smith (1979), Jackson (1981).

4 For example, Johnston (1979), Gregory (1981b).

5 In particular, in social geography. See Ley (1979), Jackson (1981).

6 For example, Buttimer (1974; 1976; 1977), Entrikin (1976), Tuan (1976: 1977a), Relph (1977).

7 For example, Gregory (1978a), Smith (1979), Eyles (1981).

8 For example, Walmsley (1974), Guelke (1978), Hay (1979), Hufferd (1980).

9 It is perhaps well to be reminded in this regard of the status of philosophical claims. In *The basic problems of phenomenology* Heidegger quotes Hegel: "The demands and standards of common sense have no right to claim any validity or to represent any authority in regard to what philosophy is and what it is not" (Heidegger, 1982, 14).

10 See the full titles of the following works: Husserl (1913; 1930; 1954).

11 In the translator's introduction to Heidegger's *The essence of reasons*, Terence Malick makes a similar point: "If Heidegger resorts to his own peculiar language, it is because ordinary German does not meet his purposes. If we cannot educate ourselves to his purposes, then clearly his work will look like nonsense. And yet we should not conclude that it *is* nonsense merely because we are not sure what it is to keep us from this conclusion" (Heidegger, 1929, xvii).

12 See, for example, Husserl (1927, 26).

13 For example, Parsons (1969) and Hägerstrand (1970).

14 A claim that Ley has subsequently been at great pains to deny as a necessary relationship.

15 Phenomenological notions have been incorporated into geography largely from social psychology in environmental perception studies (Relph, 1970, 193), and geographers have since drawn directly upon this literature and also from ethnoscience, humanistic psychology, psycholinguistics (Buttimer, 1976, 278), sociology, anthropology, theology and etiology (Relph, 1976a, preface). Specifi-

cally the work of Giorgi, Fischer, and others in the *Duquesne studies in phenomenological psychology* and Binswanger, Maslow, Rogers and Rollo May in psychology and psychotherapy (Ley and Samuels, 1978, 8) have been influential.

16 It will be important to clarify the difference between phenomena as given or as they present themselves in lived experience (generally the focus of geographers' claims) *and* as they present themselves in immediate experience. Lived experience and immediate experience are not always the same, as geographers who are concerned with issues ranging from the sedimented meanings of everyday worlds to problems of experimental space perception or physiological adaptations in complex environments should have realized. Ley has brought attention to the taken-for-granted world, but has failed to distinguish this from the immediately given world. Such a clarification is essential to understanding the claims of phenomenology, particularly of Husserl, concerning the phenomenological method itself, its relation to science, and the problematical role of lifeworld in this context.

17 Buttimer (1976, 278) argues that phenomenologists have challenged "many of the premises and procedures of positive science, they have posed a radical critique of reductionism, rationality, and the separation of 'subjects' and 'objects' in empirical research".

18 These claims will be substantiated in Chapters 5 to 8.

19 For present purposes it is perhaps significant that in treating the phenomenological method geographers – and Seamon (1979a, 48, n. 1) in particular – have most often referred to Spiegelberg (1978). Yet on page 654 Spiegelberg himself notes: "The subsequent attempt to find it [the main ingredients of a concrete phenomenology] will . . . have to be largely a personal venture. . . It seems fair to be frank about this unorthodox approach in view of some of the heresies which the subsequent presentation will reveal. This unorthodoxy will show up particularly in the treatment of the later steps of the phenomenological method."

4 *Geographical phenomenology*

1 It is at this point that methodological difficulties arise, and in their attempted solution the spectre of relativism is raised. Wood (1982) has accurately shown how methodological bankruptcy and the assumptions of geographical phenomenology underpin and influence letting the things "appear *as they are in themselves*" (Seamon, 1980b, 188–96), and how geographical phenomenologists have sought to deny the presuppositions they bring to bear on the 'phenomenological seeing'. To clarify this debate we will have to turn to hermeneutic phenomenology, in particular to show how these claims have been misunderstood.

2 Such claims are not always readily transparent, particularly because of confusion in the use of other terms. See, for example, the contradictory claims in Buttimer (1976, 291) and (1977, 183).

3 He (1970, 194) incorrectly claims that: "It follows from the concept of intentionality that there is no single, objective world; rather there is a plurality of worlds – as many as there are attitudes and intentions of man."

4 Where constructs are imposed on the world, which is forced into a priori conceptual and mathematical frameworks, whose main principles are taken from physics and biology.

5 For a philosophical treatment of Husserl's transcendental idealism see Kockelmans (1970a).

6 Billinge illustrates well the principle to which I have pointed repeatedly in Chapters

2 and 3. A phenomenology cannot be paraphrased or simplified; it must be treated as a whole, as it works itself out. Geographers have ignored this primary principle, only partially understanding the project as a result of a procedure of piecemeal adoption. Thus, Billinge follows the above statement by the following one: "phenomenology has not, in general, concerned itself with the details of implementation, but with broader aspects of conception and cogitation. It is not a 'practical' philosophy, and any attempts to make it so must face the intractability of the translation problems involved" (Billinge, 1977, 63).

7 It would be wrong to think of Schütz's *constitutive* phenomenology as a completely different phenomenology from that of Husserl, although the geographical literature gives this impression. Husserl referred to his own project of transcendental phenomenology as *constitutive phenomenology* (see for example, Husserl, 1941, 315) and regarded Schütz as one of his most understanding followers.

8 His actual claim is that: "Phenomenology, at least in Husserl's terms, is not a practical philosophy and that it has little to offer the social sciences" (Gregory, 1978b, 163).

9 See Ley (1980a, 10): "The *a priori* commitment to existence rather than essence in the study of place has extended the phenomenology of the lifeworld to the domain of value systems, interest groups, and power relations. This extension which simply works back again from Schütz to Weber is coherent both theoretically and empirically. It imbricates both lifeworld and biographical situation, both the power of culture and also the culture of power."

5 Husserlian phenomenology

1 For a consideration of this polarization in a broader context see Heidegger's *The essence of reasons* (1929).

2 See, for example, Husserl (1927).

3 This is not, however, to claim that Husserl and the empiricists agree, nor that Husserl is in agreement with logical empiricism and positivism. Husserl reserves some of his most strident attacks for empiricistic naturalism and psychologism, where naive empiricism seeks to explain its atomistic conceptions by reducing all phenomena to naturalistic or psychologistic causal explanation.

4 Such antecedents have been recognized by geographers (Mercer and Powell, 1972; Entrikin, 1976) but they have failed to draw the necessary and important distinctions between their use in the nineteenth century and their use by Husserl and subsequently in the twentieth century. Without such distinction the Husserlian sense of phenomenology has been repeatedly interpreted in geography through the Kantian categories of phenomenon and phenomenology, influenced by the strong Kantian and neo-Kantian tradition within the discipline. For Kant 'phenomenon' and 'thing-in-itself' (noumenon) are opposed. For Husserl the concept of 'phenomenon' and 'phenomenology' are not constructed out of any opposition to 'in itselfness'.

5 These include: (1) the Cartesian way (*Ideas, Cartesian meditations*) (2) the way through the sciences (*First Philosophy*) and, (3) the way through the lifeworld (*Crisis*).

6 The text followed for the 1927 article will be the Palmer translation in McCormick and Elliston (1981, 21–35). For the reasons for not using the text as published in the *Encyclopaedia Britannica* see Spiegelberg (1971).

7 Such claims have been greatly misunderstood by geographers. Ley (1980a) in

particular has misinterpreted Husserl's use of the term 'pure' in this context, assuming that it refers to pure reflection, and consequently is unrelated to the concerns of the social scientist (a reason he turns instead to Schütz). Yet Husserl himself clarifies its use:

pure phenomenology was not established to be an empirical science, and what it calls its 'purity' is not just that of pure reflection but is at the same time the entirely different sort of purity we meet in the names of other sciences.

We often speak in a general, and intelligible, way of pure mathematics, pure arithmetic, pure geometry, pure kinematics, etc. These we contrast, as *a priori* sciences, to sciences, such as the natural sciences, based on experience and induction. Sciences that are pure in this sense, *a priori* sciences, are pure of any assertion about empirical actuality. Intrinsically they purport to be concerned with the ideally possible and the pure laws thereof rather than with actualities. In contrast to them, empirical sciences are sciences of the de facto actual, which is given as such through experience. (Husserl, 1917, 16)

Unlike the empirical sciences, descriptive phenomenology is not concerned with singular facts and inductive generalizations, nor with empirically generated universal claims, including causal laws. It is interested in the 'typical', 'general' or universal structures of its objects and how these objects are primordially given.

8 Geographers have misunderstood the nature of 'phenomenon' and 'object' when claiming that there is an inherent limitation of the subject-matter of phenomenology to ontical conceptions of individual and social meaning.

9 As Gadamer (1969, 186) has argued, it was one of the claims of transcendental phenomenology to provide the sciences with "a new, clarified basis that no crisis could disturb. That was the claim Husserl made in the *Ideas* and retained and repeated in the last work, the so-called *Crisis*." Husserl's claims for a truly rational, fully rigorous science are not merely polemical. His goal is ultimately the rational reconstruction of an irrational world (in particular the world of Austria and Germany between 1890 and 1930). For Husserl, this crisis is not only a crisis of rationalism, but a crisis of European man (see Husserl, 1965). "Only rigorous science can provide us with reliable methods and sound results; it alone can thereby provide the preparatory theoretical work upon which a rational reform of culture depends" (Husserl, 1923, 327). Thus the fate of Western rationalism in general is Husserl's central concern. As his letters to Roman Ingarden show, he knew that rationalism was *always* in danger from irrationalism and relativism, and in the twentieth century also from *Lebensphilosophie* and existentialism. To overcome these challenges a new type of critical reflection is necessary – phenomenology.

10 When we turn to Heidegger and hermeneutic phenomenology it will be necessary to question this possibility, in order to understand his claims for the hermeneutic and projective character of science. Here "[it] remains doubtful whether the thingly character comes to view at all in the process of stripping off everything equipmental" (Heidegger, 1971a, 30). He continues: "The thingly feature in the work should not be denied; but if it belongs admittedly to the work-being of the work, it must be conceived by way of the work's workly nature. If this is so, then the road toward the determination of the thingly reality of the work leads not from the thing to the work but from the work to the thing" (39).

11 Within a given whole, such as the cultural world, abstractive reduction cuts out something without reducing the object of concern to another object. When all cultural factors have been thus abstracted from the realm of cultural objects, and we turn to what we have left, we retain factors characteristic of animated and physical objects only. But this is not to reduce cultural objects *to* physical entities (naturalism) or animated entities (biologism).

12 Gadamer (1975a) has shown precisely how the question of method and its relationship to truth requires a turn to hermeneutic investigation.

13 The phenomenological *epoche* (or bracketing) cannot be something like doubting the existence of the world, as in the Cartesian radical doubt. Rather it is a shift of attitude in which direct living into the world is inhibited, and the focus of attention is shifted to the cogitative types or styles through which such living into the world occurs. In the mundane or naive sciences truth and falsehood in the world is the main concern. Reflection upon this situation occurs, but the world as given is already taken for granted. In descriptive phenomenology emphasis is directed not to the world, but to the cogitative types through which the world is given. In this seeking to thematize such cogitative types the phenomenologist focuses on the *how of the givenness* of the objects as structures of such types (see Husserl, 1941, 320). Both the naive and descriptive sciences take the world and the world as given for granted, and thus remain within the natural attitude. (The transcendental attitude is constituted in questioning the possibility and form of such knowing.) Phenomenology thus has two overall aims: (1) clarifying the nature of particular cogitative types, including scientific perspectives; (2) providing apodictic grounding for such types.

  The mundane attitude is, clearly, genetically prior and one-sidedly founding for the phenomenological attitude (what Heidegger will claim in a different context to be the ontical priority of Being). Phenomenology seeks to give an explicit account and thus performs the *epoche*. In posing the question in this way, and in asking what kind of meaning this can have, phenomenology is ontologically prior to the development of the mundane sciences. In this way *both* the mundane and the phenomenological sciences can be held together, and we can see more clearly precisely why and how phenomenology is a method, not a metaphysics.

14 What Husserl (1930, 9) refers to as "the Objectively documented theoretical structures (propositions, theories) that are in fact generally accepted as sciences".

6 *Phenomenology, science and phenomenological geography*

1 With this object in view, phantasy variation, free variation or variátion in imagination is performed. Eidetic intuition through methodically guided variation in imagination, gives the eidos as the corresponding intersubjectively verifiable object.

2 Landgrebe (1981, 151) refers to regional ontologies as "the philosophical disciplines within which the categories of each region are developed, which go to make up the specific ontic-constitutions or the 'object-character' of the objects of science". But Kockelmans (1967a, 101) claims that the regional ontologies cannot be philosophical sciences because Husserl characterized the differences between philosophical and non-philosophical disciplines by pointing to the fundamental difference between the philosophical and natural attitude. The formal and material ontologies belong to the realm of the sciences in the natural attitude. Here focus of concern shifts from the world to the world as given in the how of its givenness. The cogitative types and the a priori frameworks of meaning from which they view the world are the subject of reflection.

3 For the necessity of seeing them as distinct, see Kockelmans (1978a, 182–3; 273–301).

7 *Towards a fundamental ontology of science*

1 *Existential* is used here in the sense of Heidegger (1927, 12–13) to refer to the formal or universal structures of man's being-in-the-world. It is not used as it is more commonly known under the term *existentialism*, which in the present context refers to the *existentiell*, factual existence of a concrete worldly being. Schrag (1958, 286–7) clarifies this distinction, through the original German terms, in the following way: "The German word, *Existenzielle*, has the specific denotation of the *concrete act of existing*. It refers to man's understanding of himself in his concrete–historical and ontic situation. The word, *Existential*, on the other hand, refers to the *universal conditions* present in the concrete act of existing. It denotes the universal and ontological as over against the concrete and the ontic."

2 Precisely how this can be, without reducing the ready-to-hand to merely *world-points*, will not be evident until Chapter 8, when we bring together the formal a priori character of phenomenological science and the projective character of all science, and thereby extend the claims made here about the nature of scientific concept formation to the realm of the human sciences and the ready-to-hand.

3 It is, of course, for this reason that eidetic phenomenology is a science and requires the phenomenological reductions to constitute its objects.

8 *Implications for the human sciences*

1 To interpret Kuhn's revolutionary and normal science along these lines might be a productive enterprise.

2 This is not to argue that any projection is acceptable, although in principle this cannot be rejected. All formal a priori projections are to be grounded in the appropriate realms of phenomena, and must be phenomenologically founded.

3 But see Sugiura (1983).

4 "In this context, every deeper reflection leads back to the *fundamental* questions of practical reason, which concern both the individual person and the community, and its rational life in its essential and purely formal universality, a universality which leaves far behind it all empirical matters of fact and all contingent concepts" (Husserl, 1923, 330). For an elaboration of such fundamental questions see Heidegger's (1927) existential analytic and Gadamer's (1975a; 1977) philosophical hermeneutics.

5 Husserl (1923, 328).

6 See Heidegger (1927).

7 Heidegger's concern is with the question of the meaning of being, and it is to this end that his analytic of *Dasein* is aimed. Consequently we cannot expect a complete ontology of *Dasien* which would fully ground the 'regional ontology' we seek. His interpretation will provide only some of the pieces, but important ones (Heidegger, 1927, 17). For Heidegger's treatment of hermeneutics see Heidegger (1927). For an historical treatment of hermeneutics see Gadamer (1975a). A more general text is Palmer (1969).

8 He will later ask the question of the meaning of being, not from the side of *Dasein*, but from the side of being. At that point hermeneutic phenomenology is no longer the necessary foundation for *any* ontology whatsoever, although such an ontology must still be phenomenological, and still in some way presupposes a hermeneutic phenomenology. See Heidegger's letter to Richardson in Richardson (1967, viii–xxiii).

9 In this regard see Heidegger's important note x: "But to disclose that *a priori* is not to make an '*a-prioristic*' construction . . . '*A-priorism*' is the method of every scientific philosophy which understands itself. There is nothing constructive about it. But for this very reason *a priori* research requires that the phenomenal basis be properly prepared" (Heidegger, 1927, 50). Husserl has clarified this point. This basis, as that which is closest to us, lies in *Dasein*'s average everydayness.

10 Tuan (1975a; 1975b; 1977b) in particular has used this form of recovering to show how man's primitive relationships with place and space point towards more fundamental and universal relationships.

11 In note xi, page 51, Heidegger (1927) points to Cassirer's interpretation of myth as an example of such a grounded analytic. Yet because Cassirer builds upon Kant's *Critique of pure reason*, Heidegger leaves open the question as to whether the foundations of this interpretation are sufficiently transparent, or whether a more primordial approach may not be needed. Indeed, according to Heidegger, Cassirer himself sees the possibility of such an analytic, both when he refers to the phenomenological horizons disclosed by Husserl, and in discussion with Heidegger himself (see Heidegger, 1976, 32–45).

9 Towards an understanding of human spatiality

1 See Sack (1973), Golledge (1979, 109ff), Johnston (1982, 123).

2 See Sack (1980) for a full characterization of this view of space in geography; in particular notice the categories with which space is handled – 'social space and objective meanings of space', 'social space and subjective meanings of space', 'the child's and the practical view of space', and '[spaces of] myth and magic'.

3 This is not to dismiss the Cartesian project. It cannot be seen to be fundamental for human science, as has traditionally and implicitly been assumed. But it was preparatory for the a priori comprehension of material nature used by Newton and formalized by Kant (see Heidegger, 1927, 101).

4 Heidegger (1927, 67) describes this kind of knowing: "the kind of Being which belongs to such concernful dealings is not one into which we need to put ourselves first. This is the way in which everyday Dasein always is: when I open the door, for instance, I use the latch. The achieving of phenomenological access to the entities which we encounter, consists rather in thrusting aside our interpretative tendencies, which keep thrusting themselves upon us and running along with us, and which conceal not only the phenomenon of such 'concern', but even more those entities themselves *as* encountered of their own accord *in* our concern with them."

5 The spatiality of much of Heidegger's language has been noted. On pages 299ff (1927) he says: "In the term 'situation' there is an overtone of a signification that is spatial. We shall not try to eliminate this from the existential conception, for such an overtone is also implied in the 'there' of Dasein."

6 In *What is a thing?* (80ff) Heidegger compares the Greek experience of nature with that of modern times by comparing Aristotle's and Newton's physics. One of the biggest differences is that in Newton's physics "The concept of place itself is changed: place is no longer where the body belongs according to its nature, but only a position in relation to other positions" (1967, 86).

7 In 'Language in the poem: a discussion of Georg Trakl's poetic work' Heidegger (1971d) describes a *site* in a similar way: as a place which gathers and preserves unto

itself, not by encapsulating things, but by "penetrating with its light all it has gathered, and only thus releasing it into its own nature" (159–60).

8 It is interesting to speculate on how ontical and geographical regions come to be noticeable in this regard. Geographers have long maintained that the flourishing of regional geography and the concern with *pays* in the nineteenth and early to mid-twentieth centuries was a reaction to the destruction or decline of traditional regional boundaries and affinities with changing economic, technological and social conditions. More recently, the claim has been made that the 'humanist' return to the work of de la Blache is a similar response to the breakdown of traditional regional boundaries.

The interesting point here then, is not that geographers' interests can be explained in this way, they probably cannot, but that the opening of regions and the creation of places are *always* and *everywhere* a necessary condition for man's dwelling; that they generally remain inconspicuous, becoming conspicuous only when some problem arises with them; when they fail to reflect the existing and familiar relations between places, or when social and technological change has substantially altered the conditions through which the region makes sense. We might say that only the ontical outlines of such regions change with social and technological transformations, not their ontological primacy for any people. Even in the most technologically advanced society man creates regions in this way, through which things and people are given and find their place. The character of regions and regioning in particular cases changes, but its universal nature as an on-going, fundamental process of man's being-in-the-world does not.

9 'Building dwelling thinking' was given as a lecture August 5 1951 at the *Darmstadt Colloquium* on 'Man and Space' (Heidegger, 1971b, xxiv).

10 At this point I will set to one side the important, but for our present purposes complicated, treatment of man's dwelling and its relation to the fourfold of mortals, gods, earth and sky. See Heidegger (1971b, 149–51).

11 In *Kant and the problem of metaphysics*, Heidegger (1962, 75) describes the formation of this *free-space* as the transcendence of *Dasein* toward the being of objects in theoretical understanding.

12 In 'The nature of language' Heidegger (1971c, 84) describes this process more graphically: "The neighborhood in question pervades everywhere our stay on this earth and our journey in it. But since modern thinking is even more resolutely and exclusively turning into calculation, it concentrates all available energy and 'interests' in calculating how man may soon establish himself in a worldless cosmic space. This type of thinking is about to abandon the earth as earth. As calculation, it drifts more and more rapidly toward the conquest of cosmic space. This type of thinking is itself already the explosion of a power that could blast everything into nothingness."

13 For our present purposes the rather complex relationship of temporality and spatiality will be bracketed. For discussion of this see Heidegger (1927, 367–70; 1972, 15–23). In *On time and being* (1972, 23) Heidegger says that the attempt made in *Being and time* to derive human spatiality from temporality is untenable, and that the "first, original, literally incipient extending in which the unity of true time consists" is to be called "nearing nearness" or "nearhood". True time as four-dimensional seems here to be derived from *Dasein*'s spatiality, and hints at a new possibility for considering the relation of space and time. See also Heidegger (1966).

14 See the translator's note 2, Heidegger, 1927, page 138 (English pagination).

15 See Maurice Merleau-Ponty (1964) on space and space perception and its relation to body-space and anthropological-space.

References

Ackerman, E. A. 1945. Geographic training, wartime research, and immediate professional objectives. *Annals of the Association of American Geographers*. 35 (4), December 121–43.

1958. *Geography as a fundamental research discipline*. University of Chicago, Department of Geography Research Paper 53.

Aitchison, J. 1980. Elusive encounters of the phenomenological kind. *Journal of Geography in Higher Education*. 4 (2), Autumn, 86–9.

Allen, P. M. and Sanglier, M. 1981a. A dynamic model of a central place system – II. *Geographical Analysis*. 13 (2), April, 149–64.

1981b. Urban evolution, self-organization, and decision making. *Environment and Planning* A, 13, 167–83.

Annals of the Association of American Geographers. 1979. Special Issue: Seventy-five years of American geography. 69 (1), March.

Arendt, H. 1958. *The human condition*. Chicago: The University of Chicago Press.

Bachelard, G. 1969. *The poetics of space*. Trans. Jolas, M. Boston: Beacon Press.

Barrows, H. H. 1923. Geography as human ecology. *Annals of the Association of American Geographers*. 13 (1), March, 1–14.

Bartels, D. 1973. Between theory and metatheory. In Chorley, R. J. (ed.). *Directions in geography*. London: Methuen.

1982. Geography: paradigmatic or functional change? A view from West Germany. In Gould and Olsson (1982). 24–33.

Beer, S. 1974. *Designing freedom*. Massey lectures, Thirteenth Series. Toronto: CBC Publications.

Berger, P. L. and Luckmann, T. 1967. *The social construction of reality: a treatise in the sociology of knowledge*. New York: Anchor Books.

Berkeley, G. 1965. 'Idealism'. Edited from *Principles of human knowledge*. In Hirst, R. J. *Perception and the external world*. New York: Macmillan. 247–60.

Berry, B. J. L. and Marble, D. F. (eds). 1968. *Spatial analysis. A reader in statistical geography*. Englewood Cliffs, New Jersey: Prentice-Hall.

Biemel, W. 1977. Husserl's *Encyclopaedia Britannica* article and Heidegger's remarks thereon. In Elliston and McCormick (1977). 286–303.

Billinge, M. 1977. In search of negativism: phenomenology and historical geography. *Journal of Historical Geography*. 3 (1), 55–67.

Bird, J. 1977. Methodology and philosophy: progress report. *Progress in Human Geography*. 1 (1), March, 104–110.

Blaut, J. M. 1961. Space and process. *The Professional Geographer*. 13 (4), July, 1–7.
1962. Object and relationship. *The Professional Geographer*. 14 (6), November, 1–7.

Broek, J. 1965. *Geography. Its scope and spirit*. Columbus, Ohio: Charles E. Merrill Publishing Co.

Bunge, W. 1962. *Theoretical geography*. Lund Studies in Geography, Series C.1. Lund: C. W. K. Gleerup.

Burnett, P. 1976. Behavioral geography and the philosophy of mind. In Golledge, R. G. and Rushton, G. (eds). *Spatial choice and spatial behavior. Geographic essays on the analysis of preferences and perceptions*. Columbus: Ohio State University Press. 23–48.

Burton, I. 1965. The quantitative revolution and theoretical geography. *The Canadian Geographer*. 7, 151–62.

Buttimer, A. 1969. Social space in interdisciplinary perspective. *Geographical Review*. 59 (3), 417–26.

1971. *Society and milieu in the French geographic tradition*. AAG Monograph 6. Chicago: Association of American Geographers.

1974. Phenomenology, existentialism and the study of values. *Values in geography*. Commission on College Geography Resource Paper Number 24. Washington D.C.: Association of American Geographers.

1976. Grasping the dynamism of lifeworld. *Annals of the Association of American Geographers*. 66 (2), June, 277–92.

1977. Comment in reply to Relph (1977). Humanism, phenomenology and geography. *Annals of the Association of American Geographers*. 67 (1), March, 180–3.

Buttimer, A. and Seamon, D. (eds). 1980. *The human experience of space and place*. New York: St. Martin's Press.

Cairns, D. 1976. *Conversations with Husserl and Fink*. The Hague: Martinus Nijhoff.

Carr, D. 1970. Translator's introduction. In Husserl (1954). xv–xliii.

Clark, K. 1981. *What is a masterpiece?* New York: Thames and Hudson.

Coetzee, J. M. 1982. *Waiting for the barbarians*. New York: Penguin.

Comte, A. 1830–42. *Cours de philosophie positive*. In Lenzer (1975). 69–306.

1854. Preface to the early writings. In Lenzer (1975). 3–5.

Copleston, F. 1964. *A history of philosophy. Modern philosophy, the French Enlightenment to Kant*. 6 (1). New York: Image Books.

Cosgrove, D. 1978. Review essay. Place, landscape and the dialectics of cultural geography. *The Canadian Geographer*. 22 (1), Spring, 66–72.

Couclelis, H. 1982. Positivist philosophy and research on human spatial behavior. Mimeo, Department of Geography, University of California, Santa Barbara.

Cox, K. R. and Golledge, R. G. (eds). 1969. *Behavioral problems in geography: a symposium*. Northwestern University Studies in Geography Number 17. Evanston, Ill.

1981. *Behavioral problems in geography revisited*. New York and London: Methuen.

Dardel, E. 1952. *L'homme et la terre: nature de réalité géographique*. Paris: Presses Universitaires de France.

Davis, W. M. 1906. An inductive study of the contents of geography. *Annals of the Association of American Geographers*. 67–84.

1924. The progress of geography in the United States – an analogy with astronomy. *Annals of the Association of American Geographers*. 14, December, 160–215.

Dilthey, W. 1957. The types of world views and their unfoldment within the metaphysical systems. *Dilthey's philosophy of existence. Introduction to Weltanschauungslehre*. (ed) Kluback, W. and Weinbaum, M. New York: Bookman Associates.

Downs, R. M. and Stea, D. (eds). 1973. *Image and environment. Cognitive mapping and spatial behavior.* Chicago: Aldine.

Duncan, J. 1978. The social construction of unreality: an interactionist approach to the tourist's cognition of environment. In Ley and Samuels (1978). 269–82.

Elliston, F. A. and McCormick, P. (eds). 1977. *Husserl: expositions and appraisals.* Notre Dame, Indiana: University of Notre Dame Press.

Entrikin, J. N. 1976. Contemporary humanism in geography. *Annals of the Association of American Geographers.* 66 (4), December, 615–32.

1977. Geography's spatial perspective and the philosophy of Ernst Cassirer. *The Canadian Geographer.* 21 (3), 209–22.

Eyles, J. 1981. Why geography cannot be Marxist: towards an understanding of lived experience. *Environment and Planning* A, 13, 1371–88.

Feyerabend, P. 1979. Dialogue on method. In Radnitzky, G. and Andersson, G. (eds). *The structure and development of science.* Dordrecht, Holland: Reidel. 63–131.

Fischer, E., Campbell, R. D. and Miller, E. S. 1969. *A question of place. The development of geographic thought.* Arlington, Va.: Beatty.

Gadamer, H.-G. 1963. The phenomenological movement. In Gadamer (1977). 130–81.

1969. The science of the lifeworld. In Gadamer (1977). 182–97.

1975a. *Truth and method.* New York: Continuum.

1975b. Hermeneutics and social science. *Cultural Hermeneutics.* 2, 307–16.

1977. *Philosophical hermeneutics.* Trans. and ed. Linge, E. Berkeley and Los Angeles: University of California Press.

Gale, S. 1972. Inexactness, fuzzy sets and the foundations of behavioral geography. *Geographical Analysis.* 4 (4), October, 337–49.

1977. Ideological man in a nonideological society. *Annals of the Association of American Geographers.* 67 (2), June, 267–72.

Gale, S. and Olsson, G. (eds). 1979. *Philosophy in geography.* Dordrecht, Holland: Reidel.

Gendlin, E. T. 1967. Analysis. In Heidegger, M. *What is a thing?* South Bend, Indiana: Gateway Editions. 247–96.

Gibson, E. M. 1974. Commentary on 'Values in geography'. In Buttimer (1974). 46–50.

Giddens, A. 1976. *New rules of sociological method: a positive critique of interpretative sociologies.* London: Hutchinson.

Gingerich, O. 1982. The Galileo affair. *Scientific American.* 247 (2), August, 132–43.

Golledge, R. G. 1973. Some issues related to the search for geographical knowledge. *Antipode.* 5 (2), May, 60–6.

1979. Reality, process, and the dialectical relation between man and environment. In Gale and Olsson (1979). 109–20.

1981. Misconceptions, misinterpretations, and misrepresentations of behavioral approaches in human geography. *Environment and Planning* A, 13, 1325–44.

Gould, P. R. 1981. Space and rum: an English note on espacien and rumian meaning. *Geografiska Annaler.* 63B (1), 1–3.

Gould, P. R. and Olsson, G. (eds). 1982. *A search for common ground.* London: Pion.

Gregory, D. 1976. Rethinking historical geography. *Area.* 8 (4), 295–9.

1978a. *Ideology, science and human geography.* London: Hutchinson.

1978b. The discourse of the past: phenomenology, structuralism and historical geography. *Journal of Historical Geography.* 4 (2), 161–73.

1981a. Human agency and human geography. *Transactions of the Institute of*

British Geographers. N.S. 6 (1), 1–18.

1981b. Phenomenology. In Johnston (1981). 252–4.

1982. A realist construction of the social. *Transactions of the Institute of British Geographers*. N.S. 7 (2), 254–6.

Guelke, L. 1975. On rethinking historical geography. *Area*. 7 (2), 135–8.

1977. The role of laws in human geography. *Progress in Human Geography*. 1 (3), October, 376–86.

1978. Geography and logical positivism. In Herbert, D. T. and Johnston, R. J. (eds). *Geography and the urban environment. Progress in research and applications*. Vol. 1. New York: Wiley. 35–61.

Habermas, J. 1971. *Knowledge and human interests*. Trans. Shapiro, J. J. Boston: Beacon Press.

Hägerstrand, T. 1953. *Innovation diffusion as a spatial process*. Trans. Pred, A. Chicago: The University of Chicago, 1967.

1970. What about people in regional science? *Papers of the Regional Science Association*. 24, 7–21.

1973. The domain of human geography. In Chorley, R. J. (ed). *Directions in geography*. London: Methuen. 67–87.

Haggett, P. 1965. *Locational analysis in human geography*. London: St. Martins Press, 1966.

Harbison, R. 1977. *Eccentric spaces*. New York: Avon Books.

Hartshorne, R. 1939. *The nature of geography. A critical survey of current thought in the light of the past*. Lancaster, Pa.: Association of American Geographers.

1952. On the mores of methodological discussion in American geography. *Annals of the Association of American Geographers*. 38, 113–25.

1955. "Exceptionalism in Geography" Re-examined. *Annals of the Association of American Geographers*. 45 (3), September, 205–44.

1958. The concept of geography as a science of space, from Kant and Humboldt to Hettner. *Annals of the Association of American Geographers*. 48 (2), June, 97–108.

1959. *Perspective on the nature of geography*. Association of American Geographers Monograph. Washington, D.C.

Harvey, D. 1969a. Conceptual and measurement problems in the cognitive–behavioral approach to location theory. In Cox and Golledge (1969). 35–67.

1969b. *Explanation in geography*. London: Edward Arnold.

1972. Revolutionary and counter-revolutionary theory in geography and the problem of ghetto formation. *Antipode*. 4 (2), 1–13.

1974. What kind of geography for what kind of public policy? *Transactions of the Institute of British Geographers*. 63, November, 18–24.

Harvey, M. E. and Holly, B. P. 1981. *Themes in geographic thought*. London: Croom Helm.

Hay, A. M. 1979. Positivism in human geography: response to critics. In Johnston, R. J. and Herbert, D. T. (eds). *Geography and the urban environment. Progress in research and applications*. Vol. 2. New York: Wiley. 1–26.

Heelan, P. A. 1983. *Space perception and the philosophy of science*. Berkeley and Los Angeles: University of California Press.

Heffner, J. 1974. Husserl's critique of traditional empiricism. *Journal of the British Society for Phenomenology*. 5 (2), May, 159–62.

Heidegger, M. 1927. *Being and time*. Trans. Macquarrie, J. and Robinson, E. New York: Harper and Row, 1962.

1929. *The essence of reasons*. Trans. Malick, T. Evanston: Northwestern University Press. 1969.

1959. *An introduction to metaphysics*. Trans. Manheim, R. New Haven: Yale University Press.

1962. *Kant and the problem of metaphysics*. Trans. Churchill, J. S. Bloomington: Indiana University Press.

1966. *Discourse on thinking*. Trans. Anderson, J. M. and Freund, E. H. New York: Harper and Row.

1967. *What is a thing?* Trans. Barton, W. B. and Deutsch, V. South Bend, Indiana: Gateway Editions.

1969a. *Identity and difference*. Trans. Stambaugh, J. New York: Harper and Row.

1969b. Art and space. *Man and World*. 6, 3–8.

1971a. The origin of the work of art. *Poetry, language, thought*. Trans. Hofstadter, A. New York: Harper and Row. 17–87.

1971b. Building dwelling thinking. *Poetry, language, thought*. 145–61.

1971c. The nature of language. *On the way to language*. Trans. Hertz, P. D. New York: Harper and Row. 57–108.

1971d. Language in the poem. A discussion of Georg Trakl's poetic work. *On the way to language*. 159–98.

1972. *On time and being*. New York: Harper and Row.

1976. *The piety of thinking*. Trans. Hart, J. G. and Maraldo, J. C. Bloomington: Indiana University Press.

1977a. *The question concerning technology and other essays*. Trans. Lovitt, W. New York: Harper Colophon Books.

1977b. The age of the world [as] picture. *The question concerning technology and other essays*. 115–54.

1977c. Science and reflection. *The question concerning technology and other essays*. 155–82.

1977d. The question concerning technology. *The question concerning technology and other essays*. 3–35.

1977e. The word of Nietzsche: God is dead. *The question concerning technology and other essays*. 53–112.

1982. *The basic problems of phenomenology*. Trans. Hofstadter, A. Bloomington: Indiana University Press.

Hettner, A. 1905. Das System der Wissenschaften. *Preuss. Jahrbücher*. 122, 251–77.

1927. *Die Geographie, ihre Geschichte, ihr Wesen und ihre Methoden*. Breslau.

Hufferd, J. 1980. Towards a transcendental human geography of places. *Antipode*. 12 (3), 18–23.

Hughes, H. S. 1977. *Consciousness and society. The reorientation of European social thought, 1890–1930*. New York: Vintage Books.

Hugill, P. J. 1979. The landscape paradigm in cultural geography: a review and commentary. Paper presented at the Annual Meeting of the Association of American Geographers. Philadelphia.

Husserl, E. 1891. *Philosophie der Arithmetik: psychologische und logische Untersuchungen*. Halle a. S.: Pfeffer.

1900–1. *Logical investigations*. Trans. Findley, J. N. 2 vols. New York: Humanities Press, 1970.

1907. *The idea of phenomenology*. Trans. Alston, W. P. and Nakhnikian, G. The Hague: Martinus Nijhoff, 1973.

1911. Philosophy as rigorous science. *Phenomenology and the crisis of philosophy*.

Trans. Lauer, Q. New York: Harper Torchbooks, 1965. 71–147.

1913. *Ideas: general introduction to pure phenomenology*. Trans. Boyce Gibson, W. R. New York: Collier, 1962.

1917. Husserl's inaugural lecture at Freiburg im Breisgau. Trans. Jordan, R. W. In McCormick and Elliston (1981). 9–20.

1923. Renewal: its problem and method. Trans. Allen, J. In McCormick and Elliston (1981). 326–31.

1927. Phenomenology. Edmund Husserl's article for the *Encyclopaedia Britannica*. Rev. trans. Palmer, R. E. In McCormick and Elliston (1981). 21–35.

1930. *Cartesian meditations. An introduction to phenomenology*. Trans. Cairns, D. The Hague: Nijhoff, 1973.

1931. *The Paris Lecture*. Trans. Koestenbaum, P. The Hague: Martinus Nijhoff.

1941. Phenomenology and anthropology. Trans. Schmitt, R. G. In McCormick and Elliston (1981). 315–23.

1954. *The crisis of European sciences and transcendental phenomenology: an introduction to phenomenological philosophy*. Trans. Carr, D. Evanston: Northwestern University Press, 1970.

1965. Philosophy and the crisis of European man. *Phenomenology and the crisis of philosophy*. Trans. Lauer, Q. New York: Harper Torchbooks. 149–92.

1973. *Cartesian meditations. An introduction to phenomenology*. Trans. Cairns, D. The Hague: Martinus Nijhoff.

1978. *First philosophy*. Trans. Allen, J. The Hague: Martinus Nijhoff.

Jackson, P. 1981. Phenomenology and social geography. *Area*. 13 (4), 299–305.

James, P. E. and Martin, G. J. 1978. *The Association of American Geographers. The first seventy-five years*. Washington, D.C.: Association of American Geographers.

1981. *All possible worlds. A history of geographical ideas*. New York: Wiley.

Johnston, R. J. 1978. Paradigms and revolutions or evolution: observations on human geography since the Second World War. *Progress in Human Geography*. 2 (2), June, 189–206.

1979. *Geography and geographers. Anglo-American human geography since 1945*. London: Edward Arnold.

(ed). 1981. *The dictionary of human geography*. Oxford: Blackwell.

1982. On the nature of human geography. *Transactions of the Institute of British Geographers*. N.S. 7 (1), 123–5.

Jordan, R. W. 1981. Introduction to 'Husserl's inaugural lecture at Freiburg im Breisgau (1917)'. In McCormick and Elliston (1981). 3–8.

Kaplan, A. 1968. Positivism. *International encyclopedia of the social sciences*. 12. New York: Macmillan and The Free Press. 389–95.

Kisiel, T. 1970. Phenomenology as the science of science. In Kockelmans and Kisiel (1970). 5–44.

1973. On the dimensions of a phenomenology of science in Husserl and the young Dr. Heidegger. *Journal of the British Society for Phenomenology*. 4 (3), October, 217–34.

1982. The genesis of *Being and time*. A lecture given in the series: Phenomenology, Time, and Natural Science in the early Heidegger. Summer Program in Phenomenology. The Pennsylvania State University, University Park, August 2–14.

Kockelmans, J. J. 1965. *Martin Heidegger. A first introduction to his philosophy*. Pittsburgh, Pa.: Duquesne University Press.

1966. *Phenomenology and physical science. An introduction to the philosophy of physical science.* Pittsburgh, Pa.: Duquesne University Press.

1967a. *A first introduction to Husserl's phenomenology.* Pittsburgh, Pa.: Duquesne University Press.

(ed). 1967b. *Phenomenology. The philosophy of Edmund Husserl and its interpretation.* New York: Anchor Books (Doubleday).

1969. *The world in science and philosophy.* Milwaukee: The Bruce Publishing Co.

1970a. World-constitution. Reflections on Husserl's transcendental idealism. *Analecta Husserliana.* 1, 11–35.

1970b. The mathematization of nature in Husserl's last publication, *Krisis.* In Kockelmans and Kisiel (1970). 45–67.

1970c. The era of the world-as-picture. In Kockelmans and Kisiel (1970). 184–201.

1971. Phenomenological psychology in the United States: a critical analysis of the actual situation. *Journal of Phenomenological Psychology.* 1 (2), Spring, 139–72.

1973. Theoretical problems in phenomenological psychology. In Natanson (1973b), 225–80.

1975. Toward an interpretative or hermeneutic social science. *Graduate Faculty Philosophy Journal.* 5 (1), Fall, 73–96.

1978a. *Edmund Husserl's phenomenological psychology. A historico-critical study.* Atlantic Highlands, N.J.: Humanities Press.

1978b. Reflections on social theory. *Human Studies.* 1, 1–15.

1979. Science and discipline. Some historical and critical reflections. In Kockelmans, J. J. (ed.). *Interdisciplinarity and higher education.* University Park: The Pennsylvania State University Press. 11–48.

1980. Some reflections on the meaning and function of interpretative sociology. *Tijdschrift voor Filosofie.* 42 (2), June, 294–324.

1982. On the impact of the human sciences on our conception of man and society. *Analecta Husserliana.* 14, 51–76.

Kockelmans, J. J. and Kisiel, T. J. 1970. *Phenomenology and the natural sciences. Essays and translations.* Evanston: Northwestern University Press.

Kohn, C. F. 1970. The 1960's: A decade of progress in geographical research and instruction. *Annals of the Association of American Geographers.* 60 (2), June, 211–19.

Landgrebe, L. 1940. The world as a phenomenological problem. *Philosophy and Phenomenological Research.* 1 (1), September, 38–58.

1981. *The phenomenology of Edmund Husserl.* Ithaca and London: Cornell University Press.

Lenzer, G. (ed) 1975. *Auguste Comte and positivism. The essential writings.* New York: Harper Torchbooks.

Leontieff, W. 1982. Academic economics. *Science.* 217, July 9, 104–7.

Lesse, P. F. 1982. A phenomenological theory of socioeconomic systems with spatial interactions. *Environment and Planning* A, 14, 869–88.

Ley, D. 1977. Social geography and the taken-for-granted world. *Transactions of the Institute of British Geographers.* N.S. 2 (4), 498–512.

1978. Social geography and social action. In Ley and Samuels (1978). 41–57.

1979. Social geography and the taken-for-granted world. In Gale and Olsson (1979). 215–36.

1980a. Power and the geographical lifeworld. A paper presented to the 19th annual meeting of the Society for Phenomenology and Existential Philosophy, Ottawa, November.

1980b. *Geography without man: a humanistic critique.* School of Geography Research Paper 24. University of Oxford.

1981. Behavioral geography and the philosophies of meaning. In Cox and Golledge (1981). 209–30.

1982. Rediscovering man's place. *Transactions of the Institute of British Geographers.* N.S. 7 (2), 248–53.

Ley, D. and Samuels, M. S. (eds). 1978. *Humanistic geography. Prospects and problems.* Chicago: Maaroufa Press.

Livingstone, D. N. and Harrison, R. T. 1981. Immanuel Kant, subjectivism and human geography: a preliminary investigation. *Transactions of the Institute of British Geographers.* N.S. 6 (3), 359–74.

Lowenthal, D. 1961. Geography, experience, and imagination: towards a geographical epistemology. *Annals of the Association of American Geographers.* 51 (3), September, 241–60.

Luckmann, T. (ed). 1978. *Phenomenology and sociology. Selected readings.* Harmondsworth, Middlesex: Penguin.

McCormick, P. and Elliston, F. (eds). 1981. *Husserl. Shorter works.* Indiana: University of Notre Dame Press.

Madison, G. B. 1977. Phenomenology and existentialism: Husserl and the end of idealism. In Elliston and McCormick (1977). 247–68.

May, J. A. 1970. *Kant's concept of geography and its relation to recent geographical thought.* University of Toronto Department of Geography Research Publications 4.

Mercer, D. C. and Powell, J. M. 1972. *Phenomenology and related non-positivistic viewpoints in the social sciences.* Monash University Publications in Geography. Victoria, Australia: Department of Geography.

Merleau-Ponty, M. 1962. *Phenomenology of perception.* Trans. Smith, C. London: Routledge and Kegan Paul.

1964. Cezanne's doubt. *Sense and non-sense.* Trans. Dreyfus, H. L. and Dreyfus, P. A. Evanston, Ill.: Northwestern University Press. 9–25.

Mill, J. S. 1865. *Auguste Comte and positivism.* Ann Arbor: University of Michigan Press, 1965.

Mills, W. J. 1982. Positivism reversed: the relevance of Giambattista Vico. *Transactions of the Institute of British Geographers.* N.S. 7 (1), 1–14.

Moriarty, B. 1981. Future research directions in American human geography. *The Professional Geographer.* 33 (4), 484–8.

Natanson, M. 1973a. *Edmund Husserl: philosopher of infinite tasks.* Evanston: Northwestern University Press.

(ed). 1973b. *Phenomenology and the social sciences.* Evanston: Northwestern University Press. Vol. 1.

Newton, I. 1687. Scholium to the definitions. *Mathematical principles of natural philosophy.* Reprinted in Smart, J. J. C. *Problems of space and time.* New York: Macmillan, 1964. 81–8.

Nicholson, L. J. 1980. Why Habermas? *Radical Philosophy.* 25, Summer, 21–6.

Nystuen, J. D. 1968. Identification of some fundamental spatial concepts. In Berry and Marble (1968). 35–41.

Olsson, G. 1972. Some notes on geography and social engineering. *Antipode.* 4 (1), 1–22.

1975. *Birds in egg.* Michigan Geographical Publication 15. Ann Arbor: University of Michigan Department of Geography.

1980. Hitting your head against the ceiling of language. *Birds in egg/Eggs in bird*. London: Pion. 3e–18e.

Palmer, R. E. 1969. *Hermeneutics. Interpretation theory in Schleiermacher, Dilthey, Heidegger, and Gadamer*. Evanston: Northwestern University Press.

Parsons, J. J. 1969. Toward a more humane geography. *Economic Geography*. 45 (3), July, Editorial.

Pickles, J. 1981. The hermeneutics–ideology critique debate: some implications for an interpretative social science. Paper presented at the Annual Meeting of the Canadian Association of Geographers. Cornerbrook, Newfoundland. June.

1982. 'Science' and the funding of human geography. *The Professional Geographer*. 34 (4), November, 387–92.

Radnitzky, G. 1973. *Contemporary schools of metascience*. Chicago: Gateway Edition.

Relph, E. C. 1970. An inquiry into the relations between phenomenology and geography. *The Canadian Geographer*. 14 (3), 193–201.

1973. The phenomenon of place. Unpublished doctoral dissertation. Department of Geography, University of Toronto.

1976a. *Place and placelessness*. London: Pion.

1976b. *The phenomenological foundations of geography*. University of Toronto, Department of Geography Discussion Paper.

1977. Humanism, phenomenology and geography. *Annals of the Association of American Geographers*. 67 (1), March, 177–9.

Richards, P. 1974. Kant's geography and mental maps. *Transactions of the Institute of British Geographers*. 61, March, 1–16.

Richardson, G. D. 1981. Comparing two cognitive mapping methodologies. *Area*. 13 (4), 325–31.

Richardson, W. J. 1967. *Heidegger. Through phenomenology to thought*. The Hague: Martinus Nijhoff.

Ricoeur, P. 1967. *Husserl. An analysis of his phenomenology*. Trans. Ballard, E. G., and Embree, L. E. Evanston: Northwestern University Press.

1973a. The task of hermeneutics. *Philosophy Today*. 17 (2/4), Summer. 112–28.

1973b. The hermeneutical function of distanciation. *Philosophy Today*, 17 (2/4), Summer. 129–41.

Rose, C. 1981. Wilhelm Dilthey's philosophy of historical understanding. A neglected heritage of contemporary humanistic geography. In Stoddart (1981). 99–133.

Rossides, D. W. 1978. *The history and nature of sociological theory*. Boston: Houghton Mifflin.

Sack, R. D. 1972. Geography, geometry, and explanation. *Annals of the Association of American Geographers*. 62 (1), March, 61–78.

1973. A concept of physical space in geography. *Geographical Analysis*. 5 (1), January, 16–34.

1974a. Chorology and spatial analysis. *Annals of the Association of American Geographers*. 64 (3), September, 439–52.

1974b. The spatial separatist theme in geography. *Economic Geography*. 50 (1), January, 1–18.

1979. Critical science and geography: book review essay. *Progress in Human Geography*. 3 (3), September, 443–52.

1980a. Conceptions of geographic space. *Progress in Human Geography*. 4 (3), September, 313–45.

1980b. *Conceptions of space in social thought. A geographical perspective*.

Minneapolis: University of Minnesota Press.

Samuels, M. S. 1978. Existentialism and human geography. In Ley and Samuels (1978). 22–40.

Sauer, C. O. 1965. The morphology of landscape. In Leighly, J. (ed.). *Land and life*. Berkeley: University of California Press. 315–50.

Schaefer, F. K. 1953. Exceptionalism in geography: a methodological examination. *Annals of the Association of American Geographers*. 43 (3), September, 226–49.

Schrag, C. O. 1958. Phenomenology, ontology, and history in the philosophy of Heidegger. Reprinted in Kockelmans (1967b). 277–93.

1980. *Radical reflection and the origin of the human sciences*. West Lafayette, Indiana: Purdue University Press.

Scott, A. J. 1976. Review of *Birds in egg*. *Annals of the Association of American Geographers*. 66 (4), December, 633–6.

Seamon, D. 1979a. Phenomenology, geography and geographical education. *Journal of Geography in Higher Education*. 3 (2), Autumn, 40–50.

1979b. *A geography of the lifeworld*. New York: St. Martins Press.

1980a. Concretising phenomenology: a response to Aitchison. *Journal of Geography in Higher Education*. 4 (2), 89–92.

1980b. Afterword: community, place, and environment. In Buttimer and Seamon (1980). 188–96.

1982. Philosophical directions in behavioral geography with an emphasis on the phenomenological contribution. Paper presented at the Annual Meeting of the Association of American Geographers, San Antonio, Texas.

Seebohm, T. 1982. Naturalism, historicism and the paradox of subjectivity. A lecture in the series: Introduction to Husserl's transcendental phenomenology. Summer Program in Phenomenology, The Pennsylvania State University, August 2–14.

Smith, N. 1979. Geography, science and post-positivist modes of explanation. *Progress in Human Geography*. 3 (3), September, 356–83.

Sorokin, P. A. 1962. The structure of sociocultural space. *Society, culture and personality. Their structure and dynamics: a system of general sociology*. New York: Cooper Square Publ.

1964. *Sociocultural causality, space, time. A study of referential principles of sociology and social science*. New York: Russell and Russell.

Spiegelberg, H. 1971. On the misfortunes of Edmund Husserl's *Encyclopaedia Britannica* article 'Phenomenology'. In McCormick and Elliston (1981). 18–20.

1978. *The phenomenological movement. A historical introduction*. The Hague: Martinus Nijhoff, 2nd edition. 2 vols.

Stewart, J. Q. 1947. Empirical mathematical rules concerning the distribution and equilibrium of population. *Geographical Review*. 37 (3), July 461–85.

1956. The development of social physics. *American Journal of Physics*. 18, 239–53.

Stewart, J. M. and Warntz, W. 1958. Macrogeography and social science. *Geographical Review*. 48 (2), April, 167–84.

1959. Physics of population distribution. *Journal of Regional Science*. 1 (1), Summer, 99–123.

Stoddart, D. R. (ed). 1981. *Geography, ideology and social concern*. Oxford: Blackwell.

Sugiura, N. 1983. Rhetoric and geographers' worlds: The case of spatial analysis in human geography. Unpublished doctoral dissertation. Department of Geography, The Pennsylvania State University.

Taaffe, E. J. 1970. *Geography*. Englewood Cliffs, New Jersey: Prentice-Hall.

1974. The spatial view in context. *Annals of the Association of American Geographers.* 64 (1), March, 1–16.

Talarchek, G. M. 1977. Phenomenology as a new paradigm in human geography. Department of Geography Discussion Paper 39. New York: Syracuse University.

Tuan, Y. 1965. 'Environment' and 'world'. *The Professional Geographer.* 17 (5), 6–8.

1971a. Geography, phenomenology, and the study of human nature. *The Canadian Geographer.* 15 (3), 181–92.

1971b. *Man and nature.* Commission on College Geography Resource Paper 10. Washington D.C.: Association of American Geographers.

1972. Structuralism, existentialism and environmental perception. *Environment and Behavior.* 5 (3), September, 319–31.

1973. Ambiguity in attitudes toward environment. *Annals of the Association of American Geographers.* 63 (4), December, 411–23.

1974. Commentary on 'Values in geography'. In Buttimer (1974). 54–8.

1975a. Place: an experiential perspective. *The Geographical Review.* 65 (2), April, 151–65.

1975b. Space and place: humanistic perspective. *Progress in Geography.* 6, 211–52.

1976. Humanistic geography. *Annals of the Association of American Geographers.* 66 (2), June, 266–76.

1977a. Comment in reply to Relph (1977), Humanism, phenomenology, and geography. *Annals of the Association of American Geographers.* 67 (1), March, 179–80.

1977b. *Space and place: the perspective of experience.* Minneapolis: University of Minnesota Press.

Tymieniecka, A. T. 1962. *Phenomenology and science in contemporary European thought.* New York: The Noonday Press.

Ullman, E. L. 1954. Geography as spatial interaction. *Annals of the Association of American Geographers.* 44 (3), September, 283–4.

Van den Berg, J. H. 1961. *The changing nature of man. Introduction to a historical psychology.* Trans. Croes, H. F. New York: Dell.

Van Paassen, C. 1957. *The classical tradition of geography.* Groningen: J. B. Wolters.

Waelhens, A. de. 1958. The human sciences, the ontological horizon and the encounter. In Luckmann (1978). 161–80.

Walmsley, D. J. 1974. Positivism and phenomenology in human geography. *The Canadian Geographer.* 18 (2), 95–107.

Walter, E. W. 1980–81. The places of experience. *The Philosophical Forum.* 12 (2), Winter, 159–81.

Warntz, W. 1957. Transportation, social physics, and the law of refraction. *The Professional Geographer.* 9 (4), July, 2–7.

1973. New geography as general spatial systems theory – old social physics writ large? In Chorley, R. J. (ed). *Directions in geography.* London: Methuen. 89–126.

Welte, B. 1982. God in Heidegger's thought. *Philosophy Today.* 26, Spring, 85–100.

Whitehead, A. N. 1925. *Science and the modern world.* New York: The Free Press, 1967.

Whittlesey, D. 1957. The regional concept and the regional method. In James, P. and Jones, C. F. (eds). *American geography: inventory and prospect.* Syracuse: Syracuse University Press.

Wiener, N. 1954. *The human use of human beings: cybernetics and society.* Boston: Houghton Mifflin.

Wood, D. 1982. Review of *The human experience of space and place.* Buttimer, A. and Seamon, D. (eds). *Environment and Behavior.* 14 (4), July, 503–6.

Index